AN EARNEST MINISTRY

AN EARNEST MINISTRY

THE WANT OF THE TIMES

John Angell James

THE BANNER OF TRUTH TRUST

THE BANNER OF TRUTH TRUST
3 Murrayfield Road, Edinburgh EH12 6EL
PO Box 621, Carlisle, Pennsylvania 17013, USA

First published 1847
First Banner of Truth edition 1993
ISBN 0 85151 657 2

Printed and bound at The Bath Press, Avon

CONTENTS.

AN EARNEST MINISTRY THE WANT OF
THE TIMES.

PREFACE.

HAS the modern evangelical pulpit lost, and is it still losing, any of its power? This is a question far too momentous to be asked in the spirit of mere curiosity, or to be answered in unreflecting and ignorant haste. An affirmative reply involves consequences so deeply and so painfully affecting the eternal welfare of mankind, as well as the cause of orthodoxy, that it should not be given except upon indubitable evidence; while on the other hand, a negative answer would, if the evil really exists, only perpetuate it, by superseding all measures for correcting it which might remain in our power.

In settling this question, it is necessary to define what is meant by the loss of the power of the pulpit. If it is intended to ask whether evangelical ministrations have lost any of their attractiveness in drawing people together to hear them, it may be unhesitatingly affirmed that they have not; for perhaps there never were such numbers found listening to the glad tidings of salvation as at the present time. The true meaning of the inquiry then is, whether the modern pulpit has lost any of its efficiency as regards the great ends for which the gospel is preached; that is, the conversion of sinners, and the spiritual advancement of believers. In coming to a right conclusion upon this matter, another question must be proposed and answered; with what past period of history the present is to be compared. If we go back to the time of Baxter, Howe, Owen, Bates, Manton, and Charnock, there can be little reason to believe that the moderns preach with the same results that they did. As little can it be questioned that Whitfield and Wesley, with the men called out by their labours, both in the Church of England and among Nonconformists, proclaimed the gospel of the grace of God with more power and success than the preachers of the present day. It is better, therefore, to limit the inquiry to the last quarter of a century, and to state it thus; does the preaching of the gospel now, taking all evangelical denominations into the investigation, appear to be followed with the same saving and sanctifying results, as it was then; and if not, does there appear to be a progressive diminution of its effect still going on?

This is a question for the solution of which we must depend pretty much upon general reports, not having accurate statistics relating to it. It may be asked then, whether this want of efficiency is not matter of acknowledgment and lamentation by all evangelical bodies? True it is, that, to a certain extent, similar acknowledgments and lamentations have been made in every age, by ministers of all denominations. But the admission now referred to is made chiefly by those who compare themselves with themselves; and their success at the present time, with their own success in past time. There are concurrent confessions by the Presbyterians, Congregationalists, Baptists, and Methodists of the United States, that there is a deadness in all their churches, that revivals are rare, and conversions few, and the power of godliness among professing Christians is low, among them. The Methodist body in the United Kingdom reported last year (1846) but an increase of about seven hundred members, and this year a decrease of five thousand. The evangelical clergy of the Church of England lament the rarity of conversions by their preaching, and confess that the power of Venn, Romaine, Cecil, and Newton, seems wanting to their successors. The Baptists and Independents have no better report to make. Dr. Chalmers, in a late article in the North British Review, in speaking of Scotland, and that at a time when the disruption of the Presbyterian Establishment might have been supposed to have given new activity to the ministry of the Free Church at least, uses the following mournful language: "As things stand at present, our creeds and confessions have become effete; and the Bible a dead letter; and the orthodoxy which was at one time the glory, by withering into the inert and lifeless, is now the shame and reproach of all our churches." This is strong language, and a startling opinion. But the most melancholy thing connected with it is its truth.

Assuming then the fact that the modern evangelical pulpit has lost and is losing something of its power in converting sinners and carrying forward the spiritual life of believers, it surely becomes us all to reflect upon the painful fact with the deepest seriousness, and to endeavour, with the most intense anxiety, to discover its cause. It would ill become us in a spirit of antinomian indolence or fanaticism to resolve the whole matter into Divine sovereignty, and to say, "God wills it." With the same propriety, and on as good ground,

might the impenitent sinner be satisfied with his condition, and trace it up to a withholding of the influence
necessary for his conversion. That there is a suspension
of Divine influence must be admitted, if there be a
diminished result; but as the Spirit works by appropriate means, may not this very suspension itself be
traced up to some fault of the preachers themselves?
Would not a different order of means, or more energy
in the use of them, lead to a removal of this suspension
of the Spirit's power? The question for us to ask in
all seriousness and prayerful examination, is this: Does
the diminished power of the pulpit arise from a diminished adaptation of the pulpit to the state of the people;
or is the lamented deficiency to be traced up exclusively
to the circumstances of the times that are now passing
over us? Something, no doubt, may be set down to
both these causes.

This, then, is a matter that concerns all, and deeply
concerns all; for the tendency of decline is always
downward; what is weak will become weaker, if not
arrested in its progress.

There is another consideration which may account
for the diminished effect of the pulpit, and that is an
increased power of the press and of Sunday schools.
At one time the preacher had the public mind almost to
himself. There were indeed Bibles, schools, and tracts;
but how few and uninfluential compared with what they
are in the present day! Evangelical truth now comes
before the million in every possible variety of form; the
child learns his lessons from the Sunday-school teacher,
and the poorest adult reads it at home in the tract and
the penny magazine; and though this is a help in one
respect to the preacher, it takes from him all the

advantage which novelty of representation, and something approaching an exclusive hold on the public, once gave him; for he has been forestalled on every topic by the living voice of the Sunday-school teacher, and the silent exhortations of the tract. These auxiliary means of conversion will, however, never supersede the pulpit, if the pulpit does not allow itself to be superseded; and it is evident that such competitors should increase its labours to be, what God ever intended it to be, his power to the salvation of men. That the pulpit has nothing to fear from the increase of religious knowledge by the Sunday school and the press, is evident from the fact that as science multiplies its treatises, and cheapens them down to the poorest pocket, it multiplies in equal proportion its public lecturers.

The facts thus briefly noticed will account for, and perhaps be admitted to justify, the appearance of the volume which this preface is intended to introduce. We live in an earnest age, and nothing but an earnest ministry can hope to succeed in it. When honoured by an invitation to preach last year the anniversary sermon for Cheshunt College, the author found his subject in this conviction. The publication of the discourse then preached was solicited at the time of its delivery; but as it was given to the world pretty fully in the Patriot, he abandoned all thoughts of complying with the request, though so kindly preferred. His attention was, however, called again to the subject, and his resolution changed, by the solicitation of the distinguished minister who presides with so much wisdom and dignity over that collegiate institution; and who, to all his other works, so rich in practical piety, has added another of a very different kind, which, while it lays the

world under deep obligations to its author, will associate
the name of Dr. Harris with the most profound religious
philosophers of any age or country.   May his valuable
life be spared to complete that magnificent series
of treatises, which, with such adventurous but well-
balanced intellect, he has projected, and of which the
volume lately issued is but the commencement !

When revising his manuscript for publication, the
author found that it admitted of more expansion and
amplification than at first struck him; and he resolved,
as soon as he could find time for it, to prepare a small
treatise which should have a better chance of living
than an ephemeral pamphlet.   The subject grew under
his hand, and has at length swelled into this volume.

But in undertaking to become, especially at such
length, the counsellor of his brethren, he can scarcely
acquit himself of the charge of presumption.   He feels
that he has little claim upon the attention of his
fellow-labourers in the ministry, even the youngest
of them.   True it is that he has now arrived at an
age when he takes his place among fathers; but years
do not always teach wisdom.   It is no less true that
he has now laboured two and forty years in the ministry
of the word, and has had no very limited opportunity
of observing in others, and of discovering experimentally,
what contributes to ministerial acceptableness and usefulness; still he can truly say, without a grain of vanity
concealed under a simulated modesty, that he offers the
present treatise to the notice of his brethren with fear
and trembling.   He knows that what is offered to them
should, both as to matter and manner, be worthy of
their attention; and had he to sustain a literary reputation for which he was jealous, he would feel still

more solicitude about the reception of his work; yet as he aims at nothing but usefulness, without making any pretensions to a finished style, he can only express a hope that they may not deem this offering unworthy their attention, and respectfully ask them to accept it as an affectionate endeavour to aid their usefulness, made in his own way. God has helped him to do something for his cause, and knowing how that has been done, he is anxious to draw others into the same way. And now that his shadow lengthens on the plain, and his eye is fixed on the declining sun, he feels, in the review of life, that the thought of having done any thing to save souls from death gives him far more delight than he could have derived from having made the largest acquirements in learning and science, or from having gained a reputation for genius and taste. There is a time coming to every man when the knowledge of having been the instrument of plucking a single brand from the eternal burning, will yield him more real satisfaction than the certainty of having accomplished the loftiest objects of literary ambition.

The author anticipates a remark which will be made by many of the readers of this volume, that it is in some measure, a book of extracts. They will, however, have little cause to complain of this, since what he has given from the stores of other men's thoughts is much better than any thing he could have brought from his own. Besides, in so important a matter as advice to the ministry, he was anxious to be sustained in what he advanced, by the authority of men whose names and counsels would carry far more weight than his own. Be it so that the book presents the appearance of mosaic work; the author is quite content that

his own part of the volume should be the setting
of stones so precious.

There will be found some repetitions of thought,
and even of expression in the work; and this was
hardly to be avoided from the nature of the subject.
It is a poor excuse for imperfections, to plead the
want of time for correcting them; and yet it is the
best excuse the author has to make for the many that
will be found in his little volume. His situation exposes him to a thousand vexatious interruptions, which
many in more retired nooks never suffer. These pages
have been written amidst such abounding and various
occupations, that they could be composed only during
snatches of time redeemed from other duties, and in
brief intervals of busy activity. But if this effort
should do nothing more than draw the attention of
writers in our reviews and magazines, as well as of our
more able authors, to a renewed consideration of that
most vital point, our ministry, it will, however humble
its pretensions and low its merits, have accomplished
a high and holy work.

APRIL, 1847.

PREFACE TO THE THIRD EDITION.

IT is not with vanity, but gratitude, that the author of this volume refers to the fact of a third edition of it having been called for within six months after the publication of the first: and he willingly and joyfully considers this rapid sale rather as an indication of the deep interest taken in the subject, than as a proof of approbation of the manner in which it has been here treated. Scarcely anything could be a more hopeful sign of the times, religiously viewed, than this interest in a matter so deeply involving the eternal welfare of mankind, as that of an "Earnest Ministry." Whether the author has, or has not, ability to excite and guide this earnestness, it is evident, from the sale of his volume, that there is a prevailing disposition to consider the subject: and that multitudes are prepared to be moved to greater intensity of feeling and energy of action in their high and holy vocation, if any one can be found to give the impulse.

The author has had abundantly more than enough to gratify him, and to reward him for his labour, in the private acknowledgements he has received from various quarters, and in the notice which has been taken of his treatise by the periodicals; but he is still anxious that the editors of our leading journals devoted to religious literature, should call some of their ablest writers to the subject, who would speak with a power and authority not possessed by his pen. Intently bent upon it himself, how gladly would he sink into the shadow of some of these gifted men, if they would come forward and fill the land and the age with a sense of the importance of a competent, energetic, and efficient ministry. One has already done much to accomplish this object; to Dr. Vaughan we stand indebted for his valuable work on the Modern Pulpit. May we soon see another contribution to it from his pen in the pages of the " British Quarterly !" The pulpit, notwithstanding the influence of the press, must still remain the main lever of the moral world ; how much therefore does it become all those who are concerned for the spiritual interests of the community, to endeavour to augment the force of this so powerful engine. The friends of evangelical doctrine, and the advocates of orthodoxy, have the following objects to keep ever in view in this age; they must take care of their Bibles, that they be not mutilated or curtailed by lawless criticism; they must take care of their theology, that it be not perverted by false philosophy; and they must take care of their pulpits, that they be not occupied by heretical, unspiritual, or incompetent ministers.

October 19, 1847.

CHAPTER I.

THE APOSTOLIC MINISTRY.

" Now then we are ambassadors for Christ; as though God did beseech you by us, we pray you in Christ's stead, be ye reconciled to God." 2 COR. v, 20.

IN this truly wonderful passage, viewed in connection with its context, are set before us with beautiful simplicity, yet with surpassing grandeur, the theme, the design, and the method, of the Christian ministry. The theme is God reconciling the world to himself; a subject compared with which the negotiations of hostile nations and the treaties which put an end to the horrors of war, and bind in concord the fiercest passions of humanity, are matters of only momentary and limited importance. The design of the ministry, which is strictly in harmony with its theme, is to bring sinful men into actual reconciliation with God, on the ground of that system of mediation through Christ which God himself has devised and proclaimed. And its method is the earnestness of persuasion addressed to the rebel heart of man, in order to induce him to lay aside his enmity against his offended Sovereign, and to accept this offer of a gracious amnesty. The union and the harmony of these three views of the ministry are singularly

impressive : he who leaves out the great scheme of
christian reconciliation from his habitual ministrations,
omits the divinely appointed theme ; he who does not
supremely aim to bring sinners into a state of actual
friendship with God, falls short of the design of the
sacred office ; and he who does not employ for the purpose
all the arts and means of persuasion, mistakes or
undervalues the divinely prescribed method of fulfilling
its duties.

As the apostle is writing to a Christian church, it is
perhaps a matter of surprise to some that he should
entreat them to be reconciled to God, since by their
very profession of religion they must have been supposed
to be already in that state. Upon looking attentively
at the passage as it stands in the Bible, the reader will
perceive that the pronouns of the second person are in
italics, intimating that they are not in the original
Greek, but are supplied in our English translation to
complete the sense ; consequently any other word that
would accomplish this better may be substituted for
them. If therefore we put the substantive "men,"
instead of the pronoun "you" in the first clause of the
verse, and the pronoun of the third person "them" for
the pronoun of the second person "you" in the latter
clause, we shall avoid the improbability of the apostle
calling upon professing Christians to come into a state
to which they must be supposed to have already attained,
and the text will then show what he intended to set
forth, the usual manner in which he discharged the
functions of his momentous office. With this alteration it would read thus, "As ambassadors for Christ,
as though God did beseech 'men' by us, we pray 'them'
in Christ's stead to be reconciled to God." It is as

if he had said, "wherever we go, we find men in un-
provoked hostility, inveterate enmity, and mad rebellion, against God's holy nature, law, and government :
we carry with us, as his ambassadors, the proclamation
of mercy through the mediation of our Lord Jesus
Christ : we tell them that we are appointed by God
whom they have offended, and who could overwhelm
them with the terrors of his justice, to call upon them
to lay down their arms and accept the offer of eternal
pardon and peace : but we find them every where so
bent upon their sins, and the enjoyment of their worldly
occupations and possessions, that we are compelled to
use the language of the most vehement entreaty, and
to beseech and implore them in God's name, and in
Christ's stead, to come into a state of reconciliation."

The apostle not only used the most intense earnestness of entreaty, as an expression of his own concern,
but he told the objects of his imploring anxiety that his
importunity for their welfare was but an imitation of,
and a substitute for, that of God himself; that his
beseeching solicitation to them, on behalf of their
own salvation, was uttered in Christ's stead. This is
the most wonderful scene that the universe will ever
witness ; a beseeching God, an imploring Saviour,
standing at the door of the sinner's heart with eternal
salvation in his hand, knocking for entrance and beg-
ging to be let in ; the insulted Omnipotent Creator of
the universe, beseeching a worm, whom an exercise of
his will could sink in a moment to perdition, and his
justice be glorified in the act, to accept his pardon-
ing mercy, and waiting year after year, in all long-
suffering, for the sinner's reconsideration of his obstinate
refusals. Be astonished, O heaven, at God's unutter-

able mercy, and be horribly afraid, O earth, at man's indescribable wickedness! Here is the climax of God's divine love, and man's desperate depravity. Divine benevolence did not reach its uttermost when Jesus Christ was nailed to the cross; that was reserved for the scene before us.

I might with ineffable delight expatiate at length on this scene of matchless mercy, but let me pass on to other applications of the passage appropriate to the subject before us. And what a view does it give us of the Christian ministry! It is an embassy from God to man, and therefore most dignified and honourable. I admit that it is only in a qualified sense that the title and office of an "ambassador" for Christ can be applied to the ordinary ministers of the gospel; but in a subordinate sense it may be applied to them, since they are ordained to do what he would do were he personally present; they are to propose the same blessings, to lay down the same terms of peace, as he would were he again on earth; and therefore are, so far, his ambassadors. And if the honour of an ambassador be in proportion to the power and glory of the sovereign who employs him, what is the dignity of him who is the ambassador of the King of Kings and Lord of Lords; and at the same time, what ought to be the sanctity of his conduct, and the elevation of his character? If nothing unworthy of the monarch who sends him, and the nation which he represents, should be done by him who is despatched on an embassy to a foreign court and people, how vigilant and solicitous to do nothing unworthy of God and his Christ, should he be whose business it is to negotiate with man the weighty affairs of judgment and of mercy from heaven! If he bears the dignity of his office, let him associate with it a corresponding dignity of character. How natural, how just, how necessary, the reflection, " I am an ambassador for Christ; what manner of person ought I to be in all holy conversation and godliness ; what should I be who represent, so far as my office is concerned, the majesty of heaven and earth !"

The ministry of the gospel is shown in this passage to be an embassy of peace : this is its very designation, " the ministry of reconciliation." Never was a more beautiful idea expressed or conceived : nothing could be devised to throw over the ministry the charm of greater loveliness. If in one hand the preacher of the gospel carry the sword of the Spirit, it is only to slay the sin; while he holds forth the olive branch in the other, as the token of peace and life to the sinner. He enters the scene of strife and discord to harmonize the jarring elements, and goes to the field of conflict to reconcile the contending parties. It is his to proclaim the treaty of man's peace with God, to explain its terms, to urge its acceptance, and to bring the sinner into friendship with his offended lawgiver; to carry peace into man's troubled bosom, and reconcile him to his own conscience; to cast out the enmity and prejudices of his selfish and depraved heart, and to unite him by charity to his fellows; to calm down the violence of his temper, and give him peace on earth, and at last to conduct him to the realms of undisturbed tranquillity in the celestial world. This is his business. Angels hover over him in his course, and chant over his labours their ancient song, " Glory to God in the highest, and on earth peace, good will toward men ;" redeemed men and women, saved by his instrumentality from the wrath of God, and the turbulence of passion, hail him in the language of the prophet, " How beautiful upon the mountains are the feet of him that bringeth good tidings, that publisheth peace;" while the Saviour himself pronounces upon him the beatitude, "Blessed are the peace-makers, for they shall be called the children of God." Honoured and happy man, minister of reconciliation, friend and promoter of peace, the world knows thee not, because it knew not Christ; nor, perhaps, does even the church duly appreciate, or adequately reward, thy services; but even now thy work is its own reward: peace attends upon thy steps, and blessings spring up in thy path.

But still it is an embassy of difficulty. It is to treat with those who are unwilling to be saved, and to persuade the sinful, proud, and stubborn hearts of men to capitulate to holiness and grace. The minister carries the offer of infinite and ineffable blessedness, but it is to men who have no taste for that species of felicity. His were an easy office did he find men every where predisposed to close with the proposals of infinite benevolence; but wherever he goes he meets with hearts not only indifferent, but hostile, to his message. The parable which represents the excuses made for not coming to the marriage feast, is still applicable to the children of men in reference to the invitations of the gospel: men are as they ever were, too busy, or too well satisfied with their enjoyments and possessions, to care about salvation. They are madly set upon the objects of the present world; they are asleep, and need to be roused; careless, and need to be interested; indolent, and need to be stimulated; and it is with the greatest difficulty we can engage their attention to the invisible realities of eternity. No one who leaves out of view the desperate wickedness of the human heart, can form a true estimate of the nature, design, and difficulties of the ministerial office : and the reason why there is so little of hard labour, and intense earnestness, and beseeching entreaty, in the ministers of the gospel, is, that there is the want of a deep conviction, or proper consideration, of the resistance to their endeavours in the sinner's heart, which is perpetually meeting them.

This brings me to the subject of the present discourse, and that is the necessity of an earnest ministry. Nothing less than earnestness can succeed in any cases of great difficulty, and the earnestness must of course be in proportion to the difficulty to be surmounted. Great obstacles cannot be overcome without intense application of the mind. How then can the work of the ministry be accomplished? Every view we can take of it replies, " Only by earnestness." Every syllable of the apostle's language replies, "Only by earnestness." Every survey we can take of human nature replies, " Only by earnestness." Every recollection of our own experience, as well as every observation we can make of the experience of others, replies, " Only by earnestness." This, this is what we want, and must have, if the ends of the gospel are ever to be extensively accomplished, an earnest ministry.

We have heard much of late about a learned ministry, and God forbid we should ever be afflicted by so great an evil as an unlearned one. We have been often reminded of the necessity of an educated ministry ; and in this case, as in every other, men must be educated for their vocation ; but then that education must be strictly appropriate and specific. We are very properly told from many quarters, we can do nothing without a pious ministry. This is very true, nor can any truth bearing upon this subject be more momentous; for of all the curses which God ever pours from the vials of his wrath upon a nation which he intends to scourge, there is not one so fearful as giving them up to an unholy ministry. And I trust our churches will ever consider piety as the first and most essential qualification in their pastors, for which talents, genius, learning, and eloquence, would and could be no substitutes. It will be a dark and evil day when personal godliness shall be considered as secondary to any other quality in those who serve at the altar of God. But still there is something else wanted in addition to natural talent, to academic training, and even to the most fervent evangelical piety, and that is, intense devotedness. This is the one thing, more than any or all other things, that is wanting in the modern pulpit, and that has been wanting in most ages of the Christian church. The following sentence occurs in a valuable article in a late number of the British Quarterly Review: "No ministry will be really effective, whatever may be its intelligence, which is not a ministry of strong faith, true spirituality, and deep earnestness." I wish this golden sentence could be inscribed in characters of light over every professor's chair, over every student's desk, and over every preacher's pulpit. Condensed into that one short paragraph is every thing that needs be said on this subject. I feel that every syllable I have to write would be superfluous, if all our pastors, students, and tutors, would let that one sentence take full occupation of their hearts, possess their whole souls, and regulate their conduct. The most I can hope to accomplish is to expand and enforce it.

CHAPTER II.

THE NATURE OF EARNESTNESS.

PERHAPS there is scarcely one single phrase more frequently employed, or better understood, in the sphere of human activity, than this, "Be in earnest." What distinctness of aim, what fixedness of purpose, what resoluteness of will, what diligence, patience, and perseverance in action, are implied or expressed in these three words. He who would stimulate indolence, quicken activity, and inspire hope; he who would breathe his own spirit into the soul of another, and excite there the enthusiasm which glows in his own bosom, says to his fellow, "Be in earnest:" and that short sentence, a scintillation flying off from a burning mind, has often in lighting upon another spirit, kindled the flames of enthusiasm in it also. And what else, or what less, does Jesus Christ say to every one whom he sends into the work of the Christian ministry than, "Be in earnest?"

There is something in the aspect and power of earnestness, whatever be its object, that is impressive and commanding. A man who has selected some one object of pursuit, and then yielded up himself to the desire of its attainment, with a devotion admitting of no reserve, a steadiness of aim allowing of no diversion, a diligence consenting neither to rest nor intermission; and who ever retains this purpose so far uppermost in his heart as to fill his conversation, and so entirely and constantly before his mind as to throw into its broad shadow every other subject of consideration; such an instance of decision, amounting to a ruling passion, gains a strange fascination over the feelings of others, and exerts over us, while witnessing it, an influence which we feel to be contagious. We involuntarily sympathise with a man who is thus carried away by his fervour; and if all his earnestness is for the promotion of our interests, its effect is irresistible. That man must be a stone, and destitute of the ordinary feelings of humanity, who can see another, interested, active, and zealous for his welfare, while he himself remains inert and indifferent. Even the apathetic and indolent have been kindled into ardour, and led to make efforts for themselves, by solicitude manifested by others for their welfare.

How strictly does this apply to the ministry of God's word, which relates to the most momentous matters that can engage the attention of the human understanding. Sympathy is a law of our mental being which has never been sufficiently taken into account in estimating the influences which God employs for the salvation of men. There is a silent and almost unconscious process often going on in the minds of those who are listening to the sermons of a preacher really labouring for the conversion of souls. "Is he so earnest about my salvation, and shall I care nothing about the matter? Is my eternal happiness so much in his account, and shall it be nothing in mine? I can meet cold logic with counter arguments; or at any rate, I can raise up objections against evidence. I can smile at the artifices of rhetoric, and be merely pleased with the displays of eloquence. I can sit unmoved under sermons which seem intended by the preacher to raise my estimate of himself, but I cannot stand this earnestness about me. The man is evidently intent upon saving my soul. I feel the grasp of his hand upon my arm, as if he would pluck me out of the fire. He has not only made me think, but he has made me feel. His earnestness has subdued me."

But it will be necessary now to meet and answer the question, What is meant by an earnest ministry?

I. In the first place then, earnestness implies, the selection of some one object of special pursuit, and a vivid perception of its value and importance. It is next to impossible for the mind to be intently employed, or the heart to be very deeply engaged, on a multiplicity of objects at once. We have not energy enough to be so divided and distributed. Our feelings to run with force must flow pretty much in one channel: our attention must be concentrated, our purpose settled, our energy exerted, upon one thing, or we can do nothing effectually. The earnest man is a man of one idea, and that one idea occupies possesses and fills his soul. To every other claimant upon his time, and interest, and labour, he says, "Stand by; I am engaged, I cannot attend to you; something else is waiting for me." To that one thing he is committed. There may be many subordinate matters amongst which he divides any surplus water, but the current flows through one channel, and turns one great wheel. This "one thing I do," is his plan and resolution. Many wonder at his choice, many condemn it : no matter, he understands it, approves it, and pursues it, notwithstanding the ignorance which cannot comprehend it, and the diversity of taste which cannot admire it. He is no double-minded man, unstable in all his ways, whose preference and purpose are shaken by every cross gale of opinion. It is nothing to him what others do, or what they say as to what he does: he must do that, whatever else he leaves undone. No one can be in earnest who has not thus made up his mind; and he who has, and is resolutely bent upon an object, keeps it constantly before his mind; his attention is so strongly and tenaciously fixed upon it, that even at the greatest distance, "like the Egyptian pyramids to travellers, it appears to him with a luminous distinctness, as if it were nigh, and beguiles the toilsome length of labour and enterprise by which he must reach it." It is so conspicuous before him that he does not deviate a step from the right direction, he ever hears a voice calling him onward, and every movement and every day brings him nearer to the end of his journey. Break in upon him at any moment, you know where you will find him and how he will be employed.

This is the first part of the description of an earnest minister: he too has selected his object, and made up his mind concerning it, and insulating it from all others, sets it clearly and distinctly before his mind; and what is it? What should it be? Not science, or literature, or philosophy; not a life spent in the acquisition of knowledge, or the gratification of taste; not the power of adding to the treasures of knowledge or learning accumulated during ages, or to the elegancies which embellish civilized existence, and give amenity to social intercourse. The man who has entered the sacred office merely to luxuriate in the haunts of the muses, has mistaken his vocation to the pulpit, and is no less guilty though somewhat less sordid than he who says, " Put me into the priest's office, that I may eat a morsel of bread." That a minister may to a certain extent indulge a literary or scientific taste, and that he may even make it subservient to a higher and more sacred object, is admitted. The pulpit has done, and is doing, much service in all the departments of learning and philosophy. It is in Christian countries that the valuable remains of Eastern, Greek, and Roman wisdom and eloquence have been preserved, studied, imitated, and sometimes even excelled. Christian nations have conducted philosophical inquiries with the best success, and improved them for the most useful and benevolent purposes.

" If these things are good and profitable unto society, a large portion of the honour of such usefulness belongs to men set for the defence of the gospel, desirous by sound reasoning to convince gain-sayers, and conscious what arms human literature furnishes for this holy war. And then in addition to all this, consider the effect of the pulpit upon what might be called the popular mind. To thousands who have comparatively little leisure or opportunity to form their taste, and cultivate their rational powers, by conversation with the wise and enlightened, or by reading their works, a school is thus open, established indeed for higher purposes, where men of sound understandings, though low in rank, may without expense, and almost without intending it, learn from example to distinguish or connect ideas, to infer one truth from another, to examine the force of an argument, and so to arrange and express their sentiments as deeply to impress themselves and others. As in a few years the child gradually acquires the faculty of speaking his mother-tongue with a considerable degree of ease and fluency, without any formal lessons, merely by hearing it spoken, so there is a natural logic and rhetoric which some acquire without designing it, who go to church for nobler ends, whereby they are enabled to detect the cunning craftiness which the enemies of religion or of public tranquillity, lie in wait to deceive. Indeed the culture of the talents and improvement of that respectable class of men who earn their bread by the sweat of their brow, generally rises or falls in proportion to the character and genius of their religious discourses." *

This is as true as it is beautiful, and should remind all ministers of the gospel of the necessity and importance at all times, but especially in such times as these, of keeping in mind the collateral and secondary objects of pulpit instruction, and of preparing themselves for conducting it with power and efficiency. There is not a temporal interest of man as an individual, or a member of society, on which the sermons and general influence of the ministry may not be made to bear advantageously ; but then it must never be forgotten that the things which have just been enumerated are at best only the incidental, secondary, and collateral benefits of the ministry of the word : they are among the many things that may be touched, but are not the one thing that must be grasped : they are little rills diverted from the main stream for the purposes of irrigation, but are not the river itself, bearing wealth and civilization to the nations between whom it rolls.

Nor is it the great object of our ministry merely to preside with dignity over the solemnities of public worship; to content ourselves and please our people with preparing and delivering two well studied discourses on the Sabbath; to keep all quiet and orderly in the church ; to maintain a kind of religious respectability and intellectuality in the congregation. The end and aim of the ministry are to be gathered from the apostle's solemn and comprehensive language, " they watch for your souls as they that must give account." There in that

* Discourses by Dr. John Erskine.

short, but sublime and awful sentence, the end of the pastoral office is set before us. The design of the pulpit is identical with that of the cross: and the preacher is to carry out the design of the Saviour in coming to seek and to save that which was lost. Preaching and teaching are the very agency which Jesus Christ employs to save those souls for which he died upon Calvary. If souls are not saved, whatever other designs are accomplished, the great purpose of the ministry is defeated.

You are now prepared to understand what is the nature of real earnestness in a minister of Christ; a distinct, explicit, practical recognition of his duty to labour for the salvation of souls as the end of his office. Such a man has settled with himself that this is his vocation and business. He has looked at every thing else which can be presented to his mind, has weighed the claims of all, and with intelligence and firmness has said, and is prepared to stand by his affirmation, " I watch for souls." He thus understands his errand; he is under no mistake, no uncertainty, no confusion. He has entered into fellowship with God the Father in his eternal purpose of the salvation of the human race; with the Son in the end of his incarnation and death; and with the Holy Spirit in the intent of his coming down upon our desolate world. Of this salvation which is the object of his ministry, the prophets inquired; to accomplish it prophets preached, and angels ministered; and thus justified in his choice by the Triune God and the noblest of his creatures, he leaves far below him, in the aspirations and soarings of his ambition, the scholar, the philosopher, and the poet. He has taken up an object in reference to which, if he succeed but in a single instance, he will have achieved a triumph which will endure infinite ages after the proudest monuments of human genius have perished in the conflagration of the world.

"The salvation of souls" as the great object of the ministerial office, is a generic phrase, including as its species, the awakening of the unconcerned; the guidance of the inquiring; the instruction of the uninformed; and the sanctification, comfort, and progress of those who through grace have believed; in short the whole work of grace in the soul. But the attention of the reader is directed to the first of these particulars as the most commanding object of ministerial solicitude, I mean the conversion of the unregenerate; and if without offending against the law of modesty I may refer to my own history, labours and success, I would observe, that I began my ministry, even as a student, with a strong desire after this object; and long before this, while yet a youth engaged in secular concerns, I had been deeply susceptible of the power of an awakening style of preaching, and had been wrought upon by the rousing sermons of Dr. Davies* of New Jersey. From that time to the present I have made the conversion of the impenitent the great end of my ministry, and I have had my reward. I have been sustained in this course by the remarks of Baxter, in his "Reformed Pastor," a long extract from which I must now be permitted to introduce.

* I wish these discourses were better known, and more imitated by our young ministers. They are admirable specimens of persuasive, hortatory, and impressive preaching, formed upon the model of Baxter. It is such preaching we want. In these striking discourses may be seen what I mean by earnest preaching. They are by no means scarce, and I would advise my younger brethren to buy and read them.

"We must labour in a special manner for the conversion of the unconverted. The work of conversion is the great thing we must drive at; after this we must labour with all our might. Alas! the misery of the unconverted is so great that it calleth loudest to us for compassion. If a truly converted sinner do fall, it will be but into sin which will be pardoned, and he is not in that hazard of damnation by it as others are. Not but that God hateth their sins as well as others, or that he will bring them to heaven, let them live ever so wickedly; but the spirit that is within them will not suffer them to live wickedly, nor to sin as the ungodly do. But with the unconverted it is far otherwise. They 'are in the gall of bitterness, and in the bond of iniquity,' and have yet no part nor fellowship in the pardon of their sins, or the hope of glory. We have therefore a work of greater necessity to do for them, even 'to open their eyes, and to turn them from darkness to light, and from the power of Satan unto God; that they may receive forgiveness of sins, and an inheritance among them who are sanctified.' He that seeth one man sick of a mortal disease and another only pained with the tooth-ache, will be moved more to compassionate the former than the latter, and will surely make more haste to help him, though he were a stranger, and the other a brother or a son. It is so sad a case to see men in a state of damnation, wherein, if they should die, they are lost for ever, that methinks we should not be able to let them alone, either in public or private, whatever other work we have to do. I confess I am frequently forced to neglect that which should tend to the further increase of knowledge in the godly, because of the lamentable necessity of the unconverted. Who is able to talk of controversies, or of nice, unnecessary points, or even of truths of a lower degree of necessity, how excellent soever, while he seeth a company of ignorant, carnal, miserable sinners before his eyes, who must be changed or damned? Methinks I even see them entering upon their final woe! Methinks I hear them crying out for help, for speediest help! Their misery speaks the louder, because they have not hearts to ask for help themselves. Many a time have I known that I had some hearers of higher fancies, that looked for rarities, and were addicted to despise the ministry if I told them not something more than ordinary; and yet I could not find in my heart to turn from the necessities of the impenitent for the humouring of them; nor even to leave speaking to miserable sinners for their salvation, in order to speak so much as should otherwise be done to weak saints for their confirmation and increase in grace. Methinks as Paul's 'spirit was stirred within

him,' when he saw 'the Athenians wholly given to idolatry,' so it
should cast us into one of his paroxysms to see so many men in the
greatest danger of being everlastingly undone. Methinks if by faith
we did indeed look upon them as within a step of hell, it would more
effectually untie our tongues than Crœsus' danger did his son's. He
that will let a sinner go down to hell for want of speaking to him,
doth set less by souls than did the Redeemer of souls; and less by
his neighbour than common charity will allow him to do by his
greatest enemy. O therefore, brethren, whomsoever you neglect,
neglect not the most miserable! Whatever you pass over, forget not
poor souls that are under the condemnation and curse of the law, and
who may look every hour for the infernal execution if a speedy
change do not prevent it. O call after the impenitent, and ply this
great work of converting souls, whatever else you leave undone!"

The editor of Baxter says :

"These powerful and impressive observations we cannot too
earnestly recommend to the attention of ministers. We have no
hesitation in saying that the most of preachers whom we have known
were essentially defective in the grand and primary object of the
Christian ministry, labouring for the conversion of souls. From the
general strain of some men's preaching, one would almost be ready
to conclude that there were no sinners in their congregations to be
converted. In determining the proportion of attention which a
minister should pay to particular classes of his congregation, the
number of each class, and the necessities of their case, are unquestionably the principal considerations which should weigh with him.
Now in all our congregations we have reason to fear the unconverted
constitute by far the majority; their situation is peculiarly pitiable;
their opportunities of salvation will soon be for ever over; their
danger is not only very great, but very imminent; they are not
secure from everlasting misery, even for a single moment. Surely
then the unconverted demand by far the largest share of the christian
minister's attention, and yet from many they receive but a very
small share of attention; their case, when noticed at all, is noticed
only, as it were, by the bye. This, no doubt, is a principal cause
that amongst us there are so few conversions by the preaching of the
word, and especially in the congregations of particular ministers.
We feel this subject to be of such transcendent importance that we
trust we shall be excused for here introducing a quotation connected

with it, from another work of our author, which has been introduced
into the series of 'Select Christian Authors.'"

"It is not', says he, in his 'Mischiefs of Self-Ignorance,' 'a general
dull discourse, or critical observations upon words, or the subtle
decision of some nice and curious questions of the schools, nor is it a
neat and well-composed speech, about some other distant matters,
that is like to acquaint a sinner with himself. How many sermons
may we hear that are levelled at some mark or other which is very
far from the hearers' hearts, and therefore are never likely to convince
them, or open and convert them! And if our congregations were in
such a case as that they needed no closer quickening work, such
preaching might be borne with and commended. But when so many
usually sit before us that must shortly die, and yet are unprepared
for death; and that are condemned by the law of God, and must be
pardoned or finally condemned; that must be saved from their sins
that they may be saved from everlasting misery; I think it is time
for us to talk to them of such things as most concern them, and that
in such a manner as may most effectually convince, awaken, and
change them.

"A man that is ready to be drowned is not at leisure for a song
or a dance; and a man that is ready to be hanged, methinks, should
not find himself at leisure to hear a man show his wit and reading
only, if not his folly and malice, against a life of holiness. Nor
should you think that suitable to such men's case that doth not
evidently tend to save them. But alas! how often have we heard
such sermons as tend more to diversion than direction, to fill their
minds with other matters, and find them something else to think
of, lest they should study themselves, and know their misery! A
preacher that seems to speak religiously by a dry, sapless discourse,
that is called a sermon, may more plausibly and easily ruin him. And
his conscience will more quietly suffer him to be taken off the
necessary care of his salvation, by something that is like it, and
pretends to do the work as well, than by the grosser avocations or
the scorn of fools. And he will be more tamely turned from religion
by something that is called religion, and which he hopes may serve
the turn, than by open wickedness or impious defiance of God and
reason. But how often do we hear sermons applauded, which force
us in compassion to men's souls to think, 'O what is all this to the
opening of a sinner's heart unto himself, and showing him his unregenerate state? What is this to the conviction of a self-deluding
soul, that is passing into hell, with the confident expectations of

heaven? What is this to show men their undone condition, and the absolute necessity of Christ, and of renewing grace? What is in this to lead men up from earth to heaven, and to acquaint them with the unseen world, and to help them to the life of faith and love, and to the mortifying and pardon of their sins?' How little skill have many miserable preachers in the searching of the heart, and helping men to know themselves, whether Christ be in them, or whether they be reprobates? And how little care and diligence is used by them to call men to the trial, and help them in the examining and judging of themselves, as if it were a work of no necessity? 'They have healed the hurt of the daughter of my people slightly, saying, Peace, peace, when there is no peace, saith the Lord.'"

Oh what preachers we should be, could we drink into the spirit of these powerful passages! May God impress them on our hearts, and lead us to mould our discourses after their fashion. We should, however, by no means be unmindful of the importance of building up the believer on his holy faith. Not only must the children of the redeemed family be born, but they must also be fed, watched, guided, and nourished up to manhood. The growth of the heirs of immortality in grace and knowledge must be an object of deep solicitude with the faithful pastor. His children in the faith are not glorified as soon as converted, but are carried through a probation, and often a long one, of conflict, trial, and temptation; and it is his business, by the instrumentality of the truth, deeply searched, carefully expounded, and appropriately applied, to conduct them through the perplexities and the dangers of the divine life. Hence, therefore, it is the duty of the minister, not to be always dwelling on first principles, and teaching the mere alphabet of Bible knowledge, but to lead his people " on unto perfection;" yet still he is never to forget that by far the greater number of those who are before him do not experimentally know these first principles, and have not learnt even this alphabet of practical piety. I once had a member of my church, who had been brought out of the literary world to a deep, experimental knowledge of divine truth. She was a woman of uncommonly fine and tasteful mind. After her conversion she dwelt for a season in London, and on her return from the metropolis, in giving an account of the various preachers she had heard, expressed her surprise and regret that their sermons, however excellent, seemed to be addressed almost exclusively to true believers, as if they took it for granted that their congregations were composed wholly of such, and contained none who were dead in trespasses and sins. And I know a devoted and consistent Christian, who, upon leaving a minister whom he had attended for several years, declared he had scarcely ever heard one thoroughly practical sermon from him during the whole time: there had been much doctrinal statement, much theological science, much religious comfort; but no vivid and pungent appeals either to saints or sinners: no wonder he knew of no conversions there: and yet this preacher is not an Antinomian.

II. Earnestness implies that the subject has not only been selected, but that it has taken full possession of the mind, and has kindled towards it an intense desire of the heart.

It is something more than a correct theory and logical deductions; more than mere exercise of the intellect, and the play of the imagination: earnestness means that the understanding having selected and appreciated its object, has pressed all the faculties of both mind and body to join in the pursuit of it. It urges the soul onward in its career of action at such a speed that it is set on fire by the velocity of its own motion. The object of an earnest man is never for any long period of time absent from his thoughts. He meditates on it by day, and dreams of it by night: it meets him in his solitary walks as some bright vision which he loves to contemplate, and it comes over him in company with such power that he cannot avoid making it the topic of his conversation, till he appears in the eyes of those who have no sympathy with him, in the light of an enthusiast.

Foster, in his "Essay on Decision of Character," has alluded to Howard as supplying a fine illustration of this mental quality. I furnish one extract bearing more directly than perhaps any other on our present theme. It relates to the singular fact that this great philanthropist turned not a moment from his course, when traversing scenes most calculated to awaken curiosity, and to enkindle enthusiasm by the associations of ancient glory with which they are connected, even Rome itself.

"The importance of his object held his faculties in a state of excitement which was too rigid to be affected by lighter interests, and on which, therefore, the beauties of nature and art had no power: like the invisible spirits who fulfil their commission of philanthropy among mortals, and care not about pictures, statues, and sumptuous buildings. It implied an inconceivable severity of conviction that he had one thing to do; and that he who would do some great thing in this short life, must apply himself to the work with such a concentration of his forces, as, to idle spectators, who live only to amuse themselves, looks like insanity. It was thus he made the trial, so seldom made, what is the utmost effect which may be granted to the last possible effort of a human agent; and therefore what he did not accomplish, he might conclude to be placed beyond the sphere of mortal activity, and calmly leave to the disposal of Omnipotence."

There, again, is the representation of the really and

intensely earnest minister of Jesus Christ, and of the manner in which he regards the object of his ministry, the salvation of immortal souls. He has drunk in the inspiration of those inexpressibly sublime and solemn words, so often already quoted, "They watch for your souls, as they that must give account, that they may do it with joy, and not with grief." This declaration has come over him like a spell, from the fascination of which he neither tries nor wishes to escape. Whether seated in his chair in his study, or carrying on the exercises of devotion in the closet, or preaching the gospel in the pulpit, or enjoying the pleasures of Christian friendship in the social circle, or recreating his energies amidst the beauties of creation, the words of Solomon stand conspicuously before his mind's eye, "He that winneth souls is wise." While, ever and anon, the thunder of Christ's awful inquiry comes pealing over his ear; "What shall it profit a man if he gain the whole world, and lose his own soul; or what shall a man give in exchange for his soul?" To be useful in converting souls is his constant and practical aim : and his texts are chosen, his sermons are composed and delivered, and his language, figures, and illustrations are selected, with a view to this. That word, usefulness, has the same meaning in his ear, the same power over his soul, as the word "victory" has over the mind of the hero : and the preparation and delivery of the most eloquent sermons, with all the plaudits that follow them, will no more satisfy his ambition, than the skilful evolutions, the military splendour, and the martial music of a field-day, however they may be admired by the multitudinous spectators, will content the desires of the patriot warrior who burns to defeat his country's foe upon the field

of battle, and to rescue the liberties of his enslaved
nation from the grasp of its tyrant.   By the earnest
minister, the salvation of souls is sought with the obligation of a principle, and the ardour of a passion.   It
is impressed upon his whole character, and is inseparable from his conduct.   It distinguishes him among,
and from, many of his brethren.   When congregations
either at home or abroad go to hear him, they know
what to expect, and consequently do not look for the
flowers of rhetoric, but for the fruit of the tree of life;
not for a dry crust of philosophy, or a petrifaction
of criticism, but for the bread which comes down from
heaven ; not for a display of religious fireworks, splendid
but useless, but for the holding up of the torch of eternal
truth in all its brightness to guide wandering and
benighted souls to the refuge of the lost.   He has by
the usual style of his pulpit discourses established his
character as a useful preacher, and those who go to hear
him would as soon expect to hear from a physician
whom they consulted when sick, a mere poetical effusion
or classical dissertation, instead of directions for their
health, as to hear such matters from this servant of
Christ, instead of a sermon calculated and designed to
do good to their souls.   He could possibly be eloquent,
profound, or learned ; and when such qualities can aid
him in securing his one great end, he does not scruple
to use them.   His aim is at the heart and conscience,
and if any thing poetic, literary, logical, or scientific,
will at any time polish and plume his shafts or sharpen
the points of his arrows, he will not reject them, but
will avail. himself of their legitimate use, that he may
the more certainly hit and pierce the mark.   This is his
motto, " If by any means I might save some."

III. But this touches a third thing implied in genuine earnestness, and that is the studious invention and diligent use of all appropriate means to accomplish the selected object. An earnest man is the last to be satisfied with mere formality, routine, and prescription. He will often survey his object, his means, and his instruments : will look back upon the past to review his course, to examine his failure and success, with the causes of each; to learn what to do, and what to avoid, for the future. His inquiries will often be, What next? What more? What better? And as the result of all this, new experiments will be tried, new plans will be laid, and new courses will be pursued. With an inextinguishable ardour, and with a resolute fixedness of purpose, he exclaims, " I must succeed. And how is it to be ?"

And shall we ministers possess nothing of this earnestness, if we are seeking the salvation of souls? Shall dull uniformity, still formality, wearisome repetitions, and rigid routine, satisfy us? Shall we never institute the inquiry, " Why have I not succeeded better in my ministry? How is it that my congregation is not larger, and my church more rapidly increasing? In what way can I account for it that the truth as it is in Jesus, which I believe I preach, is not more influential, and the doctrine of the cross is not, as it was intended to be, the power of God unto the salvation of souls? Why do I not more frequently hear addressed to me, by those who are constantly under my ministry, the anxious inquiry, ' What shall I do to be saved?' I am not wanting, as far as I know, in the regular discharge of my ordinary duties, and yet I gather little fruit of my labours, and have to utter continually the prophet's complaint, 'Who hath believed our report, and to whom is the arm of the Lord revealed?'" Do we indeed indulge in such complaints! Have we earnestness enough to pour forth such lamentations? Or is it of little consequence to us, whether the ends of the ministry are accomplished or not, provided we get our stipends, keep up our congregations to their usual size, and maintain tranquillity in our churches? Are we often seen by God's omniscient eye pacing our studies in deep thoughtfulness, solemn meditation, and rigorous self-inquisition; and after an impartial survey of our doings, and a sorrowful lamentation that we are doing no more, questioning ourselves thus? " Is there no new method to be tried, no new scheme to be devised, to increase the efficiency of my ministerial and pastoral labours? Is there nothing I can improve, correct, or add? Is there any thing particularly wanting in the matter, manner, or method of my preaching, or in my course of pastoral attention?" Surely it might be supposed that such inquiries would be often instituted into the results of a ministry so momentous as ours; that seasons would be not unfrequently set apart, especially at the close or beginning of every year, for such a purpose. The result could not fail to be beneficial.

Here it may be proper for us to look out of our own profession, and ask if the earnest tradesman, soldier, lawyer, philosopher, and mechanician, are satisfied to go on as they have done, though with ever so little success? Do we not see in all other departments of human action, where the mind is really intent on some great object, and where success has not been obtained in proportion to the labour bestowed, a dissatisfaction with past modes of action, and a determination to try new ones? And should we who watch for souls, and labour for immortality, be indifferent to success, and to the plans by which it might be secured? In calling for new methods, I want no new doctrines; no new principles; no startling eccentricities; no wild irregularities; no vagaries of enthusiasm, no phrensies of the passions; no, nothing but what the most sober judgment and the soundest reason would approve; but I do want a more inventive, as well as a more fervid, zeal in seeking the great end of our ministry. Respectable but dull uniformity, and not enthusiasm, is the side on which our danger lies. I know very well the contortions of an epileptic zeal are to be avoided, but so also is the numbness of a paralytic one; and after all, the former is less dangerous to life, and is more easily and frequently cured, than the latter. We may, as regards our preaching for instance, examine whether we have not dwelt too little on the alarming, or on the attractive, themes of revelation : whether we have not clothed our discourses too much with the terrors of the Lord : and if so, we may wisely determine to try the more winning forms of love and mercy : or whether we have not rendered the gospel powerless by a perpetual repetition of it in common-place phraseology : whether we have not been too argumentative, and resolve to be more imaginative, practical, and hortatory : whether we have not addressed ourselves too exclusively to believers, and determine to commence a style of more frequent and pungent address to the unconverted : whether we have not been too vague and general in our descriptions of sin, and become more specific and discriminating : whether we have not been too neglectful of the young, and begin a regular course of sermons to them : whether we have not had too much sameness of topic, and adopt courses of sermons on given subjects : whether we have not been too elaborate and abstract in the composition of our discourses, and come down to greater simplicity : whether we have not been too careless, and bestow more pains : whether we have not been too doctrinal, and in future make all truth bear, as it was intended to do, upon the heart, conscience, and life.

Nor must the enquiry stop here. There ought to be the same process of rigid scrutiny instituted as to the labours of the pastorate. We must review the proceedings of this momentous department, for here also is most ample scope for invention as to new plans of action. Perhaps upon inquiry we shall find out that we have neglected various channels through which our influence might have been brought to bear upon the flock committed to our care, and shall discover many ways in which we can improve upon our former plans, in the way of meeting inquirers after salvation, giving our aid to Sunday schools, setting up Bible classes, or visiting the flock. What is needed is an anxious wish to be wanting in nothing that can conduce to our usefulness, a diligent endeavour to make up every deficiency, and a mind ever inquisitive after new means and methods of doing good. Did we but adopt the plan of setting apart a day at the close of every year for solemn examination into our ministerial and pastoral doings, with the view of ascertaining our defects and neglects, to see in what way we could improve, to humble ourselves before God for the past, and to lay down new rules for the future, we should all be more

abundantly useful than we are. And does not earnestness require all this? Can we pretend to be in earnest
if we neglect these things? The idea of a minister's
going on from year to year with either little success, or
none at all, and yet never pausing to inquire how this
comes to pass, or what can be done to increase his
efficiency, is so utterly repugnant to all proper notions
of devotedness, that we are obliged to conclude, the
views such a man entertains of the design and end
of his office are radically and essentially defective.

IV. Earnestness implies a purpose and power of
subordinating every thing it meets with, selects, or
engages in, to the accomplishment of its one great
object.

An earnest man has much sagacity in discerning
even at a distance, the objects which are favourable to
his purpose; much power in seizing them as they
approach; and much tact in pressing them into his
service, and making them subserve his schemes. He
avoids at the same time the folly of letting go his main
object in pursuit of inferior ones: and of converting
what ought to be only means into ends. The operations of his mind resemble those of a vast machine, in
which the ruling power subjects to itself the thousand
little wheels and spindles that are set in motion, and
makes them all accomplish the purpose for which the
engine has been set up. Or the current of his thought
and feeling may be compared to the majestic flow
of some noble river, which receives into its stream,
numerous rivulets by which its waters are swollen, and
its power increased. So acts the earnest minister.
There are various matters which he may attend to, and

ought not to neglect, which may with great propriety be considered as means, but which cannot be viewed as the end of his high and holy calling.

The first of these which I mention is learning, and indeed general knowledge of all kinds. Literature, science, and philosophy, however excellent in themselves, and however subservient they may be rendered as means to accomplish the great ends of the ministerial office, must never be exalted into the place of those ends themselves. Viewed as subordinate and subsidiary, they cannot be too highly valued, or too diligently sought. There is not any kind or degree of knowledge which may not be made tributary to the ends of gospel ministrations. All other things being equal, he is likely to be the most useful preacher, who is the most learned one. There is nothing, there can be nothing, in literature and science, which of itself can be'injurious to a minister of Christ: the pride and vanity which produce such a result are but the weeds which flourish in a shallow and sandy soil, but wither and die in a rich deep loam. The man who decries learning as in itself mischievous to the ministry, is fit only to be torch-bearer to another Caliph Omar, and to act the part of an incendiary to all the libraries of the world. A minister may have too little piety, too little solicitude for the salvation of souls, too little devotedness, too little care to render his acquisitions subservient to the ends of his vocation, but he can never have too much knowledge.

How beautiful is the following language of Dr. Wiseman, and how correct the sentiment which it clothes and adorns.

"Perhaps the best answer that can be given to those inconsiderate Christians who say that religion needs not such foreign and meretricious aids as human learning, is that of South, 'If God hath no need of our learning, he can have still less of your ignorance.' In the spiritual temple, as well as in the ark of the covenant, there is room not only for those humbler gifts, the skins and hair cloth, but also for the gold and silver of human learning: and even the sciences themselves, daughters as they are of the uncreated wisdom, may receive consecration from seraphic piety, and be made priestesses of the Most High, by the very service in which we employ them."

"You all, I doubt not have often admired those exquisite paintings in the ceilings in the Borgia apartments of the Vatican, wherein the sciences are represented as holding their separate courts ; each enthroned upon a stately chair, with features and mien of the most noble and dignified beauty, surrounded by the emblems and most distinguished representatives of its power on earth, and seeming to claim homage from all that gaze upon it. And judge what would have been the painter's conception, and to what a sublimity of expression he would have risen, had it been his task to represent the noblest of all sciences, our divine religion, enthroned as ever becomes her to receive the fealty and worship of these her handmaids. For if, as hath been proved, they are but ministers to her superior rule, and are intended to furnish the evidences of her authority, how much above theirs must be the comeliness, and grace, and majesty, and holiness, with which she must be arrayed ! And what honour and dignity must be conferred on him who feels himself deputed to bear the tribute of these fair vassals ; and how must his admiration of their graces be enhanced, by finding himself brought so near her presence." *

This splendid passage expresses what I would urgently enforce, that literature and science may be subservient, but must be only subservient to the ends of the ministerial office.

Having thus quoted a passage from a Roman Catholic author, let me subjoin to it another from a Protestant, of a different kind indeed, but by no

* "Lectures on the Connexion between Science and Revealed Religion." Vol. 2, p. 317.

means inharmonious with it. The amiable and pious Doddridge, in his incomparable sermon on "The Evil and Danger of Neglecting Souls," says,

" Oh my brethren, let us consider how fast we are posting through this dying life, which God has assigned to us, in which we are to manage concerns of infinite moment: how fast we are passing on to the immediate presence of our Lord, to give up our account to him. You must judge for yourselves, but permit me to say for my own part, I would not for ten thousand worlds be that man, who when God shall ask him at last how he has employed most of his time, while he continued a minister of his church and had the care of souls, shall be obliged to reply, ' Lord, I have restored many corrupted passages in the classics, and illustrated many which were before obscure ; I have cleared up many intricacies in chronology or geography ; I have solved many perplexed cases in algebra ; I have refined on astrono-mical calculations, and left behind me many sheets on these curious and difficult subjects ; and these are the employments in which my life has been worn out, while preparations for the pulpit, and minis-trations in it, did not demand my more immediate attendance.' Oh Sirs, as for the waters that are drawn from these springs, how sweetly soever they may taste to a curious mind that thirsts after them, or to an ambitious mind that thirsts for the applause they sometimes procure, I fear there is too often reason to pour them out before the Lord, with rivers of penitential tears, as the blood of souls which have been forgotten, whilst these trifles have been remembered and pursued."

This is the language of a scholar, a critic, and a man of varied knowledge, whose piety as a Christian, and whose devotedness as a minister, were equal to his other attainments.

In a very elaborate and able critique on Hagenbach's " History of Doctrines," contained in the Eclectic Re-view, for September, I find the following just and ad-mirable remarks.

" We trust that among the rising ministry no one will allow himself to be tempted to the task for the mere reputation of learning. The real value of learning, in the estimate of a faithful servant of Christ, lies solely in the use that can be made of it. He who employs time and toil in rendering himself a learned man, which employed otherwise, would more effectually render him a useful man, is unfaithful to his Master. There are few things more important than the right appreciation of learning. There are some who spend their whole lives in acquiring it, in amassing hoard upon hoard; as if it were the object of life to try how much may be got in a given time ; not how much good may be done with it, or to what uses it may be turned as it is acquired. It is get, get, get; all getting and no giving. This is of a piece with the mania by which some are possessed in the mercantile world, the mania of money-making : with whom life's problem is, how they may die rich, how much they can be worth in the world, before the moment comes when they must leave it. There is one material difference between the two cases ; and, strange to say it is in favour of the rich rather than of the learned man. The rich man leaves his amassed treasures behind him ; so that, although to himself they have been of little use while he lived, and now are of none, they are not lost ; others may use them, and use them well. But he who has been acquiring learning all his days without expending it in its appropriate uses, leaves nothing behind him. He carries all with him. There is no bank for deposits of learning, as there is for lodging silver and gold. So far as his fellow-men are concerned, therefore, the money-hoarding miser does most good. And should it be thought an advantage on the side of the miser in learning, that he carries his mental stores away with him, as being treasures that belong to the immortal mind, there are two serious deductions to be made from this advantage : the first that the large proportion of what he had acquired, is of a nature to be of little use to him, in all likelihood, in the world to which he is going; and the second, that in common with the man of wealth, he carries with him to that world, the guilt, (unthought of by him here, it may be, but noted in his account with his Divine Master,) of not having laid out his acquisitions for the good he might have accomplished by them, where and when alone they could be available. Let it not be forgotten that mere learning is not wisdom ; that wisdom is learning or knowledge in union with the disposition and ability to make a right use of it. Neither let it be forgotten that there is an opposite extreme to that which has just been described. If there are some who are ever getting and never giving, there are some too who would fain be ever giving while they are never getting. They are fond of preaching, but not of reading and study. Such young ministers may be well-meaning ; but they are under the influence of a miserable mistake. Itinerants they may be, and useful ones : but efficient pastors they can never be. They may preach the simple elements of the gospel, from place to place; but for the constant regular instruction of the same flock they are utterly unfit. He must be an extraordinary man who has resources in himself for such a work, that render him independent of reading and study. Barrenness, tameness, sameness, triteness, irksome and unprofitable repetition, must be the almost invariable result of such presumption. There are some too, who, by way of honouring the Bible, make it their rule to study nothing else, not even such human helps as may fit them for understanding and illustrating its contents. This also, though a better extreme than his, who neglecting the Bible itself, studies only human opinions about it, yet is still an extreme, and an extreme which, while it professes to put honour upon the Bible, indicates no small measure of self-sufficiency. We put most honour upon the Bible, when we manifest our impression of the value of a full and clear comprehension of its contents, in the diligent application of all accessible means for the attainment of it." *

It may be conceded, that we live in an age when to carry out the main purpose of the christian ministry, and to render it efficient for the salvation of souls, higher ministerial qualifications, and larger acquirements of general knowledge are required, than at any former period.

It will be clearly seen from all this, that I am not decrying education, or learning, or the greatest diligence in ministers for the acquisition of knowledge. Quite the contrary : but I am enforcing, with all the earnestness I can command, the indispensable necessity

* The whole critique, of which this is a quotation, is of inestimable value, and makes one rejoice that we have periodicals, and able writers in them, to use this writer's own remark, " too old-fashioned and puritanical to endure" much of what is now coming from even the orthodox German school of theology ; periodicals and writers, that will continue, it is ardently hoped, to use their critical and evangelical sieve to winnow the works now being, in such numbers, translated from German into English, which though they have much wheat, have also some chaff.

of rendering all acquirements subordinate to the great work of saving souls. Learning as an ultimate object and for its own sake, is infinitely below the ambition of a holy and devoted servant of Christ; but learning employed to invigorate the intellect, to enrich the imagination, to cultivate the taste, to give power to thought, and variety to illustration; to add to the skill and energy with which we wield the weapons of our warfare, is in some cases indispensable, and in all invaluable. Unhappily it is not uncommon for those who have made acquisitions in varied learning, or acquired a scientific, philosophic, or literary taste, to yield to the seductions of these pursuits, and to allow themselves to be led astray from the simplicity that is in Christ Jesus. Their eye is not single, and their whole body is not full of light. If there is one man to be admired, envied, and imitated above all others, it is he who has baptized all his classic and scientific acquirements at the font of Christianity, has presented them at the foot of the cross, and has used them only as the instruments and materials of that divine art by which he is enabled to give a richer colouring, stronger light, and greater power to those facts and scenes, of which the cross is the centre and the symbol. To hear such a man chastening and guiding, but not checking or freezing, the gushing utterances of a full heart, by the standard of genuine eloquence; and warming and sanctifying the finest rhetoric by the glow of a soul on fire with love to God and souls; to see the genius of Tully or Demosthenes, embuing itself with the spirit of Paul, Peter, or John, and under the constraining love of Christ, employing all its resources of diction, dialectics, and metaphor, to persuade men to be reconciled to God, teaches the earnestness

which the pulpit deserves and demands. Such a minister is a polished shaft in Jehovah's quiver, and to such
a preacher we can almost fancy that not only men but
angels must listen with delight. Such preachers we
have had, and by the divine blessing may have again :
only let us use the means, and look to have our tongues
touched with the live coal from the divine altar.

There is, however, too much truth in the following
remarks of Dr. Vaughan.

"The effect of learning and elegant scholarship, in the modern
pulpit, has commonly been to render men incapable of producing
impression of this nature in any degree. In the case of such
preachers, neither the diction they use, nor the mould into which
they cast their expressions and sentences, nor the comparisons they
introduce, nor anything belonging to their rhetoric, has been an
object of study with a view to its fitness to secure attention, and to
move the thoughts and passions of such assemblies as are generally
convened by the preacher, assemblies made up from the popular,
much more than from the thoroughly educated, classes of society.
The great object of this class of preachers has been to acquit themselves learnedly, or to acquit themselves elegantly. It is grievous to
witness the mischiefs which have resulted from this conventionalism
in pulpit taste. If our pulpit lessons must be veiled in the language
of a particular kind of scholarship, then the people generally, and
even men of good natural parts, who have not been initiated into that
scholarship, will fail to perceive our meaning, and will begin as the
consequence, to cast about for some better employment than listening
to the utterance of our unknown tongue."*

I go on now to mention another qualification for the
sacred office, which the earnest minister will anxiously
cultivate with a view to the great object of his life and
labours, and to this I advance with a praying mind, an
anxious heart and a trembling hand, ardently desirous
to set it forth in such manner as shall secure for it the
attention which its importance demands ; I mean per-

* Modern Pulpit, pp. 23, 24.

sonal religion. We are weak in the pulpit, because we are weak in the closet. An earnest man will not only train his mind to understand his object, and draw around him the resources requisite for its accomplishment, but will discipline his heart : for there, within, is the spring of energy, the seat of impulse, and the source of power. There the life that quickens must reside, and thence it must be felt to emanate. If the heart beat feebly, the whole circulation must be sluggish, and the frame inert. So it is with us ministers : our own personal religion is the mainspring of all our power in the pulpit. We are feeble as preachers, because we are feeble as Christians. Whatever other deficiencies we have, the chief of them all lies in our hearts. The apostle said, " We believe and therefore speak." We not only speak what we believe, but as we believe : if our faith be weak, so will be our utterance. In another place the same inspired writer said, " Knowing the terrors of the Lord, we persuade men." It was as standing amidst the solemnities of the last judgment, that apostles besought men to be reconciled to God. The flame of zeal which in their ministrations rose to such a height and intensity as to subject them to the charge of insanity, is thus accounted for, " The love of Christ constraineth us." We have too much forgotten that the fount of eloquence is in the heart ; and that it is feeling which gives to words and thoughts their power. An unrenewed man, or one of lukewarm piety, may preach elaborate sermons upon orthodox doctrines, but what are they for power and efficiency when compared with even the inferior compositions of the preacher who feels as well as glories in the cross, but as the powerless gleams of the aurora borealis to the warm and vivifying rays of the sun?

The Christian minister sustains a double relation, and has a double duty to perform; he is a preacher to the world, and a pastor to the church; and it is impossible he can fulfil, or be in earnest to fulfil, the obligations he is under to either, without a large measure of personal godliness. As regards the church which is committed to his care, and of which he is made by the Holy Ghost the spiritual overseer, he has to increase not their knowledge only, but also their holiness, love, and spirituality; to aid them in performing all the branches of duty, and in cultivating all the graces of sanctification. And what is the present spiritual condition of the great bulk of the professors of religion? Amidst much that is cheering, there is on the other hand much that is discouraging and distressing to the pious observer. We behold a strange combination of zeal and worldly-mindedness; great activity for the extension of religion in the earth, united with lamentable indifference to the state of religion in a man's own soul; apparent vigour in the extremities, with a growing torpor at the heart. Multitudes are substituting zeal for piety, liberality for self-mortification, and a merely social for a personal religion. No careful reader of the New Testament, and careful observer of the present state of the church, can fail to be convinced, one should think, that what is now wanting is a higher tone of spirituality. The Christian profession is sinking in respect of personal piety; the line of separation between the church and the world becomes less and less perceptible: and this is taking place, less through the elevation of the world, than through the depression of the church. The character of genuine Christianity, as expounded from pulpits, and delineated in books, has too rarely a counterpart in the lives and spirit of its professors.

How is this to be remedied, and by what means is the spirit of piety to be revived? May we not ask a previous question, How came the spirit of slumber over the church? Was it not from the pulpit? And if a revival is to take place in the former, must it not begin in the latter? Are the ministers of the present day possessed of that earnest piety which is likely to originate and sustain an earnest style of preaching, and to revive the lukewarmness of their flocks? I do not mean for a moment to insinuate that the ministers of the present day among the Dissenters, or Methodists, or the Evangelical clergy of the Church of England, are characterised by immorality, or even by a want of substantial holiness; or that they would suffer, as regards their piety, in comparison with those of some other periods in the history of their denominations: but what I am compelled to believe, and what I now express is, that our deficiencies are great, when we are compared not only with what ministers have ever been required to be, but especially with what we are required to be by the circumstances of the times in which we live. Amidst the eager pursuit of commerce, the elegance and soft indulgence of an age of growing refinement, the high cultivation of intellect, and the contests of politics, the church needs a strong and high barrier to keep out the encroachment of tides so adverse to its prosperity, and to keep in and to raise higher its spiritual life. And where shall it find this, if not in the pulpit? It is not to be expected in the nature of things that the church will in spirituality ever be superior to

the ministry; or will ever consider itself without excuse
for its inferiority. It will not tread a path which its
spiritual guides are slow to pursue; and will deem it
an affectation of sanctity and presumptuous ambition
to attempt to advance beyond them. How else than
by admitting a deficiency of our piety can we account
for the fact of a diminished efficiency in our ministry?

I cannot resist the temptation of giving here a long
extract from a beautiful tract entitled "A Revived
Ministry our only Hope for a Revived Church;" a tract
so eminently excellent, and so adapted to promote the
end of the pious and accomplished writer, that the fact
of such a heart-searching, soul-reviving production
having as yet reached only a second edition, is a proof
that we have little wish to be raised to higher attainments in piety.

"And for such a revived ministry there would be the most hopeful
preparation of mind. The object to be aimed at would be distinctly
conceived; it would be loved and cherished as the noblest to which a
redeemed being can consecrate himself; and there would be a readi-
ness to yield everything to the urgency and grandeur of its claims,
together with a simplicity and guilelessness of intention, which
would mightily aid the judgment in seeing its best way to the best
methods of achieving it. In such circumstances, all the distracting
influences arising from indistinct views, a divided heart, and infirmity
of purpose, would be withdrawn, and leave the minister of Christ free
to take a decided and energetic course. The subjection of the church
and the world to the dominion of the truth, in a pure heart and holy
life, would be ever present to his mind as the sole and sublime end
of his ministry : and drawing after it the full tide of his sympathies,
and permitting no diversion of his strength to any inferior object, it
would command all his powers, and dispossess him of every wish but
that of living and dying for it. And that moment would be the dawn
of an era of prosperity.

"Everything which he did would be enlivened by the presence of
a warmer and holier zeal; but it would be the public administration
of divine truth, in the ordinance of preaching, in which the stronger

and healthier pulsations of spiritual life would be most signally displayed, and from which the largest results might be expected. In this he would be prepared for acting a new part. Himself saved, and eminently sanctified, as well as possessed of the whole treasury of sacred knowledge in the inspired volume, he would be well versed in the respective truths best calculated for awakening the unconverted, and promoting the highest sanctification of the church, and administer them with improved wisdom and force. The wretchedness of the soul as guilty, depraved, and hastening to the judgment-seat; the blessedness of arresting it in its downward course, and of exalting it once more to the glory of the Divine image and favour; the ample means provided for all this in the mediation of Christ; the experience of the efficacy in himself, and the conviction of their undiminished power to do as much for others; the rapid flight of time, and the possibility of all the mercy overshadowing that hour being trifled with and lost for ever, these thrill his soul with mingled commiseration, hope, and fear, and urge him to improve to the utmost the fleeting opportunity of snatching sinners from perdition, and adding to the brightness of the Redeemer's crown. How well chosen is his theme, no matter of curious speculation, but some one or more of the solemn verities which concern the instant faith and obedience of every hearer, and bring life or death, as accepted or rejected! Away with those artificial rules which some have prescribed, as if to prepare a sermon were something like composing an epic! He has a truth to enforce, a moral effect to produce, and the sense of its unutterable importance brings to bear upon it all the resources of a judicious, intelligent, and impassioned mind. Bent on winning souls to God, or quickening them to higher obedience, this one desire possesses and inflames him, and gives a unity and completeness to his subject, a force and compactness of argument, a felicity of speech and manner, an ardour and impressiveness of appeal, which the art of the rhetorician could never have supplied. He feels moreover, that his strength is in God, and that the pleadings of human wisdom and pity never availed apart from a higher inspiration. Would there not be more than hope from a ministry like this? In itself so convincing and persuasive, rendered still more so by the practical exhibition of all the faith, uprightness, benevolence, and spirituality which it inculcates, looking to God, and owning its weakness without his blessing, it would have all the characteristics from which the susceptibilities of the human mind, and the solemn promises of the Almighty, authorise the expectation of enlarged success. When was such a ministry known to be long in contact with the minds of men, without producing the happiest effects? 'The word of the Lord would have free course and be glorified,' converts press into the church, and the church be raised to a higher renovation.

" And the minister thus revived would have unwonted power in individual intercourse with the members of his flock. Living only for their advancement in faith and holiness, the warmth and tenderness of his concern for it would make him prompt to seize every opportunity of promoting it, and give an appropriateness and weight to his sayings, which a colder and less earnest piety would never have dictated : while the objects of his solicitude, feeling the point and force of his words, and impressed with his singleness of purpose, and still more with that uniform display of the Christian virtues, which was the best voucher of his deep sincerity, would find themselves drawn along by a combination of influences so pure and commanding, that they must tread in the steps of his piety, and bend to his hallowed purpose of extending the limits of the church, and giving it a holier aspect. Every faithful minister can look back upon seasons when under the kindlings of a warmer love and zeal, and a more affecting sense of eternal things, he was animated to increased exertion ; and he has found that not only did his preaching fix the attention and touch the souls of his hearers more than at other times, but that, when he went among them in private, the elevation of his spirit, the seriousness of his converse, and the solemnity and unction pervading his petitions, produced an evident impression, and that he left them with improved feelings and resolves. All emotion is contagious, and easily propagates itself to other bosoms ; but, besides this, the wakefulness of his zeal, and his steadiness of purpose, made him eager to extract the highest amount of good from every opportunity, stimulated ingenuity, and gave an aptness and charm to all that he said, which fell with happy effect on the understanding and the heart. And had the ardour and determination of those seasons been permanent, the equable and healthy excitement of every day's labour, instead of soon relapsing into the feebler sensibility of other times, his ministry would doubtless have told a different history, and be far more richly laden with precious fruit."

Happy shall I feel if this feeble tribute, not only of the recommendation of my pen, but of my heart's gratitude for the benefit I have derived from this production, shall induce any of my brethren to peruse this precious gift, which has been offered to them by a writer who veils himself under the modest title of "One of the least among the Brethren."

Do we want examples and patterns of eminent and earnest piety, how richly are they supplied both in number and in quality in the pages of our own denominational history! Where is the deep, ardent, experimental religion of our ancestors, the fathers and founders of Protestant nonconformity? What a theologian was Owen, when he wrote his "Exposition of the Hebrews;" what a polemic when he penned his "Controversy" with Biddle; what an ecclesiastic when he drew up his "Treatise on Church Government;" but what a Christian when he indulged in his "Meditations on the Glory of Christ," and gave us his treatise "On Spirituality of Mind and the Mortification of Sin." What a logician and divine was Howe, when he produced his "Living Temple;" but what a Christian, when in the shadow of this noble structure of his holy genius, he poured out his heart in his work on "Delighting in God," and the "Blessedness of the Righteous." And then think of holy Baxter, who gained repose from the labours of polemic strife, and relief from the tortures of the stone, in the believing anticipations of "The Saint's Rest." Was their piety the result of their sufferings? Then for one I could be almost content to take the latter, so that I might be possessed of the former. Lead me to the spots, I do not say where they trimmed their midnight lamp, and continued at their studies till the morning star glittering through their casement chided them to their pillow; but to those more hallowed scenes, where they held their nightly vigils, and wrestled with the angel till the break of day. Mighty shades of Owen and Baxter, Howe and Manton, Henry and Bates, Goodwin and Nye, illustrious and holy men, we thank you for the rich legacy you have bequeathed to us in your immortal works: but O where has the mantle of your piety fallen? "God of our fathers! be the God of their succeeding race."

Here then let us begin, where indeed we ought to begin, with our own spirits; for what should be the piety of that man on the state of whose heart depends in no small degree the spiritual condition of a whole Christian community? If we turn to any department of human action we shall learn that no one can inspire a taste, much less a passion, for the object of his own pursuit, who is not himself most powerfully moved by it. It is a scintillation of his zeal flying off from his own glowing heart, and falling upon their souls, which kindles in them the fire which burns in himself. Lukewarmness can excite no ardour, originate no activity, produce no effect: it benumbs whatever it touches. If we enquire what were the sources of the energy, and the springs of the activity, of the most successful ministers of Christ, we shall find that they lay in the ardour of their devotion. They were men of prayer and of faith. They dwelt upon the mount of communion with God, and came down from it like Moses to the people, radiant with the glory on which they had themselves been intently gazing. They stationed themselves where they could look at things unseen and eternal, and came with the stupendous visions fresh in their view, and preached under the impression of what they had just seen and heard. They drew their thoughts and made their sermons from their minds and from their books, but they breathed life and power into them from their hearts, and in their closets. Trace either Whitfield or Wesley in their career, and you will see how beaten was the road between their pulpits and their closets: the grass was not allowed to grow in that path. This was in great part the secret of their power. They were mighty in public, because in their retirement they had clothed themselves, so to speak, with Omnipotence. They reflected the lustre they had caught in the Divine presence; and its attraction was irresistible. The same might be said of all others who have attained to eminence as successful preachers of the gospel. If then we would see a revival of the power of the pulpit, we must first of all see a revival in the piety of those who occupy it: and when this is the case, then, "he that is feeble among us shall be as David, and the house of David shall be as God, as the angel of the Lord before them."

CHAPTER III.

THE NATURE OF EARNESTNESS (CONTINUED).

V. Earnestness will manifest itself by energetic and untiring action in use of those means by which its object is accomplished. It does not satisfy itself with contemplation, however enraptured; schemes, however well concerted; wishes, however fervent; or anticipations, however lively; but proceeds to vigorous, well arranged, and well adapted exertion. An earnest man must of necessity be an active one: he is the opposite and the contrast of an idle dreamer. "I see my object," he exclaims; "it stands out in bold relief, clearly defined before my eyes, and I will leave no effort untried to accomplish it. I have made up my mind to labour, self-denial, and fatigue; and if I do not succeed, it shall not be for want of determined and continuous effort." Such is his resolution, and his practice fulfils it. He is always at work. You know where to find him, and how he will be employed. He is the very type of diligence. Labour is pleasure. No difficulties deter him, no disappointments dishearten him. The ignorant do not understand him, the indolent pity him, but the intelligent admire him. There is something in his earnestness commanding, attractive, and inspiring, especially when the object of it is worthy.

Apply this to the ministry; there are two means by which this accomplishes its end, preaching and the pastorate.

In reference to the former, I advert first to the matter of our ministrations. And this must consist of course of those topics which bear most obviously and directly upon the great ends we are seeking to accomplish. Earnestness will take the nearest and most direct road to its object; nor will it be seduced from its path by beautiful prospects and pleasant walks, that lie in another direction. "I want to reach that point, and I cannot allow myself to be attracted by scenes, which however agreeable and interesting to others, would, if I stayed or turned to contemplate them, only hinder me in my business." Such is the language of one intent upon success in any particular scheme. Now what is the end of our office? The reconciliation of sinners to God, and their ultimate and complete salvation, when so reconciled. It is easy then to see that the matter of our instruction and persuasion must be the ministry of reconciliation. Of course it must be our purpose to declare the whole counsel of God, and to remember " that all Scripture is given by inspiration of God, and is profitable for doctrine, for reproof, for correction, for instruction in righteousness; that the man of God may be perfect, thoroughly furnished unto all good works." In the way of exposition, a minister should go through the greater part of the whole Bible, fairly and honestly explaining and enforcing it. But since the whole Bible, as explained by the more perfect revelation of the New Testament, directly or indirectly points to Christ, or may be illustrated and enjoined by considerations suggested by his mission and work, our preaching should have a decidedly evangelical character. The divinity, incarnation, and death of Christ; his atonement for sin; his resurrection, ascension, intercession, and mediatorial reign; his spiritual kingdom, and his second coming; the offices and work of the Holy Spirit in illuminating, regenerating, and sanctifying the human soul; the doctrine of justification by faith, and the new birth; the sovereignty of God in the dispensation of his saving gifts; these and their kindred and collateral topics should form the staple of our ministrations and teaching. It surely must be this which the apostle meant when he said, "I determined to know nothing among you save Jesus Christ and him crucified." "The Jews require a sign, and the Greeks seek after wisdom, but we preach Christ crucified, to the Jews a stumbling-block, and unto the Greeks foolishness; but unto them which are called, both Jews and Greeks, Christ the power of God and the wisdom of God." If there be any meaning in language, this must imply that the apostle in his ministry dwelt chiefly upon the work of Christ. His epistles all sustain this view of his meaning. They are all full of this great subject. We may perhaps smile at the simple piety of the individual who was at the trouble of counting the number of times that the apostle Paul mentions the name of Jesus in his epistles; but at the same time, something is to be learnt from the fact that he found it to reach between four and five hundred. This teaches us how thoroughly christian, how entirely imbued with evangelism, his mind and his writings were. His morality was as evangelical as his doctrine, for he enforced all the branches of social obligation by motives drawn from the cross. His ethics were all baptised with the spirit of the gospel, so that the believer who has imbibed the spirit of his writings, will have his eye as constantly kept upon the crucified One, in the progress of his sanctification, as the sinner's eye is turned towards the same object, for his justification. This then was the earnestness of the apostle; one constant, uniform, and undeviating endeavour to save men's souls by the truth as it is in Jesus.

A question now arises whether it is the duty of modern preachers to adopt the same method, and whether, inasmuch as their ends are the same with those of the apostle, they are to seek them by the same means. One would suppose there can be no rational doubt of this. If the apostles were the inspired teachers of Christianity, and have given us in their writings a full exhibition of what Christianity really is; and if it is our business to explain and enforce their writings, it seems to follow, as a thing of course, that our teaching, as to the matter of our discourses, must resemble theirs: and will any one pretend that this resemblance can be established, unless our preaching is richly and prevailingly evangelical? I am aware it is sometimes said that times have altered since the apostles' days, that the state of the world is different from what it then was. But is not human nature in all its essential elements the same? Is it not the same in its moral aspect, impotency, and necessities? Does it not as much need, and as much depend upon, the gospel scheme now, as it did then? Is not the gospel as exquisitely and fully adapted to its miserable condition now as it was then? Can sin be pardoned in any other way than through the atonement of Christ; or the sinner be justified by any other means than faith in the Lord our Righteousness;

or the depraved heart be renewed and sanctified by any
other agency than that of the Holy Spirit? Are not
all the motives supplied by evangelical doctrine as
powerful and as efficacious now, as they were then?
No alteration of the subjects of preaching then can be
called for now, to meet the advancing state of society,
since the gospel is intended and adapted to be God's
instrument for the salvation of man, in all ages of the
world, in all countries, and in all states of society. The
moral epidemic of our nature is always and every where
the same, in whatever various degrees of virulence it
may exist, and the remedial system of salvation by
grace, through faith, is God's own and unalterable
specific for the disease, in every age of time, in every
country of the world, and in every state of society.
Men may call in other physicians than Christ, and try
other methods of cure, as they have done; but they
will all fail, and leave the miserable patient hopeless
and helpless, as regards any other means of health
than that which the cross of Christ presents. I reject alike as delusive and fatal the ancient practice
of conforming the evangelical scheme to systems of
philosophy, and the modern Puseyite notion of the
progressive developement of Christian doctrine by the
church. To the men who would revive the former, I
say, "Beware lest any man spoil you, through a vain
and deceitful philosophy, after the tradition of men,
after the rudiments of the world, and not after Christ:"
to the latter I say, "Jesus Christ, the same yesterday,
and to-day, and for ever. Be not carried about with
divers and strange doctrines; for it is a good thing that
the heart be established with grace." It appears to me
that something like the same attempts are being made

in this day to corrupt the gospel by superstitious additions on the one hand, and by philosophic accommodations on the other, as were made in the early days of Christianity. Our danger lies in the latter.

It should never be forgotten that the time when the apostles discharged their ministry was only just after the Augustan era of the ancient world. Poetry had recently bestowed on the lettered world the works of Virgil and Horace. The light of philosophy, though waning, still shed its lustre over Greece. The arts still exhibited their most splendid creations, though they had ceased to advance. It was at such a time, and amidst such scenes, the gospel began its course. The voices of the apostles were listened to by sages who had basked in the sunshine of Athenian wisdom, and were reverberated in startling echo from temples and statues that had been shaken by the thunders of Cicero and Demosthenes; yet they conceded nothing to the demands of philosophy, but held forth the cross as the only object they felt they had a right to exhibit. They never once entertained the degrading notion that they must accommodate themselves to the philosophy or the taste of the age in which they lived, and the places where they ministered. It is true the philosophy of that day was a false one, but it was not known or acknowledged to be such at the time. It was admired as true, though like many systems that have succeeded it, it gave place to another, and was doomed, like some that now prevail, to wane before new and rising lights. Whether the apostle addressed himself to the philosophers on Mars Hill, or to the barbarians on the island of Melita; whether he reasoned with the Jews in their synagogues, or with the Greeks in the school of Tyran-

nus, he had but one theme, and that was Christ, and
him crucified. And what right, or what reason have
we for deviating from this high and imperative example?
Be it so, that we live in a literary, philosophic, and
scientific age, what then? Is it an age that has out-
lived the need of the gospel for its salvation; or for the
salvation of which any thing else can suffice but the gospel? The supposition that something else than pure
Christianity, as the theme of our pulpit ministrations, is
requisite for such a period as this, or that it must be
presented in a philosophic guise, appears to me a most
perilous sentiment, as being a disparagement to the
gospel itself, a daring assumption of wisdom superior to
God's, and containing the germ of infidelity. The
gospel sustains the nature of a testimony which must be
exhibited in its own peculiar and simple form; a testimony to certain unique and momentous facts which
must be presented as they really are, without any
attempt or wish to change their nature or alter their
character, in order to bring them into nearer conformity
to the systems of men. Let the taste be cultivated as
it may by literature, or the mind be enlightened by
science, or the reason be disciplined by philosophy, the
heart is still deceitful and wicked, the conscience still
burdened with guilt, and the whole soul in a state of
alienation from God. The moral constitution is mor-
tally diseased, and nothing but the gospel can convey
God's saving health, which is as much required for his
spiritual restoration by the polished son of science, as by
the savage of New Zealand, or the Hottentot of South
Africa. All else is but pretence and empiricism; and
the man who would be successful in the salvation of
souls must have a clear conviction and a deep impression

of these facts. Philosophy must never be allowed to dilute the elixir of life, nor to evaporate it into the clouds of metaphysics.

But perhaps the danger to which the evangelical ministry of the present age is exposed is not so much a philosophising spirit, or an attempt to make the gospel conform to any metaphysical theory, as an effort to attain to a high intellectuality in setting forth received truths. We hear a great deal about this in modern times. It is become a kind of cant term, (for there is high as well as low cant,) to speak of some men as very intellectual preachers. If by an intellectual preacher be meant a man who applies the acquirements of a well furnished and well trained understanding to explain and enforce the great topics of evangelical truth; or the application in the most attractive form to the great end of the Christian ministry, of whatever knowledge such a mind can obtain in its pursuit of all kinds of information; or the employment of sound logic and natural eloquence to make the doctrines which are unto salvation bear upon men's hearts and consciences, if this be meant, a man cannot be too intellectual, the great and glorious doctrines of revealed truth deserve and demand the mightiest energies of the noblest intellects : but if, as is too generally the case, intellectuality means the cold, dry, argumentative discussion of metaphysical subjects rather than of evangelical truths, or the discussion of such truths in an abstract and essay-like form ; a mere heartless exercise of the reason of the preacher, intended and adapted only to engage the understanding of his hearers, without either interesting their affections or awakening their conscience ; such intellectuality will do nothing but empty the places of worship in which it is

exhibited, or at best draw together a congregation of
persons, who, though they cannot as yet bring themselves
to do without some kind of religion, yet prefer the cold
abstractions of the head to the warm affections of the
heart. Such hearers assemble to listen to a metaphysical lecturer on spiritual subjects, and not to a publisher
of glad tidings to sinners.

Here I would not be misconstrued to mean that
every sermon must be on strictly evangelical themes;
but that these must be the prevailing topics of the man
who is in earnest for the salvation of souls. Nor would
I go so far as to say that each sermon must contain as
much of the gospel as would make every hearer of it
acquainted with the way of salvation, even if he never
should listen to another discourse. There is such a
thing as treating these subjects so carelessly, so familiarly, and so frequently, as to deprive them of all their
power to interest and impress. A man whose soul is
possessed with the passion for doing good, will make
almost any and every topic connected with the gospel
tend to usefulness. Subjects, which in other hands
would be dry and uninteresting, will in his be invested
with the glow and warmth which live in his own soul,
and which he imparts to every thing he touches. His
heart beats with an action so strong, steady, and healthful, that his fervid and holy intelligence circulates an
evangelical vitality through what in others would be a
cold and torpid frame of mind, and thus causes the
principle of gospel life to reach to the very extremities
of the system of general truth. Still even he, though
he dwell occasionally on every topic which can with propriety be brought into the pulpit, will like the apostle,
"glory only in the cross of Christ." Resisting the

temptations to neglect the plain gospel, and to go in quest of airy speculations and unprofitable novelties, his aim will not be to gratify the imaginative by what is tasteful and poetic, the philosophical by what is profound, the metaphysical by what is subtle, or the curious by what is strange; but·by manifestation of the truth, to commend himself to every man's conscience in the sight of God. Alas, that any preacher of the gospel should take any other aim, and seek any other object, than this! Do we want subjects for eloquence, where can we find them in such abundance, grandeur, and sublimity, as in the gospel theme? The cross is a fount of the purest, most impassioned and most pathetic eloquence in the world, from which genius may be ever drawing, without fear of exhausting it. Compare the most finished orations and sermons of Massillon, Bossuet, or Bourdaloue, with McLaurin's discourse on "Glorying in the Cross;" and though they are more perfect as models of composition, and more decorated by the artifices and graces of rhetoric, yet how far below that incomparable sermon in the sublimity of its theme, and the grandeur of its evangelical eloquence, are those boasted masterpieces of the French pulpit! Even the soul of the polished but pointless Blair kindled into something like a glow of pious warmth when he came, which he did but rarely, within the attraction of this object; and though but as moonlight compared with the ardour of his colleague Walker, yet in his sermon on "The Death of Christ," his frigid elegance becomes enlivened by his theme, and furnishes a standing proof that the heathen morals of Epictetus are a barren source of eloquence, compared with the Christian doctrines of the apostle Paul. I make no apology here

for re-quoting a passage from an American author,
which I have already given to the public in my " Address to Students."

" My dear brethren, why are we not more inpressive ? Theology
affords the best field for tender, solemn and sublime eloquence. The
most august objects are presented ; the most important interests are
discussed ; the most tender motives are urged. God and angels ; the
treason of Satan ; the creation, ruin and recovery of a world ; the
incarnation, death, resurrection, and reign of the Son of God ; the day
of judgment ; a burning universe ; an eternity ; a heaven and a hell ;
all pass before the eye. What are the petty dissensions of the
states of Greece, or the ambition of Philip ? What are the plots and
victories of Rome, or the treason of Catiline, compared with this ?
If ministers were sufficiently qualified by education, study and the
Holy Ghost ; if they felt their subject as much as Demosthenes and
Cicero did, they would be the most eloquent men on earth, and would
be so esteemed wherever congenial minds were found." *

To know what themes have the greatest potency over
the public mind, and should form the subject of an
earnest ministry, we have only to consult the pages
of ecclesiastical history. It is unnecessary to dwell
again upon the matter of apostolic preaching. It was
by the purest evangelism that Christianity was planted
in the earth, and it was when this gave place to a
religion of forms and ceremonies that the power and
vitality of true godliness declined, and a mass of splendid corruption grew up, in the dark shadow of which
the man of sin erected his throne, and the Papacy
commenced its bloody reign. During the long night
of the middle ages the sound of the faithful preacher
was not heard, and the voice of Zion's watchman was
silent, except in a few obscure nooks and corners
of the earth ; but wherever it was then heard, the
same effects followed. It was this subject with which

* Dr. Griffin's Sermon on the Art of Preaching.

Claude of Turin, when nearly all the world was wandering after the beast, awakened in the ninth century the inhabitants of Piedmont, and commenced that glorious work which was more or less carried on for centuries, amid the seclusion of Alpine rocks and vallies; and which the concentrated power and fury of the Papacy could never entirely subvert. It was this evangelism which our Wickliff preached in England in the fifteenth century, and by it kindled a fire, amidst the smouldering ashes of which lay concealed embers which were again to ignite when fanned by the breath of other reformers, a century afterwards. By what means did Luther achieve his immortal triumph over the powers of the Vatican, and strike off the fetters which had enslaved the judgment, heart, and conscience of man? By the potency of what theme did he lift up into freedom and dignity the prostrate intellect of the human race? What was the instrument with which he struck the empire of darkness, and inflicted a blow which resounded through Christendom? the great evangelical doctrine of justification by faith. By what means did Whitfield and Wesley rouse the slumbering piety of our nation, and call up a spirit which is going on from strength to strength to this day? By the evangelical system of Divine truth. What called forth the missionary enterprise, and constructed all that moral machinery which is at work to effect the world's conversion? Before what system of truths have the inhabitants of Polynesia and New Zealand surrendered their licentious habits and bloody rites; and the Hottentots and Esquimaux dropped their barbarism, and risen up in the form and manners of civilized men? What is the doctrine by which our missionaries are taking possession of India and China? I answer in each case, the doctrine of the cross.

It is then a fact attested by authentic history, and uncontradicted by any one acquainted either with the present or the past, that all the great moral revolutions of our world, since the Christian era, have been effected by one simple process, by one set of means, and by one grand truth, and that process is preaching, those means are earnest men, and that truth is the gospel of the grace of God. Providential events may have prepared the way, by levelling mountains, and filling up vallies, and making smooth the course of the herald of the cross; but it is that herald's mighty voice proclaiming, "Behold the Lamb of God, that taketh away the sins of the world," which by the power of God's Spirit has changed the moral aspect of our dark and dreary world. This has not been done by learning, science, or philosophy, it is not the result of profound speculations on any theory of morals, or of fine processes of reasoning, or of splendid creations of poetic genius, or of the subtleties of metaphysical discussion: no, but of the simple testimony of the gospel. While the philosopher has been theorizing in his closet, and the statistical philanthropist has been carrying on his calculations in his study, the preacher has gone forth into the midst of the people, ignorant, wicked, and wretched, as they were, has lifted up the great truth of the loving God, the dying Saviour, and the regenerating Spirit, and has by these means, as an instrument of God, changed the aspect of society, and revolutionized the moral habits of nations.

Strange that with the knowledge of these facts, any of our preachers should think of replacing the glorious truths which have wrought such wonders in the world, by any other themes; or should act as if weapons that have proved their adaptation and their power, should now be wielded with a doubtful mind and with a hesitating and wavering hand! If we would know how we are to convert souls to God, we have only to ask how has God converted them. Nor is it necessary to go back to past ages, or abroad to other countries. Let us only look round upon our own country; let us go to our largest congregations and our most numerous churches, and ask what kind of preaching has done all we see: what doctrine, and how handled, has drawn those multitudes together; what magnet has put forth its attractions there? The secret will be soon discovered, and it will be found that there is an exemplification of our Lord Jesus Christ's words, "And I, if I be lifted up from the earth, will draw all men unto me." Go into other places where religious intellectuality is substituted for the vital truths of the gospel, where philosophical abstractions take the place of popular addresses on great fundamental doctrines, and cold, logical essays are read, instead of heart-stirring sermons being preached; and the attenuated and still declining congregations will proclaim the want of adaptation in the pulpit ministrations, and prove that for the popular mind there can be no substitute for the cross of Christ. Nor does this apply exclusively to the uneducated or partially educated classes. Human nature in all its prevailing features, tastes, necessities, and enjoyments, is the same in the king and in the peasant; in the savage and the sage. All men are susceptible of emotion, as well as capable of reasoning; and all men love to feel, as well as to think. A commercial or professional man, who has been at work all the week, having had his mind strained with hard thinking, as well as his body by hard labour, when he takes his seat in his pew on a Sabbath morning, wants something for his heart, as well as for his head. With a sermon, however intellectual it may be, which has nothing that comes home to his affections, and causes him to feel, he is sure to be disappointed and dissatified. A dry essay on some gospel subject which only proves a point he never doubted, or starts a difficulty he never dreamt of, is like giving him a stone when he asks for bread. He wants to be made to feel and to realize that there is something higher and better than this world. He desires to enjoy the luxury of hallowed emotion, he covets the joy and peace of believing, and the anticipations of that world where the weary are at rest, and the din of business will be for ever hushed. That man, tired and jaded by the cares, anxieties, and toils of six days, wants to lie down and take repose on the soft green of evangelical truth, and not on the hard rocks of abstract speculation. It is true that being a man of education and reading, his heart must be reached through his intellect, and he must be fed with the substantial bread of evangelical truth, which, though his taste is healthful, must not be coarse and chaffy; must not only be made of the finest wheat, but it must also be well prepared, mixed and made by a skilful hand.

It is however said that though the same gospel is to be preached, and the matter of sermons is in substance to be ever the same, in all the varying states of society, yet that the mode of exhibiting it is to be accommodated to the circumstances of the age, and that a different mode of presenting the truth must be adopted in an age of advancing knowledge, to what is pursued in one of less refined and cultivated habits. If by this be meant that there must be more vigorous thinking, more profound analysis, more accurate criticism, more varied illustration from the fields of science, more pains to show the harmony of sound theology with sound philosophy, then it may and must be admitted, that the mode of preaching should be adapted to the circumstances of an advancing age. But even with this admission, it must still be remembered that the essential nature of the gospel, as a testimony from God, to be received on the ground of its own evidence and authority, must not be altered; nor any attempts made to shift the obligation to receive it from this ground to its apparent reasonableness or conformity with the principles of any system of human philosophy. Nor must this adaptation to the circumstances of the age be carried so far either in the way of logic, criticism, or illustration, as to obscure the light, or corrupt the simplicity, of the evangelical system. The substitution of a dry, abstract, and philosophical mode of preaching the gospel, for a lively, forcible, and heart-affecting, conscience-rousing method, so far from being adapted to this age of excitement, is quite opposed to it. This is a busy, active, glowing period of time's history, as well as a thinking one. The heart is yearning, as well as the intellect. The abstractions of the intellect are dealt with now in such a manner as to kindle the affections to a blaze, and no method of exhibiting the gospel can be successful, if not adapted to produce this result. If flimsy thought, thread-bare common-places, will not do; so neither will mere airy speculation, hard logic, cold metaphysics, or mere philosophy. It must be the

gospel, preached with manly, vigorous thinking, in good
Saxon words, and with classic simplicity and perspicuity
of style. I am somewhat jealous about this idea of
accommodating our method of preaching to the taste
and circumstances of the age, till the meaning of the
expression be accurately settled and thoroughly understood. Without great care, the spirit of accommoda-
tion and the attempt at adaptation will go on from
manner to matter, and even our creeds will be somewhat curtailed and altered, to establish a harmony
between our theology and our philosophy. Already the
process has begun, and the neology of Germany, like a
beacon gleaming upon us from its dreadful rock,
should warn us of the danger we are in on such a coast,
of making shipwreck of our faith. Perhaps the best
mode of making this subject understood, and showing
to what extent this adaptation may be carried, would be
to select and compare the sermons of two different
periods of the history of the pulpit. Take, then, for
example, a sermon of Dr. Owen, or Dr. Manton, with
all its numberless divisions and sub-divisions, quaint
phraseology, and violations of taste, and put it by the
side of a sermon by Dr. Chalmers, Mr Bradley, or
Dr. Wardlaw; and by the comparison you will see that
the power of adaptation has increased in the moderns,
and that they exhibit the same glorious verities as
their predecessors with improvements of style and
arrangement.

Before I pass from this part of the subject, it may
be proper to remark that perhaps there are few expressions more misunderstood, and with respect to which
more mistakes have been made, than " preaching the
gospel." Many by the use of this phrase aim to exclude

from the pulpit almost every topic but a perpetual and almost unvarying exhibition of the death of our Lord, and consider this, and this only, as specifically preaching Christ. But it is strangely forgotten by the preachers of this school, that as the scheme of mediation by the Saviour is founded on the eternal obligation and immutable nature of the law of God, and was intended not to subvert, but to uphold, its authority, the moral law must be explained and enforced in all its purity, spirituality, and extent. Repentance towards God is no less included in the apostolic ministry, than faith in our Lord Jesus Christ; and a sinner cannot repent of his transgressions against the law, which he has violated, if he know it not: for "sin is the transgression of the law;" and "by the law is the knowledge of sin." No man can know sin without knowing the law: and herein appears to me one of the prevailing defects of modern preaching: I mean the neglect of holding up this perfect mirror, in which the sinner shall see reflected his own moral image. It is true that some are melted down at once into a sense of wickedness, and brought to the exercise of both repentance and faith, by an exhibition of divine love in the death of Christ; but this is not so usual a method of conversion as the first awakening of the sinner by an exposition and application of the perfect law. Dr Dwight says,

"Few, very few, are ever awakened or convinced by the encouragements and promises of the gospel; but almost all by the denunciation of the law. The blessings of immortality, the glories of heaven, are usually, to say the least, preached with little efficacy to an assembly of sinners. I have been surprised to see how dull, inattentive, and sleepy, such an assembly has been, amidst the strongest representations of these divine subjects, combining the most vivid images with a vigorous style and an impressive elocution." *

* Vol. II, p. 417.

This is a strong testimony, and it is perhaps a little overstated. Still I am persuaded there is much truth in it, for it seems to stand to reason, that men will care little about pardon, till they are convinced of sin; and as the apostle says, it is by the law that they come to the knowledge of sin. In this particular there appears to me a greater adaptation to the work of conviction in American preaching than in the British pulpit: it has more of this exposition of the law, and of the application of it to the sinner's conscience; more that is calculated to make him feel at once his obligations and his guilt; more of that which silences his excuses, unravels the deceitfulness of his heart, strips him of self-righteousness, makes him thoroughly acquainted with himself, and his intense need of a Saviour: in short, more of what the apostle calls commending himself to every man's conscience in the sight of God; though it has, however, I think a want of evangelical fulness and tenderness. I remember a discussion by a large company of ministers in my vestry, on one occasion, as to the style of preaching which in their own experience they had found most useful; and it was pretty generally admitted, (and some of them had been among our most successful preachers,) that sermons on alarming and impressive texts had been most blessed in producing conviction of sin, and the first concern about salvation. At the same time it must be recollected that though descriptions of sin may affect, the exhibition of its consequences may affright, vehement censures of it may alarm, and reasoning concerning it may open the gloomy road to despair, these methods alone will not convert. Law without the gospel will harden, as the gospel without the law will only lead to

carelessness and presumption: it is the union of both
that will possess the sinner with loathing of himself,
and love to God. Still our danger in this age lies not
so much in neglecting the gospel, as in omitting to
associate with it the preaching of the law. It is worthy
of remark, that Jesus Christ, who was incarnate love
itself, the living gospel, yea the way, the truth, the life,
was the most alarming preacher that was ever in our
world. It is, however, incumbent upon us not to mistake grossness for fidelity; nor harshness for earnestness.
The remarks of Mr. Hall on this, are as correct as they
are beautiful:—

"A harsh and unfeeling manner of denouncing the threatenings
of the Word of God, is not only barbarous and inhuman, but calculated, by inspiring disgust, to rob them of all their efficiency. If the
awful part of our message, which may be styled the burden of the
Lord, ever fall with due weight upon our hearers, it will be when it
is delivered with a trembling hand and faltering lips."

The look, the tone, the action, when such subjects
are discussed, should be a mixture of solemnity and
affection; the awfulness of love. To hear such topics
dwelt upon in strong language, vehement action, and
boisterous tones, strikes me as being an utter violation
of all propriety, and is likely to excite horror and
revulsion in every hearer of the least discernment.
Real earnestness is the result of deep emotion, and the
emotion excited by the sight of a fellow-creature perishing in his sins, is that of the tenderest commiseration,
which will express itself not in stormy declamation and
thundering denunciations, but in solemnly chastened
expostulation and appeal.

CHAPTER IV.

EARNESTNESS IN THE MANNER OF PREACHING.

I NOW pass from matter to manner; and when I say manner, I wish to be understood as including in that term, not simply the method of communicating truth by voice and gesture, but the cast of thought and the style of composition in reference to the truth enunciated. What is wanted for the pulpit is a vivacious, in opposition to a stiff formal and dull, method. Style must of course, to a considerable extent, vary with the subject matter, and be regulated by it. In exegetical preaching, or in that part of a sermon which is merely expository, all that is required is calm perspicuity and a flow of clear, limpid, quiet thought, which shall instruct the understanding, and gently draw after it the heart, without being intended or expected in any great degree to move the passions. We have some beautiful specimens of this in the elegant discourses of Dr. Wardlaw. Well would it be if, after his manner, we could be critical without being pedantic; exegetical without being scholastic; and invest exposition with charms which would make it attractive to all our congregations. But though a careful analysis of the text should form the basis of almost all our sermons, there must be something more than mere exegesis, however clear, correct, and instructive. We have to do not only with a dark intellect that needs to be informed, but with a hard heart that needs to be impressed, and a torpid conscience that needs to be awakened; we have to make our hearers feel that in the great business of religion, there is much to be done, as well as much to be known. We must impart knowledge, for light is as essential to the growth of piety in the spiritual world, as it is to the growth of vegetation in the natural one: and the analogy holds good in another point, we must not only let in light, but add great and vigorous labour to carry on the culture. We must therefore rise from exegesis into exhortation, warning, and expostulation. The apostle's manner is the right one, " Whom we preach, warning every man and teaching every man in all wisdom, that we may present every man perfect in Christ Jesus." We must not only direct but impel our hearers. They all know far more than they practise of the Bible: the head is generally far in advance of the heart; and our great business is to persuade, to entreat, to beseech. We have to deal with a dead heavy vis inertiæ of mind; yea more, we have to overcome a stout resistance, and to move a reluctant heart. If all that was necessary to secure the ends of our ministry were to lay the truth before the mind; if the heart were pre-disposed to the subject of our preaching, then like the lecturer on science, we might dispense with the hortatory manner, and confine ourselves exclusively to explanation. Logic unaccompanied by rhetoric would suffice; but when we find every sinner we address, acting in opposition to the dictates of his judgment, and the warnings of his conscience, as well as to the testimony of Scripture;

sacrificing the interests of his immortal soul to the
vanities of the world, and the corruptions of his heart;
madly bent upon his ruin, and rushing to the precipice from which he will take a fatal leap into
perdition ; can we, in that case, be satisfied with
merely explaining, however clearly, and demonstrating,
however conclusively, the truth of revelation ? Should
we think it enough coldly to unfold the sin of suicide,
and logically to arrange the proofs of its criminality,
before the man who had in his hand the pistol or the
poison with which he was just about to destroy himself ?
Would a definition of the sin, however clear and accurate, be enough in this case? Should we not entreat,
expostulate, beseech? Should we not lay hold of the
arm uplifted for self-destruction, or snatch the poison
cup from the hand that was about to apply it to the
lip ? What are the impenitent sinners to whom we
preach, but individuals bent upon self-destruction, not
indeed the destruction of their bodies, but of their
souls ? There they are before our eyes, rushing in
their sins and their impenitence to the precipice that
overhangs the pit of destruction; and shall we content
ourselves with sermons, which however excellent they
may be for elegance, for logic, for perspicuity, and even
for evangelism, have no hortatory power, no moving
tendency, none of the apostle's beseeching entreaty ?
Shall we merely lecture on theology, and deal out
religious science, to men, who with a flood of light
already pouring over them care for none of these
things ?

It is a question of not a little difficulty, how far the
rules and methods of secular eloquence may be observed
in the composition of sermons. The language of the

apostle in reference to his own preaching, has been thought to forbid all elaboration; "Christ sent me to preach the gospel, not with wisdom of words, lest the cross of Christ should be made of none effect." A right understanding of his circumstances and ours, will show us that there are differences which forbid too rigid and literal an application of this sentiment to our own case. Miracles gave a potency to his preaching, which is wanting in ours. Besides, the wisdom here forbidden was not the selection of the best words, and placing them in the best order for the statement of divine truth, but that combination of false philosophy and artificial rhetoric which were the usual practice of the Grecian schools; what he forbade was such a method of setting forth evangelical doctrine as would have brought it into conformity, both as to matter and manner, with the fashionable systems of philosophy. Provided the effect of elaboration is to make a sermon at once perspicuous and impressive, to give it power to command the attention, and at the same time to instruct the judgment, engage the affections, and awaken the conscience; to render the subject clearly understood, and at the same time deeply felt, it cannot be too perfect. No preparation which causes the hearer to forget the preacher, and even the sermon, as a production of art, and to think only of himself and the subject; which rivets attention, and makes every one feel that he is in the presence not only of man, but of God; which declares the way of salvation so clearly that the most obtuse understanding can comprehend it, and at the same time so forcibly and touchingly that the dullest heart must feel it, cannot be wrong. If a preacher of the power of Demosthenes were to arise, he would, and must, carry that power into the pulpit, and ought to do so. But on the other hand, an elaboration which makes it but too evident to every serious and observant mind that it was the preacher's aim not to convert souls, but to catch the applause of the fashionable, the giddy, and the frivolous ; which fills the discourse with flowery diction and gaudy metaphors, with elegant declamations, or startling apostrophes, with fanciful descriptions, and beautiful pictures; which though it takes the cross for its subject, almost instantly leaves it and runs into the fields of poetry or the labyrinths of metaphysics, for subtle arguments, or sparkling and splendid illustrations; which to sum up all, exercises the judgment or amuses the imagination, but never moves the heart, or calls the conscience to discharge its severe and awful functions : such preaching may render a minister popular, secure him large congregations, and procure for him the plaudits of the multitude; but where are the sinners converted from the error of their way, and the souls saved from death? Verily if such a preacher has his reward only in the applause of the multitude, whose object and aim were as low as his own, it was what he sought, and all he sought, and let him not complain if he gain this, and nothing else. From such preachers may God Almighty preserve our churches, and may he give us men who better know their business in the pulpit, and better do it !

A simple, as opposed to an artificial and rhetorical style, is then essential to earnestness; for who can believe that man to be intent on saving souls, who seems to have laboured in his study only to make his sermon as fine as glittering imagery and high sounding diction could render it. I could as soon believe a physician to be intent on saving his fellow-creatures from death, who, when the plague was sweeping them into the grave, spent his time in scattering over his patients flowers or perfumes, or writing his prescriptions in beautiful characters and classical latinity.

There are some judicious remarks on the style of the pulpit in two papers which appeared some time since, one in the Edinburgh Review, and the other in the Quarterly, on Hare's "Village Sermons," those admirable models of simplicity. The object of the reviewer in the Quarterly is to illustrate the nature, to prove the necessity, and to urge the cultivation, of simplicity, especially in sermons to congregations composed in great measure of the poor. After giving a quotation or two in which Mr Hare had made mention of "smugglers and poachers," "tea and wheaten bread," the critic remarks,

"We have preachers in our time who would have flinched from expressions so natural and straightforward, and would infallibly have warned their poor people against holding any intercourse with the nocturnal marauder on the main or the manor; and have suggested to them the gratitude they owed for a fragrant beverage and farinaceous food. And so might Mr Hare, if his taste had been less correct, and his desire of doing good less earnest. Affectation is bad enough anywhere; in the pulpit it is intolerable."

In speaking of illustrations, the writer goes on to advert to the excessive quaintness which was one of the vices of sermons before, and about the time of, the Reformation :

"Accordingly within a century after the Reformation we find Thomas Fuller, the last man from natural temperament one would have thought likely to offer a caution upon such a subject, saying of the faithful minister, 'His similes and illustrations are always familiar, never contemptible. Indeed reasons are the pillars of the fabric of a sermon, but similitudes are the windows which give the best light. He avoids such stories whose mention may suggest bad thoughts to the auditors, and will not use a light comparison to make thereof a grave application, for fear lest his poison go further than his antidote.' Preaching therefore now took an opposite tack, and from having been certainly once too succulent, by the time of John Wesley had become sapless. This was one cause which rendered the new style of preaching adopted by him and his followers so attractive. The standard according to which the character of the imagery and diction of the pulpit of modern days was regulated, was not fixed before the divines of Queen Anne's time; as the vocabulary of poetry, according to Johnson, was not determined before the age of Dryden. In both cases the restraint has been injurious to the subject of it. There was a Doric simplicity, 'wood-notes wild,' in the poets before Dryden, for which the greater correctness, it may be, of those who have since lived is but a poor substitute; and there was a homely vigour in the sentiments and phraseology of the pulpit of the first and second Charles, which has been ill replaced by the decorous tameness of later times. Surely it is a morbid taste, and one that requires correction, which would kick at images that satisfied a Barrow; and yet we could point to numbers in his sermons which would now be rejected by the preacher, even the village preacher too, as mean and pedestrian. The familiar illustration, therefore, by which a subject is rendered clear to persons slow to apprehend, and interesting to persons hard to be excited, is a figure not lightly to be renounced in deference to the false refinement of the magnates of a congregation, though doubtless capable of abuse. We say false refinement, for there are parables both in the prophets and in the gospels, against which the same parties might raise the same objection." *

In a similar strain and with a like object, though with still more expansion of thought, a masterly writer in the Edinburgh Review remarks :

"We have long felt that the eloquence of the pulpit in its general character has never been assimilated so far as it might have been, and ought to have been, to that which has produced the greatest effects elsewhere, and which is shewn to be of the right kind, alike by the success which has attended it, and by an

* Quarterly Review, No. 117. [Now republished among the writings of the Rev. J. J. Blunt, late Margaret Professor of Divinity at Cambridge.]

analysis of the qualities by which it has been distinguished. If we were compelled to give a brief definition of the truest style of eloquence, we should say it was 'practical reasoning,' animated by strong emotion; or if we might be indulged in what is rather a description than a definition of it, we should say that it consisted in reasoning on topics calculated to inspire a common interest, expressed in the language of ordinary life, and in that brief, rapid, familiar style, which natural emotion ever assumes. The former half of this description would condemn no small portion of the compositions called sermons, and the latter half a still larger portion.

"We would not be misunderstood. It is far, very far, from our intention to speak in terms of the slightest depreciation of the immense treasures of learning, of acute disquisition, of profound speculation, of powerful controversy, which the literature of the English pulpit exemplifies. In these points it cannot be surpassed. In vigour and originality of thought, in argumentative power, in extensive and varied erudition, it as far transcends all other literature of the same kind, as it is deficient in the qualities which are fitted to produce popular impression. We merely assert that the greater part of 'sermons' are not at all entitled to the name, if by it be meant discourses especially adapted to the object of instructing, convincing, or persuading the common mind."

After some admirably judicious remarks on the topics of the pulpit, designed to prove that these should be such as are calculated to inspire a common interest in the mass of a common audience, the writer goes on to speak of the manner of discussing them, and observes:

"Where the topics are not such as are fairly open to censure, a large class of preachers, especially amongst the young, grievously err by investing them with the technicalities of science and philosophy; either because they foolishly suppose they thereby give their compositions a more philosophical air, or because they disdain the homely and the vulgar. We remember hearing of a worthy man of this class, who having occasion to tell his audience the simple truth that there was not one gospel for the rich and another for the poor, informed them, 'that if they would not be saved on general principles, they could not be saved at all!' With such men it is not sufficient to say, that such and such a thing must be, but there is always 'a moral or physical necessity for it.' The 'will' is too old fashioned a thing to be mentioned, and every thing is done by 'volition;' duty is expanded into 'moral obligation;' man not only ought to do this, that, or the other, it is always 'by some principle of their moral nature;' they not only like to do so and so, but 'they are impelled by some natural propensity;' men not only think and do, but they are never represented as thinking and doing without some parade of their 'intellectual processes and active powers.' Such discourses are full of 'moral beauty,' and 'necessary relations,' and 'philosophical demonstrations,' and 'laws of nature,' and 'a priori,' and 'a fortiori' arguments. If some simple fact of physical science is referred to in the way of argument or illustration, it cannot be presented in common language, but must be exhibited in the pomp of the most approved scientific technicalities. If there be a common and scientific name for the same object, ten to one that the latter is adopted. Heat straightway becomes 'caloric;' lightning, 'the electric fluid;' instead of plants and animals, we are surrounded by 'organised substances;' life is nothing half so good as 'the vital principle.' Not only is such language as this obscurely understood, or not understood at all; but even if perfectly understood, must necessarily be far less effective than those simple terms of common life, which for the most part may be substituted for them. The sermons of Augustus William Hare may serve to show how the abstract terms of philosophy may be advantageously translated into simple, racy English." *

So harmonious are the judgments, on the best style of preaching, of two writers belonging to very different schools of literature and religion, whose keen sarcasm it may be hoped will correct the pedantry at which it is aimed, and convince many an ambitious aspirant after popularity that whatever methods may secure the applause of the frivolous and the ignorant, simplicity is the only way to attain usefulness and to secure the approbation of the serious, the wise, and the good. An affectation of learning and science in the pulpit, is not only a sin against good taste, but betrays an utter want of that watching for immortal souls, which is or ought

* Edinburgh Review, No 145. "On the British Pulpit." [Now republished by the Rev. H. Rogers, Professor in the Lancashire Independent College.]

to be, the preacher's steady and constant aim. To borrow the homely, but forcible language of Doolittle,

"The eyeing of eternity should make us ministers painful and diligent in our studies to prepare a message of such weight as we come about, when preaching to men concerning everlasting matters, and should especially move us to be plain in our speech, that even the capacity of the weakest in the congregation, that hath an eternal soul that must be damned or saved, might understand in things necessary to salvation, what we mean, and aim, and drive at. It hath made me tremble to hear some soar aloft, that knowing men might know their parts, whilst the meaner sort are kept from the knowledge of it; and put their matter in such a dress of words, in such a style, so composed, that the most stand looking at the preacher in the face, and hear a sound, but know not what he saith, and while he doth pretend to feed them, doth indeed starve them. Would a man of any bowels of compassion go from a prince to a condemned man, and tell him in such a language that he should not understand the condition upon which the prince would pardon him, and then the poor man lose his life because the proud and haughty messenger must show his knack in delivering his message in fine English, which the condemned man could not understand?"

I shall introduce here a quotation from that great master of chaste eloquence, Robert Hall; whose opinion on any subject, but especially on that of the art of preaching, in which he was himself so extraordinary a proficient, is entitled to peculiar deference.

"A great diversity of talents must be expected to be found amongst them (the evangelical clergy); but it has not been our lot to hear of any, whose labours a good man would think it right to treat with indiscriminate contempt. As they are called for the most part, to address the middle and lower classes of society, their language is plain and simple: speaking in the presence of God, their address is solemn; and, 'as becomes the ambassadors of Christ,' their appeals to the conscience are close and cogent. Few, if any, among them aspire to the praise of consummate orators: a character which we despair of ever seeing associated, in high perfection, with that of a Christian teacher. The minister of the gospel is called to declare

the testimony of God, which is always weakened by a profuse employment of the ornaments of secular eloquence. Those exquisite paintings and nice touches of art, in which the sermons of the French
preachers excel so much, excite a kind of attention, and produce a
species of pleasure, not in perfect accordance with devotional feeling.
The imagination is too much excited and employed, not to interfere
with the more awful functions of conscience; the hearer is absorbed
in admiration, and the exercise which ought to be an instrument of
conviction, becomes a feast of taste. In the hand of a Massillon, the
subject of death itself is blended with so many associations of the
most delicate kind, and calls up so many sentiments of natural tenderness, as to become a source of theatrical amusement, rather than of
religious sensibility. Without being insensible to the charms of eloquence, it is our decided opinion that a sermon of Mr Gisborne's is
more calculated to 'convert a sinner from the error of his way,' than
one of Massillon's. It is a strong objection to a studied attempt at
oratory in the pulpit, that it usually induces a neglect of the peculiar
doctrines of Christian verity, where the preacher feels himself re-
strained, and is under the necessity of explaining texts, of obviating
objections, and elucidating difficulties, which limit the excursions of
imagination, and confine it within narrow bounds. He is therefore
eager to escape from these fetters, and, instead of 'reasoning out of
the Scriptures,' expatiates in the flowery fields of declamation."

A want of powerful, eloquent, yet simple and unaffected exhortation, is among the greatest deficiencies of
the modern pulpit. Let any one read the sermons of
our great nonconformist predecessors, Clarkson, Doolittle, Manton, Howe, Owen, Bates, Flavel, and especially Baxter, and mark the all but overwhelming force
of persuasion which is put forth in the application of
their discourses; let him see how these great men
exerted the mightiness of their strength to make all
they said to the judgment, reach the heart and awaken
the conscience. And to come to more modern times,
let him read the sermons of Whitfield, Jonathan Edwards, and Davies of New Jersey; and to advance to

still more modern productions, let him peruse the sermons of Mr. Parsons, Dr. Chalmers, and the best
preachers on the other side of the Atlantic, Spring,
Barnes, Skinner, Beecher, Griffin, Clarke, and Sprague:
also Robert Hall's sermon on "Marks of Love to God,"
and Bradley's sermon on "Our Lamps are Gone Out,"
for fine specimens of this hortatory method; this
bearing down with the whole power of the truth on the
sinner's heart and conscience; this beseeching men to
be reconciled to God. Some specimens of this method
will be given in the following chapter. This is earnestness in preaching: when it is evident to the hearer that
the preacher feels the truths he discusses; when it is
manifest to all that he believes what he says, in affirm-
ing that his hearers are sinking into perdition, and that
he is labouring to persuade them to forsake their evil
courses: when his sermons are full of close, pointed,
personal addresses; when, in short, through the whole
discourse, he is seen moving onward from the understanding to a closer and closer approximation to the
heart in the conclusion, and the hearer feels at length
his hand seizing him with a mysterious and resistless
power, and bearing him away, almost whether he will
or no, to Christ, salvation, and heaven. The conviction
of the judgment is not the ultimate object of good
preaching; though it is the chief, if not the exclusive
end of some preachers, if we are to judge by their
manner of preaching; but they ought to know that
the persuasion of the heart does not follow as a matter
of course; that has still to be effected, and they have
to undertake it as a distinct purpose, and to aim at it
with a different sort of skill, and with a different in-

strumentality from that by which they chiefly work. Compel them to come in, was the method prescribed to the servants of the Lord who made a great feast, and sent out his invitations to the poor and needy. It is this compulsion we want; this earnest entreaty, this laying hold of the sinner, and making him feel that his salvation is with us an object of intense desire, and that we shall be bitterly disappointed if it be not accomplished.

CHAPTER V.

ILLUSTRATIONS OF EARNESTNESS COLLECTED FROM
VARIOUS AUTHORS.

FAMILIAR as most readers of this work are with examples of the kind of manner intended, it will help to illustrate and enforce its nature, if a few extracts from different authors are here introduced, by way of specimens. Those which are here presented are not selected as possessing any thing very extraordinary, or as being the best of the kind that could be selected from the same authors; but they are sufficient to answer the purpose. Nor are they exhibited as models, to be in every particular imitated in modern composition, but as being pervaded by that one quality of intense earnestness, which it is the object of this work to recommend.

The first extract which shall be quoted is from a sermon of Mr. Doolittle. This eminent minister of Christ was ejected by the Act of Uniformity in 1662, from the church of St. Alphage, London Wall. He was a man of extraordinary courage, power, and success, in preaching; and, after his expulsion from his living, educated young men for the ministry. The extract which follows is taken from a discourse contained in that valuable series called "The Morning Exercises," and is entitled "How we should eye Eternity, so that it may have its influence on all we do." It is perhaps the most solemn and awful sermon in the English or any other language; it is sadly overcharged with terminology, which should be sparingly introduced, though it ought not to be altogether excluded from the pulpit, even in this fastidious age. The sickly sentimentalism which would "never mention hell to ears polite," should be abjured with as much disgust as gross familiarity with such awful realities. It was not only Doolittle's fault, but it was the vice of the age, to approach somewhat too near to the latter extreme. But then, after this admission is made, let us look at the burning and overwhelming earnestness of the sermon.

" Is there an eternal state : such unseen eternal joys and torments? Who then can sufficiently lament the blindness, madness, and folly of this distracted world, and the unreasonableness of those that have rational and eternal souls, to see them busily employed in the matters of time, which are only for time, in present honours, pleasures, and profits, while they do neglect everlasting things; everlasting life and death is before them, everlasting joy or torment is hard at hand; and yet poor sinners take no care how to avoid the one, or obtain the other. Is it not matter of lamentation to see so many thousands bereaved of the sober serious use of their understandings? That while they use their reason to get the riches of this world, they will not act as rational men to get the joys of heaven, and will avoid temporal calamities, yet not escape eternal misery. Or if they be fallen into present afflictions, they contrive how they may get out of them: if they be sick, reason tells them they must use the means if they would be well: if they be in pain, nature puts them on to seek after a remedy; and yet these same men neglect all duty, and cast away all care concerning everlasting matters: they are for seen pleasures and profits which are passing from them in the enjoyment of them; but the unseen eternal glory in heaven they pray not for, they think not of. Are they unjustly charged? Let conscience speak what thoughts they lie down withal upon their pillow; if they wake, or sleep fly from them in the silent night, what a noise doth the care of the world make in their souls? With what thoughts do they rise in the morning? Of God, or of the world? Of the things of time, or of eternity? Their thoughts are in their shops before they have been in heaven; and many desires after visible temporal gain, before they have had one desire after the invisible, eternal God, and treasures that are above. What do they do all the day long? What is it that hath their endeavours, all their labour and travel? Their most painful industry and unwearied diligence? Alas! their consciences will tell themselves, and their practices tell others, when there is trading, but no praying; buying and selling, but no religious duties performed: the shop-book is often opened, but the sacred book of God is not looked into all the week long.

"O Lord! forgive the hardness of my heart that I can see such insufferable folly among reasonable creatures, and can lament this folly no more: good Lord, forgive the want of compassion in me that can stand and see this distraction in the world, as if the most of men had lost their wits and were quite beside themselves, and yet my bowels yearn no more towards immortal souls that are going to unseen miseries in the eternal world; to see distracted men busy in doing things that tend to no account, is not such an amazing sight as to see men that have reason for the world, to use it not for God, and Christ, and their own eternal good: to see them love and embrace a present dunghill world, and cast away all serious, affecting, and effectual thoughts of the life to come: to see them rage against the God of heaven, and cry out against holiness as foolish preciseness, and serious godliness as madness and melancholy.

"Let us call the whole creation of God to lament and bewail the folly of man that was made the best of all God's visible works, but now by such wickedness is bad beyond them all; being made by God for an everlasting state, and yet minds nothing less than that for which he was principally made.

"O sun! why is it not thy burden to give light to men to do those works and walk in those ways that bring them to eternal darkness? O earth! why dost thou not groan to bear such burdensome fools that dig into thy bowels for gold and silver, while they do neglect everlasting treasures in the eternal world? O ye sheep and oxen! fish and fowl! why do ye not cry out against them that take away your present life to maintain them in being, but only mind present things, but forget the eternal God that gave them dominion over you, to live upon you, while they had time to mind eternal things, but do not? O ye angels of God, and blessed saints in heaven, were ye capable of grief and sorrow, would not ye bitterly lament the sin and folly of poor mortals upon earth? Could ye look down from that blessed place where ye do dwell and behold the joy and glory which is to us unseen, and see how it is basely slighted by the sons of men, if ye were not above sorrow and mourning, would not ye take this up for a bitter lamentation? O ye saints on earth! whose eyes are open to see what the blind deluded world doth not see, do ye bitterly take on, let your heads be fountains of water, and your eyes send forth rivers of tears for the great neglect of eternal joys and happiness of heaven. Can you see men going out of time into eternity in their sin and in their blood, in their guilt and unconverted state, and your hearts not be moved? your bowels not yearn? Have ye spent all your tears in bewailing your own sin, that your eyes are dry when you behold such monstrous madness and unparalleled folly of so many, with whom daily ye converse? Ye sanctified parents, have ye no pity for your ungodly children? Nor sanctified children, for ungodly parents?"

The next extract I shall present is from holy Baxter, under whose ministry Doolittle was converted, and from whom he appears to have borrowed his own manner of preaching.

"O sirs, they are no trifles or jesting matters that the gospel speaks of. I must needs profess to you that when I have the most serious thoughts of these things, I am ready to wonder that such amazing matters do not overwhelm the souls of men: that the greatness of the subject doth not so overmatch our understandings and affections as even to drive men besides themselves, but that God hath always somewhat allayed it by distance; much more do I wonder that men should be so blockish as to make light of such things. O Lord, that men did but know what everlasting glory and everlasting torments are! Would they then hear us as they do? Would they read and think of these things as they do? I profess I have been ready to wonder when I have heard such weighty things delivered, how people can forbear crying out in the congregation; and much more do I wonder how they can rest till they have gone to their ministers, and learned what they shall do to be saved, that this great business should be put out of doubt. O that heaven and hell should work no more upon men! O that eternity should work no more! O how can you forbear when you are alone to think with yourselves what it is to be everlasting in joy or torment! I wonder that such thoughts do not break your sleep, and that they do not crowd into your minds when you are about your labour! I wonder how you can almost do any thing else! How can you have any quietness in your minds? How can you eat, or drink, or rest, till you have got some ground of everlasting consolations? Is that a man or a corpse that is not affected with matters of this moment; that can be readier to sleep than to tremble when he hears how he must stand at the bar of God? Is that a man or a clod of clay that can rise up and lie down without being deeply affected with his everlasting state; that can follow his worldly business and make nothing of the great business of salvation or damnation, and that when he knows it is so hard at hand? Truly, sirs, when I think of the weight of the matter, I wonder at the best saints upon earth that they are no better, and do no more, in so weighty a case. I wonder at those whom the world accounts more holy than needs, and scorns for making so much ado, that they can put off Christ and their souls with so little; that they do not pour out their souls in every prayer; that they are not more taken up with God; that their thoughts are not more serious in preparation for their last account. I wonder that they are not a thousand times more strict in their lives, and more laborious and unwearied for the crown than they are. And for myself, as I am ashamed of my dull and careless heart, and of my slow and unprofitable course of life, so the Lord knows I am ashamed of every sermon that I preach: when I think what I am, and who sent me, and how much the salvation and damnation of men is concerned in it, I am ready to tremble lest God should judge me a slighter of the truth and the souls of men, and lest in my best sermons I should be guilty of their blood. Methinks we should not speak a word to men in matters of such consequence without tears, or the greatest earnestness that possibly we can. Were we not too much guilty of the sin which we reprove, it would be so. Whether we are alone or in company, methinks our end, and such an end, should still be in our mind, and as before our eyes; and we should sooner forget any thing, or set light by any thing, or by all things, than by this."

The third extract is from the works of that great and serene spirit, John Howe; whose surpassing grandeur of thought and expression places him far above all his compeers. His sermon on the "Inquiry whether or no we truly love God," is one of the finest pieces of

solemn, heart-searching expostulation, which can be
found in the whole range of English theology : I give
from it the following pages, the spirit of which should
enter into the soul of every minister and student who
reads them.

"For further direction take heed of passing a false judgment in
this case, a judgment contrary to the truth: for,

"First, That is to no purpose, it will avail thee nothing, you
cannot be advantaged by it, for yours is not the supreme judgment.
There will be another and superior judgment to yours, that will
control and reverse your false judgment, and make it signify nothing;
it is therefore to no purpose.

"Secondly, It is a great piece of insolency, for it will be to oppose
your judgment to his certain and most authorized one ; who, if this
be your case, hath already judged it, and tells you, 'I know you, that
you have not the love of God in you.' It belongs to him by office to
judge: 'The Father hath committed all judgment to the Son,' as a
little above in this chapter; From which will you depose him ?
dethrone him ? disannul his judgment ? condemn him ? that you
may be righteous ? (to borrow that, Job xl, 8.)

"Thirdly, It is most absurd, supposing such characters as you
have heard do conclude a man in this case, yet to judge himself a
lover of God. If against the evidence of such characters a man
should pronounce the wrong judgment, it would be the most un-
reasonable and absurd thing imaginable ; for then let us but suppose
how that wronged judgment must lie related to those fore-mentioned
characters, that have been given you. Let me remind you of some
of them, he that never put forth the act of love to God cannot say
he hath the principle, he that is not inclined to do good to others,
for the sake of God, 1 John iii, 17: he that indulges himself in
the inconsistent love of this world, 1 John ii, 15: he that lives
not in obedience to his known laws, John xiv, 14, 1 John v, 3,
with many more. Now if you will pass a judgment of your case
against the evidence of such characters, come forth then, let the
matter be brought into clear sight, put your sense into plain
words, and this it will be : 'I am a lover of God, or I have the
love of God in me, though I cannot tell that ever I put forth one
act of love towards him in all my life ; I have the love of God in me,
though I never knew what it meant to do good to any for his sake,

against the express words of Scripture: How dwelleth the love of God in such a man? I have the love of God in me, though I have constantly indulged myself in that which he maketh an inconsistent love, 'Love not the world, nor the things which are in the world: if any man love the world, the love of the Father is not in him.' I have the love of God in me, though I would never allow him to rule me, though I never kept his commandments with a design to please him, and comply with his will. I have the love of God in me, though I never valued his love. I have the love of God in me, though I never cared for his image, for his presence, for his converse, for his interest and honour.' I beseech you consider how all this will sound! Can any thing be more absurdly spoken? and shall it be upon such improbabilities or impossibilities as these, that any man will think it fit to venture his soul? 'I will pawn my soul upon it, I will run the hazard of my soul upon it; I am a lover of God for all this!' Would you venture any thing else so besides your soul? Would you venture a finger so, an eye so? It is to place the name where there is nothing of the thing; it is to place the name of a thing upon its contrary. The soul of man cannot be an indifferency towards God; but if there be not love and propension, there is aversion, and that is hatred. And what! is hatred to be called love? If you bear that habitual disposition of the soul towards God, to go all the day long with no inclination towards him; no design to please him, to serve him, to glorify him; if this be your habitual temper and usual course, will you call this love? Shall this contrariety to the love of God be called love to him? You may as well call water fire, or fire water, as so grossly misname things here; and therefore again,

"That we may advance somewhat; plainly and positively pass the true judgment. If the characters that you have heard do carry the matter so, come at last plainly and positively to pass the true judgment of your own case, though it be a sad one: and tell your own souls, 'Oh my soul! though I must sadly say it, I must say it, all things conclude and make against thee: the love of God is not in thee.' Why is it not as good this should be the present issue at your own bar, and at the tribunal of your own conscience, as before God's judgment seat? Why should you not concur and fall in with Christ, the authorized Judge, whose judgment is according to truth? Why this is a thing that must be done, the case requires it, and God's express word requires it, 1 Cor. xi, 31. Other previous and preparatory duty plainly enjoined, doth by consequence enjoin it, and requires that it follow, 2 Cor. xiii, 5. What is examination for, but in order to judgment? It must therefore be done, and I shall show how it must be done, and proceed to some further directions.

First, You must do it solemnly. Take yourselves aside at some fit season or another, inspect your own souls, review your life, consider what your wonted frame, and your ordinary course has been. And if you find by such characters as heretofore were given, this is the truth of your case, then let judgment pass upon deliberation: 'Oh my soul! thou hast not the love of God in thee, whatsoever thine appearances hitherto have been; and whatsoever thy peace and quiet hath been, thou hast not the love of God in thee." Let it be done with solemnity.

"Secondly, Do it in the sight of God, as before him, as under his eye, as under the eye of Christ. That eye that is as a flame of fire, that searches hearts, and tries reins; arraign thyself before him. 'Lord, I have here brought before thee a guilty soul, a delinquent soul, wretchedly and horridly delinquent, a soul that was breathed into me by thee, an intelligent, understanding soul, a soul that hath love in its nature, but a soul that never loved thee.'

"Thirdly, Judge thyself before him as to the fact, and as to the fault. As to the fact: 'I have never yet loved thee, O God, I own it to thee; Lord, I accuse, I charge my soul with this before thee, this is the truth of the fact, I have not the love of God in me.' And charge thyself with the fault. 'Oh horrid creature that I am! I was made by thee, and don't love thee; thou didst breathe into me this reasonable, immortal spirit, and it doth not love thee; it is thine own offspring, and does not love thee. It can never be blessed in any thing but thee, and it does not love thee!' And then hereupon,

"Fourthly, Join to this, self-judging and self-loathing. That we are to judge ourselves is a law laid upon us by the supreme Lawgiver, the one Lawgiver, that hath power to save and to destroy. And his word that enjoins it, as plainly tells us what must go with it, that this self-judging must be accomplished with self-loathing, Ezek. vi, 9; xx, 43, and xxxvi, 31. Do God that right upon thyself that thou mayest tell him, 'Blessed God! I do even hate myself, because I find I have not loved thee; and I cannot but hate myself, and I never will be reconciled to myself, till I find I am reconciled to thee.' This is doing justice, doth not the Scripture usually and familiarly so represent to us the great turn of the soul to God; when poor sinners become penitents and return, that they are brought to hate themselves, and loathe themselves in their own eyes? And is there any thing that can make a soul so loathsome in itself, or ought to make it so loathsome to itself, as not to love God, to be destitute of the love of God? And then,

"Fifthly, Hereupon too, pity thyself, pity thy own soul. There is cause to hate it, to loathe it, and is there no cause to pity it, to lament it? Doth not this look like a lamentable case, 'Oh! what a soul have I that can love any thing else, that can love trifles, that can love impurities, that can love sin; and cannot love God, Christ, the most desirable good of souls? What a soul have I! What a monster in the creation of God is this soul of mine!' Methinks you should set yourselves, if any of you can find this to be the case, to weep over your own souls. Some may see cause to say, 'Oh, my soul! thou hast in thee other valuable things, thou hast understanding in thee, judgment in thee, wit in thee; perhaps learning, considerable acquired endowments in thee; but thou hast not the love of God in thee. I can do many other commendable or useful things, I can discourse plausibly, argue subtlely, I can manage affairs dexterously, but I cannot love God. Oh my soul, how great an essential dost thou want to all religion, to all duty, to all felicity! The one thing necessary thou wantest; thou hast every thing but what thou needest more than any thing, more than all things; and oh my soul, what is like at this rate to become of thee? Where art thou to have thy eternal abode? To what regions of horror and woe art thou going? What society can be fit for thee? No lover of God no lover of God! what, but of infernal, accursed spirits, that are at utmost distance from him, and to whom no beam of holy vital light shall ever shine to all eternity! Thou, oh my soul, art self-abandoned to the blackness of darkness for ever. Thy doom is in thy breast, thy own bosom, thy no love to God is thy own doom, thy eternal doom; creates thee a present hell, and shows whither thou belongest.'

"Sixthly, * * * All disobedience and rebellion is summed up in this one word, Having been no lover of God; and won't it make any man's heart to meditate terror, to think of having such a charge as this likely to lie against him in the judgment of that day; that day, when the secrets of all hearts are to be laid open? Every work must then be brought into judgment, and every secret thing, whether it be good or evil, Eccles. xii, 14. And it will be to the confusion of many an one. It may be your no love of God was heretofore a great secret, you had a heart in which was no love of God, but it was a secret, you took not care to have it writ on your forehead; you conversed with men so plausibly, nobody took you to.

be no lover of God, to have a heart disaffected to God. But now out comes the secret, that which you kept for a great secret all your days, out comes the secret ; and to have such a secret as this disclosed to that vast assembly, before angels and men. Here was a creature, a reasonable creature, an intelligent soul, that lived upon the divine bounty and goodness so many years in the world below, and hid a false disloyal heart by a plausible show and external profession of great devotedness to God, all the time of his abode in that world : oh, what a fearful thing would it be to have this secret so disclosed ! And do you think that all the loyal creatures that shall be spectators and auditors in the hearing of that great day will not all conceive a just and loyal indignation against such an one when convicted of not loving God ; convicted of not loving him that gave him breath, him whose he was, and to whom he belonged, whose name he bore ? What a fearful thing will it be to stand convicted so upon such a point as this ! And sure in the meantime there is great reason for continual fear, why a man's heart should meditate terror ! One would even think that all the creation should be continually every moment in arms against him ! One would be afraid that every wind that blows should be a deadly blast to destroy me : that when the sun shines upon me, all its beams should be turned into vindictive flames to execute vengeance upon me ! I would fear that even the very stones in the streets should fly against me, and every thing that meets me be my death ! For what ? I have not the love of God in me ! What, to go about the streets from day to day with a heart void of the love of God !"

The next extract is from Jonathan Edwards' sermon, on "Pressing into the Kingdom of God." This extraordinary man presents a remarkable proof and illustration that the most acute logician and the most subtle metaphysician may be at the same time the most earnest preacher. His sermons are some of the most impressive and alarming we have, but certainly not a little wanting in the tenderness and melting pathos of the gospel of salvation. They may be read with admirable effect to teach us how to expound the nature and enforce the obligations of the moral law so as to awaken the slumbering conscience of the unconverted sinner. His astonishing usefulness shows the adaptation of his preaching to the age and state of society in which he lived, but this method could not be rigidly followed, except in its earnestness, in the present day.

"1. I would address myself to such as yet remain unawakened. It is an awful thing that there should be any one person remaining secure amongst us at such a time as this; but yet it is to be feared that there are some of this sort. I would here a little expostulate with such persons.

"When do you expect that it will be more likely that you shall be awakened and wrought upon than now? You are in a Christless condition; and yet without doubt intend to go to heaven; and therefore intend to be converted some time before you die; but this is not to be expected till you are first awakened, and deeply concerned about the welfare of your soul, and brought earnestly to seek God's converting grace. And when do you intend that this shall be? How do you lay things out in your own mind, or what projection have you about this matter? Is it ever so likely that a person will be awakened, as at such a time as this? How do we see many who before were secure, now roused out of their sleep, and crying, What shall I do to be saved? But you are yet secure! Do you flatter yourself that it will be more likely you should be awakened when it is a dull and dead time? Do you lay matters out thus in your own mind, that though you are senseless when others are generally awakened, that yet you shall be awakened when others are generally senseless? Or do you hope to see another such time of the pouring out of God's Spirit hereafter? And do you think it will be more likely that you should be wrought upon then than now? And why do you think so? Is it because then you shall be so much older than you are now, and so that your heart will be grown softer and more tender with age, or because you will then have stood out so much longer against the calls of the gospel, and all means of grace? Do you think it more likely that God will give you the needed influences of his Spirit then than now, because then you will have provoked him so much more and your sin and guilt will be so much greater? And do you think it will be any benefit to you to stand it out through the present season of grace, as proof against the extraordinary means of awakening there are? Do you think that this will be a good preparation for a saving work of the Spirit hereafter?

"2. What means do you expect to be awakened by? As to the awakening awful things of the Word of God, you have had those set before you times without number, in the most moving manner that the dispensers of the word have been capable of. As to particular solemn warnings, directed to those that are in your circumstances, you have had them frequently, and have them now from time to time. Do you expect to be awakened by awful providences? Those also you have lately had, of the most awakening nature, one after another. Do you expect to be moved by the deaths of others? We have lately had repeated instances of these. There have been deaths of old and young: the year has been remarkable for the deaths of young persons in the bloom of life, and some of them very sudden deaths. Will the conversion of others move you? There is indeed scarce any thing that is found to have so great a tendency to stir persons up as this; and this you have been tried with of late in frequent instances; but are hitherto proof against it. Will a general pouring out of the Spirit, and seeing a concern about salvation amongst all sorts of people, do it? This means you now have, but without effect. Yea, you have all these things together; you have the solemn warnings of God's word, and awful instances of death, and the conversion of others, and see a general concern about salvation; but altogether do not move you to any great concern about your own precious, immortal, and miserable soul. Therefore consider by what means it is that you expect ever to be awakened.

"You have heard that it is probable some who are now awakened, will never obtain salvation; how dark then does it look upon you that remain stupidly unawakened! Those who are not moved at such a time as this, come to adult age, have reason to fear whether they are not given up to judicial hardness. I do not say they have reason to conclude it, but they have reason to fear it. How dark doth it look upon you, that God comes and knocks at so many persons' doors, and misses yours! that God is giving the strivings of his Spirit so generally amongst us, while you are left senseless!

"3. Do you expect to obtain salvation without ever seeking it? If you are sensible that there is a necessity of your seeking in order to obtaining, and ever intend to seek, one would think you could not avoid it at such a time as this. Inquire therefore whether you intend to go to heaven, living all your days a secure, negligent, careless life; Or,

"4. Do you think you can bear the damnation of hell? Do you imagine that you can tolerably endure the devouring fire and everlasting burnings? Do you hope that you shall be able to grapple with the vengeance of God Almighty, when he girds himself with strength, and clothes himself with wrath? Do you think to strengthen yourself against God, and to be able to make your part good with him? 1 Cor. x, 22, 'Do we provoke the Lord to jealousy? are we stronger than he?' Do you flatter yourself that you shall find out ways for your ease and support, and to make it out tolerably well, to bear up your spirit in those everlasting burnings that are prepared for the devil and his angels? Ezek. xvii, 14. 'Can thine heart endure or can thine hands be strong, in the days that I shall deal with thee?' It is a difficult thing to conceive what such Christless persons think, that are unconcerned at such a time."

The following extract is from that first of all preachers, Whitfield; and who that considers the circumstances under which these flaming periods were enunciated, and the feeling and action which accompanied their delivery, can wonder at the effects they produced?

"Beseeching Sinners. O my brethren, my heart is enlarged towards you. I trust I feel something of that hidden but powerful presence of Christ, whilst I am preaching to you. Indeed it is sweet, it is exceedingly comfortable. All the harm I wish you, who without cause are my enemies, is, that you felt the like. Believe me, though it would be hell to my soul to return to a natural state again, yet I would willingly change states with you for a little while, that you might know what it is to have Christ dwelling in your hearts by faith. Do not turn your backs; do not let the devil hurry you away; be not afraid of convictions; do not think worse of the doctrine because preached without the church walls. Our Lord, in the days of his flesh, preached on a mount, in a ship, and in a field; and I am persuaded many have felt his gracious presence here. Indeed, we speak what we know. Do not reject the kingdom of God against yourselves; be so wise as to receive our witness. I cannot, I will not, let you go; stay a little, let us reason together. However lightly you may esteem your souls, I know our Lord has set an unspeakable value on them. He thought them worthy of his most precious blood. I beseech you therefore O sinners, be ye reconciled to God. I hope you do not fear being accepted in the Beloved. Behold, he calleth you: behold, he prevents and follows you with his mercy, and hath sent forth his servants into the highways and hedges, to compel you to come in. Remember then, that at such an hour of such a day, in such a year, in this place, you were all told what you ought to think concerning Jesus Christ. If you now perish, it will not be for lack of knowledge: I am free from the blood of you all. You cannot say I have, like legal preachers, been requiring you to make bricks without straw. I have not bidden you to make yourselves saints, and then come to God; but I have offered you salvation on as cheap terms as you can desire. I have offered you Christ's whole wisdom, Christ's whole righteousness, Christ's whole sanctification and eternal redemption, if you will but believe on him. If you say you cannot believe, you say right; for faith, as well as every other blessing, is the gift of God: but then wait upon God, and who knows but he may have mercy upon thee? Why do we not entertain more loving thoughts of Christ? Or do you think he will have mercy on others, and not on you? But are you not sinners? And did not Jesus Christ come into the world to save sinners? If you say you are the chief of sinners, I answer, that will be no hindrance to your salvation; indeed it will not, if you lay hold on him by faith. Read the evangelists, and see how kindly he behaved to his disciples, who fled from and denied him: 'Go tell my brethren,' says he. He did not say, Go tell those traitors: but 'Go tell my Brethren, and Peter;' as though he had said, Go tell my brethren, in general, and poor Peter in particular, that I am risen:' O comfort his poor drooping heart, tell him I am reconciled to him; bid him weep no more so bitterly; for though with oaths and curses he thrice denied me, yet I have died for his sins, I am risen again for his justification; I freely forgive him all. Thus slow to anger and of great kindness was our all-merciful High Priest. And do you think he has changed his nature, and forgets poor sinners, now he is exalted on the right hand of God? No, he is the same yesterday, to-day, and for ever, and sitteth there only to make intercession for us. Come then, ye harlots; come, ye publicans; come, ye most abandoned of sinners, come and believe on Jesus Christ. Though the whole world despise you and cast you out, yet he will not disdain to take you up. O amazing, O infinitely condescending love! even you he will not be ashamed to call his brethren. How will you escape, if you neglect such a glorious offer of salvation? What would the damned spirits, now in the prison of hell, give, if Christ was so freely offered to their souls! And why are not we lifting up our eyes in torments? Does any one out of this great multitude dare say, he does not deserve damnation? If not, why are we left, and others taken away by death? What is this but an instance of God's free grace, and a sign of his good-will towards us? Let God's goodness lead us to repentance! O let there be joy in heaven over some of you repenting! Though we are in a field, I am persuaded the blessed angels are hovering now around us, and do long, 'as the hart panteth after the water-brooks,' to sing an anthem at your conversion. Blessed be God, I hope their joy will be fulfilled. An awful silence appears amongst us. I have good hope that the words which the Lord has enabled me to speak in your ears this day, have not altogether fallen to the ground. Your tears and deep attention are an evidence that the Lord God is amongst us of a truth. Come ye pharisees, come and see, in spite of your fanatical rage and fury, the Lord Jesus is getting himself the victory. And, brethren, I speak the truth in Christ, I lie not: if one soul of you by the blessing of God be brought to think savingly of Jesus Christ this day, I care not if my enemies were permitted to carry me to prison, and put my feet fast in the stocks, as soon as I have delivered this sermon. Brethren, my heart's desire and prayer to God is, that you may be saved. For this cause I follow my Master without the camp. I care not how much of his sacred reproach I bear, so that some of you be converted from the error of your ways. I rejoice, yea and I will rejoice. Ye men, ye devils, do your worst: the Lord who sent will support me. And when Christ, who is our life, and whom I have now been preaching, shall appear, I also, together with his despised little ones, shall appear with him in glory. And then what will you think of Christ? I know what you will think of him. You will think him to be the fairest among ten thousand; you will then think and feel him to be a just and sin-avenging Judge. Be ye then persuaded to kiss him lest he be angry, and so you be banished for ever from the presence of the Lord. Behold I come to you as the angel did to Lot. Flee, flee for your lives; haste, linger no longer in your spiritual Sodom, for otherwise you will be eternally destroyed. Numbers no doubt there are amongst you that may regard me no more than Lot's son-in-law regarded him. I am persuaded I seem to some of you as one that mocketh: but I speak the truth in Christ, I lie not; as sure as fire and brimstone was rained from the Lord out of heaven, to destroy Sodom and Gomorrah, so surely at the great day shall the vials of God's wrath be poured on you, if you do not think seriously of, and act agreeably to, the gospel of the Lord's Christ. Behold, I have told you before; and I pray God, all you that forget him may seriously think of what has been said, before he pluck you away, and there be none to deliver you."

Not to multiply these extracts unnecessarily, I give one more from a preacher, who is, perhaps without any exception, the most impressive living example of earnestness, both in matter and manner, I mean Mr. Parsons, of York.

"Oh, do not deceive yourselves! I would strive to tear away the veil. I tell you, O ye whose 'goodness has been as a morning cloud, and as the early dew that goeth away,' if unchanged you die, and if unchanged you stand before the dread tribunal where an account must be rendered of all providences, all immunities, and all feelings, you will be found fatally wanting, and will hear a sentence of condemnation that will consign you to realms of everlasting despair. As true as that Jehovah lives, is it that he will thus execute the fierceness of his indignation. Abodes of sorrow await you, where every past benefit will but be an instrument of torture; where memory and conscience will hold up the mirror of bygone privilege and promise, of abused mercy, of foresworn and perjured vows, only that remorse may strike upon the soul its more than scorpion sting, and where grace and hope can never alleviate the wailings that will reverberate through the dungeons of outer darkness for ever and for ever! Your doom will be more tremendous precisely in proportion to the means you possessed, and the signs you gave, of averting it: Can any doom be worse than yours? When these 'terrors of the Lord' are expounded, say if there be not an argument of mighty force why you should now beware, and why you should now hear the voice of God, lest you should be hardened by the deceitfulness of sin, and lest he should swear in his wrath that you shall not enter into his rest."

"But once more, to appeal to those for whom this address has been particularly designed. That such there are, I know, I could turn round and fix my eye, and rest my hand, on persons by whom, if so arraigned, the accusation of the text could not be denied or evaded. You have been again visited by the instrumentality which is adapted for the impression of the heart. Do not reject it; do not let it have that insufficient influence which is but to be dissipated for the world, and which makes the end worse than the beginning. No, nothing will avail but the entire surrender of the soul to him who gave it, the determination to live to Christ, and to glory only in his cross. In the name of the great God, who is not willing that any should perish, but that all should come to repentance, I do now adjure you, that you trifle not a moment longer, that you delay not a moment longer, that you resist not a moment longer: 'Come and return unto the Lord:' let this be a season of consideration; let this be a season of repentance; let this be a season of prayer; let this be a season of dedication to your God. Now, my hearers, now!

"Ministers and people must part once more. The book must be closed again; the voice must be silent again; the congregation must retire again. O, Spirit of God, perform thy work! 'Come from the four winds, O breath, and breathe upon these slain, that they may live!' Let there not be one here before thee, of whom, when yonder heavens shall be on fire, and when this earth shall be burned up, it shall be found that their 'goodness was as a morning cloud, and that as the early dew it went away.'

These extracts will illustrate what I mean by earnestness better than any language which I have employed or could select, and they appear to me to answer well to the apostolic method of beseeching entreaty. I do not of course insist that the pulpit should be restricted to the specific variety of preaching which we designate the hortatory method, under which classification these specimens must all be placed. There should be exegesis, as well as application; exposition, as well as expostulation. The judgment must be enlightened, in order that the heart may be impressed, and the conscience awakened; and the believer edified, no less than the sinner converted; and for this a less impassioned strain of preaching will not only suffice, but will indeed be more appropriate. Yet with regard to that portion of our public ministrations, and it should be no small portion of it, which has reference to the conversion of the impenitent, where shall we find better models on which to construct our sermons, than the Doolittles, the Howes, the Baxters, and the Whitfields of former times, so far at least as their intense earnestness is concerned. It is true the moderns have improved upon these men in matters of taste, in reference to which we do not of course hold them up for imitation. In their numerous and complicated divisions and subdivisions, through which, as so many little rills and channels, they poured the current of their thought, instead of causing it to roll onward in the channel of their sermon with the majestic flow of a noble river; in their quaintnesses and quirks; in their fantastic imagery and uncouth diction; in the occasional grossness and vulgarity, in which some of them were but too prone to indulge; they mark errors to be avoided. Yet even in reference to some of these things, it may be affirmed, that though in their free and reckless resort to every mode of stimulating attention, they were often betrayed into great violations of taste, the very same audacity of genius often produced felicities of imagery and diction, with which the blameless common place and the accurate insipidity of many modern discourses will not bear any comparison either for beauty or effect. For pregnancy of thought, for knowledge of the Word of God, for raciness of style, for evangelical sentiment, for anatomy of the human heart, for closeness of application, and especially for intensity of feeling, where shall we find their equals? They preached to their congregations, and not merely before them: they felt that the objects of their addresses were immortal souls in danger of being lost, and knew their business in the pulpit was to save those souls from perdition: they preached as if they expected there and then to achieve the great work of conversion; and felt as if the eternal destinies of their hearers were suspended on the manner in which they discharged their duties,

and as if they were to ascend the next moment after
they had finished their sermons to give an account of
them at the bar of God. Do not the extracts given,
(and they are but a very inadequate sample of their
works,) bear out these asertions? The power they exhibit, the heart-searching appeals in which they abound,
are the very things now wanting. There may be, and
there should be, more of classic elegance, more of logical
arrangement, of philosophic precision, of vigorous and
clear argumentation, than we find in the old writers;
but still, combined with this, there should also be in
our sermons, as there were in theirs, the pointed interro-
gation, the pungent appeal, the bold apostrophe, the
gush of feeling, the forcible expostulation, and the
tender invitation; now the gentle flow of deep, and
solemn, and placid thought, and then the torrent-rush
of impassioned sentiment: the beautiful and harmonious combination of reason, imagination, and affection;
and all employed to carry out the purpose for which
the gospel is to be preached, even to win souls to Christ.
Especially should there be the direct personal address
which characterises all the extracts which I have introduced. Our hearers must be made to feel that they are
not merely listening to the discussion of a subject, but
to an appeal to themselves: their attention must be
kept up, and a close connection between them and the
preacher maintained, by the frequent introduction of
the pronoun "you;" so that each may realise the
thought that the discourse is actually addressed to him.
Many preachers do not come near enough to their
congregations. Those who were privileged to hear
Mr Hall deliver, in his best days, some of his most
popular and powerful discourses, will not fail to recollect

how strikingly he combined the intense earnestness of
the passages just quoted, with the chaste and classic
elegance of our best writers; and thus, considering the
evangelical strain of his preaching he may be said to
have poured forth a torrent of the water of life, clear
as crystal. He reminded you of one, who in his yearn-
ings for the salvation of sinners seemed to feel that language was too feeble an instrument for such a purpose :
and who, notwithstanding his sovereign command and exquisite selection of terminology, was struggling to burst
the barrier by which words limit the communication of
thought, in order that he might by a still more direct
and facile method reach and grasp the soul of his
hearers.

There is, however, hope that our old theological
writers will not be quite forgotten or neglected, while
such men as Professor Stowell, of Rotherham College,
employ their talents in writing prefaces to reprints of
works such as those of Thomas Adams, and lend their
authority to recommend the perusal of such monuments
of sanctified genius. Beautifully and no less correctly
has he said, "As Edwards constrains to closeness of
thought; as Howe inspires sublimity of sentiment; as
Bates lights up the soul with a soft and silvery light;
as Owen loads the mind with a harvest of rich knowledge; as Taylor cheers the imagination with a vintage
of delicious grapes; as Baxter fires the soul with longings for salvation, first of ourselves and then of others;
even so does Adams lead to those springs of graphic
power, of dramatic grandeur, and of subduing pathos,
which it is the fear of many are dried up. We believe
they are not. We cannot but think there are minds
now opening on the awful solemnities of the Christian

ministry, to whom this example will be inciting; let them look at the things with their own eyes, ponder them in silent and lonely thought, pray over the fruits of such meditations, till they kindle into living pictures; and so let them pour out their feelings into the best words they can find; there will then be no just complaint of the want of power and originality in the English pulpit."

Happy will it be for this, and for all coming ages, if the men of the present day will study, with all the advantages, checks, and guides of modern education, the divines of the seventeenth century, both of the Episcopalian and Nonconformist churches: not indeed as models of style or logic, but of intense earnestness; not as writers who should teach us in all things how to think, but how to feel. I would not have the modern mind, so much as the modern heart, cast in the mould of these great-hearted writers. Even their theology is not to be rigidly copied; but O! their unction; their mighty power of realization; their nearness to God; their views, so intent, so clear, so piercing, of eternity; their thorough understanding of the object of their ministry, and their entire consecration of themselves to its awful functions. Would we could transcribe and make all these our own.

CHAPTER VI.

EARNESTNESS OF MANNER CONTINUED, AS MANIFESTED IN THE DELIVERY OF SERMONS.

DEMOSTHENES, on being asked what was the first excellence of an orator, replied, " Delivery : " what the second, " Delivery : " what the third, " Delivery." An impressive admonition this, from such an authority, to all preachers, on the importance of that part of our subject which we are now considering.

After the death of that seraphic man Mr McCheyne, there was found upon his desk an unopened note from one who had heard his last sermon, to this effect ; " Pardon a stranger for addressing to you a few lines. I heard you preach last Sabbath evening, and it pleased God to bless that sermon to my soul. It was not so much what you said, as your manner of speaking it, that struck me. I saw in you a beauty of holiness I never saw before."

This is only one instance out of ten thousand, in which the earnestness of a preacher's manner has secured that attention to his matter, which would not otherwise have been paid to it. The power of oratory has its foundations in the principles of our nature. It is not merely that ideas are conveyed by articulate language through the ear to the mind, but also that emotion is awakened by agreeable tones and pleasant modulations of the voice. Hence the power of music : and what is human speech but music ? No instrument has ever yet been constructed which can emit sounds so exquisitely moving as the human voice. Art is in this respect still below nature. True it is that we must go to the best voices for this superiority ; but even in voices far below the best, there is an expression of the various passions which no instruments can equal. All nations, therefore, savage as well as civilised, have confessed the power of oratory, not only as a vehicle of instruction, but as a means of impression. It is vain to pretend that matter is or ought to be every thing and manner nothing. Truth, it may be said, ought to make its own way, independently of the accompaniments of good elocution and graceful action. So it should, but these things are necessary, in many cases, to gain for it attention, and to secure that due consideration, without which it can make no impression. Manner is, so to speak, the harbinger and herald of matter, summoning the faculties of the soul to give audience to the truth to be communicated, and holding the mind in a state of abstraction from all other subjects that would divert the thoughts and prevent impression. It is not only the more illiterate and feeble-minded, not only the multitude who are led by feeling more than by reason, that are influenced by good oratory, but also men of the sturdiest intellect, and of the most philosophic cast of mind. The soul of the sage as well as of the savage, is formed with a susceptibility to the power and influence of music, and therefore to the power and influence of elocution. The importance of manner is consequently great, yea, far greater than either tutors or preachers have been disposed to admit. It is true that a good voice is necessary to good speaking, but not always to earnest speaking. Nature must do much to make a graceful and finished orator; but in the absence of this, a man of ardent mind, burning for the salvation of immortal souls, can, by an impressive earnestness of manner, be a more intense and effective speaker, notwithstanding naturally weak and unimpressive organs of speech, than the possessor of the finest voice, if destitute of life and feeling in his delivery; just as an exquisite performer can bring better music out of a bad instrument, than a bad musician can out of a good one. What may be done, for supplying deficiencies and correcting faults in elocution, where the mind is resolutely bent upon accomplishing this, Demosthenes has taught us; and were a tenth part of the pains taken by us to obtain a powerful and effective method of pulpit address which this prince of orators bestowed that he might become an effective speaker; did we exert the same determination to over-come every obstacle, we too should be orators in our better cause. And if ambition or patriotism, prompted Athenian and Roman orators to such studies and efforts for self-improvement, ought not love for souls, and zeal for God, to prompt us to similar endeavours? Did they cultivate elocution with such unwearied perseverance to counteract the designs of Philip, or to defeat or destroy Cataline; and shall we not use it to destroy the works of the devil, and to advance the kingdom of the Redeemer?

It is impossible not to observe how much the popularity of some preachers depends upon their manner; they do not say better or more striking things than other men; but they say them in a better and more striking manner. There is passion in their tones, power in their looks, and gracefulness in their gestures, which other men have never studied, and therefore have never acquired. This was eminently the case with Whitfield, the greatest of preachers. Much of the wondrous power of that extraordinary man lay in his voice and action. I have already given an extract from his sermons to illustrate his manner as regards style of composition, but who that never heard him, or indeed who that had, could illustrate his manner of delivery? Think of such paragraphs as those just quoted, delivered with an utterance appropriate to their nature; with an eye melting into tears; a voice tremulous with emotion, shrill yet full, now swelling into thunder, and then dying away again in soft whispers; one moment apostrophising God, and the next piercing the sinner's conscience with an appeal that was as sharp arrows of the Almighty; at one time pouring out a stream of impassioned pity for the sinner, and the next moment a torrent of burning indignation against his sin; his very hands, and every gesture all the while seconding his matchless elocution and seeming to help his labouring soul; all this being not the trickery of an artificial rhetoric to catch applause, but only the expression of his burning desire to produce conviction in his hearers; not the acting of a man striving after popularity, but the spontaneous gushing forth of a heart agonizing for the salvation of immortal souls! What oratory must that have been which extorted from the sceptical and fastidious Hume the confession that it was worth going twenty miles to hear, which interested the infidel Bolingbroke, and warmed even the cold and cautious Franklin into enthusiasm? In those discourses which roused a slumbering nation from the torpor of lukewarmness, and breathed new life into its dying piety, you will find no profound speculation, no subtle reasoning, no metaphysical disquisition; for these never formed, and never can form, the staple of pulpit eloquence: but you will find "thoughts that breathe, and words that burn;" and that when delivered with the magic of his wondrous voice, spoke, by the blessing of God, life into thousands dead in trespasses and sins. As a proof of the all-subduing power of his oratory, take the following scene from his Life by the Rev. Robert Philip.

"In February, 1742, Whitfield returned to London, where 'life and power soon flew all around him again; the Redeemer getting himself victory daily in many hearts.' The renewed progress of the gospel at this time in London, he calls emphatically, 'the Redeemer's stately steps.' Well he might; for during the Easter holidays, 'Satan's booth' in Moorfields poured out their thousands to hear him. This determined him to dare all hazards on Whit-Monday, the great gala-day of vanity and vice there. Gillies' account of this enterprise, although not incorrect nor uninteresting, is very incomplete, considering the fame of the feat at the time. The following account is from the pen of Whitfield himself.

"For many years, from one end of Moorfields to the other, booths of all kinds have been erected for mountebanks, players, puppet-shows, and such like. With a heart bleeding with compassion for so many thousands led captive by the devil at his will, on Whit-Monday, at six o'clock in the morning, attended by a large congregation of praying people, I ventured to lift up a standard amongst them in the name of Jesus of Nazareth. Perhaps there were about ten thousand in waiting, not for me, but for Satan's instruments to amuse them. Glad was I to find that I had, as it were for once, got the start of the devil. I mounted my field-pulpit; almost all flocked immediately around it. I preached on these words, 'As Moses lifted up the serpent in the wilderness, so shall the Son of Man be lifted up,' etc. They gazed, they listened, they wept; and I believe that many felt themselves stung with deep conviction for their past sins. All was hushed and solemn. Being thus encouraged, I ventured out again at noon; but what a scene! The fields, the whole fields, seemed in a bad sense of the word, all white, ready not for the Redeemer's but Beelzebub's harvest. All his agents were in full motion, drummers, trumpeters, merryandrews, masters of puppet shows, exhibiters of wild beasts, players, etc., etc., all busy in entertaining their respective auditories. I suppose there could not be less than twenty or thirty thousand people. My pulpit was fixed on the opposite side, and immediately to their great mortification, they found the number of their attendants sadly lessened. Judging that like Saint Paul, I should now be called as it were to fight with beasts at Ephesus, I preached from these words: 'Great is Diana of the Ephesians.' You may easily guess that there was some noise among the craftsmen, and that I was honoured with having a few stones, dirt, rotten eggs, and pieces of dead cats thrown at me, whilst engaged in calling them from their favourite but lying vanities. My soul was indeed among lions: but far the greatest part of my congregation, which was very large, seemed for awhile to be turned into lambs. This encouraged me to give notice that I would preach again at six o'clock in the evening. I came, I saw, but what? Thousands and thousands more than before, if possible, still more deeply engaged in their unhappy diversions; but some thousands amongst them waiting as earnestly to hear the gospel.

"This Satan could not brook. One of his choicest servants was exhibiting, trumpeting on a large stage; but as soon as the people saw me in my black robes and my pulpit, I think all to a man left him and ran to me. For a while I was enabled to lift up my voice like a trumpet, and many heard the joyful sound. God's people kept praying, and the enemy's agents made a kind of roaring at some distance from our camp. At length they approached nearer, and the merry-andrew (attended by others, who complained that they had taken many pounds less that day on account of my preaching,) got up upon a man's shoulders, and advancing near the pulpit attempted to slash me with a long heavy whip several times, but always with the violence of his motion tumbled down. Soon afterwards they got a recruiting sergeant with his drum, etc., to pass through the congregation. I gave the word of command, and ordered that way might be made for the king's officer. The ranks opened, while all marched quietly through, and then closed again. Finding these efforts to fail, a large body quite on the opposite side assembled together, and having got a large pole for their standard, advanced towards us with steady and formidable steps, till they came very near the skirts of our hearing, praying, and almost undaunted congregation. I saw, gave warning, and prayed to the Captain of our salvation for present support and deliverance. He heard and answered; for just as they approached us with looks full of resentment, I know not by what accident, they quarrelled among themselves, threw down their staff, and went their way, leaving, however, many of their company behind, who before we had done, I trust were brought over to join the besieged party. I think I continued in praying, preaching, and singing, (for the noise was too great at times to preach) about three hours.

"We then retired to the Tabernacle, with my pockets full of notes from persons brought under concern, and read them amidst the praises and spiritual acclamations of thousands, who joined with the holy angels in rejoicing that so many sinners were snatched, in such an unexpected, unlikely place and manner, out of the very jaws of the devil. This was the beginning of the Tabernacle society. Three hundred and fifty awakened souls were received in one day, and I believe the number of notes exceeded a thousand; but I must have done, believing you want to retire to join in mutual praise and thanksgiving to God and the Lamb."

I venture to pronounce this the greatest achievement of elocution which the history of the world presents, next to the splendid triumph of the apostle Peter's sermon over the murderers of Christ on the day of Pentecost. Who that considers the spot on which Whitfield then stood; the scenes by which he was surrounded; the discordant noises of the motley crew, which rung in his ears, and the ears of his audience; who, in short, that recollects what the wild uproar and the hurly burly of a London popular fair is, must not stand astonished, first at the courage of the man who could erect his pulpit, and preach a sermon in such a scene; and then still more at the marvellous success of his effort in the conversion of hundreds of souls by that one discourse? What, I ask, was the effect on the Athenians of the orations of Demosthenes, in rousing them against Philip of Macedon, compared with this?

The illustrious Greek had on his side every advantage which the scenery, and the historic associations connected with it, and the prepared mind of his audience, could give to his splendid argument and declamation; but the Christian orator had to combat with, and to triumph over, every thing that seemed inharmonious with his theme, and opposed to the accomplishment of his object: and what must have been the magic power of that elocution which could blind the eyes of an audience to the sights, and deafen their ears to the sounds so near them, and produce such fixedness of attention, and such power of abstraction, as to leave them at liberty for those processes of thought, which resulted in the conversion of hundreds to God !*

And to what, in the way of instrumentality, shall we attribute this astonishing effect, but to the power of his wonderful oratory, combined with the simplicity and power of the truths he enforced? This fact has stood for a century upon record, and yet we have been slow to learn from it the lessons which it is adapted to teach, and among them, the effect produced by a commanding

---

* Since the publication of the former editions of this work, I have been favoured with the following testimony to the power of Whitfield's oratory by Dr. Dewar, Principal of Marischal College Aberdeen. "When a lad," said the late Dugald Stewart, "about eighteen years of age, I went to hear Whitfield preach on the Calton Hill. I listened to him with amazement. The fascination was such as I had never felt before. I had then, and I have since, formed in my mind the idea of the perfect orator: but it was never realized, except in the case of Whitfield. He came fully up to my ideal standard of a faultless and perfect orator." "Professor Dugald Stewart," writes Principal Dewar, "was between sixty and seventy years of age when he communicated to me this opinion regarding the matchless power of Whitfield. The testimony of a philosopher so distinguished is worthy of being recorded."

method of address, in circumstances apparently the most unlikely for such a result. I am not calling upon my brethren to imitate this daring attack upon the very citadel of Satan: even Whitfield never, I believe, repeated it, and perhaps ought never to have attempted it; but my object is to show the power of voice and action, and the nature of ministerial earnestness.

We shall now contemplate another instance of the power of oratory, which if it be less grand and commanding in itself, is perhaps more likely to be useful to the readers of this little work, because it is an instance brought nearer to their own times, and to the level of their own circumstances: I mean Mr Spencer, of Liverpool. In reference to this transcendent young preacher, Mr Hall remarks, "The writer of this deeply regrets his never having had an opportunity of witnessing his extraordinary powers: but from all he has heard from the best judges, he can entertain no doubt that his talents in the pulpit were unrivalled; and that had his life been spared, he would, in all probability, have carried the art of preaching to a greater perfection than it ever attained, at least in this kingdom. His eloquence appears to have been of the purest stamp, effective, not ostentatious; consisting less in the preponderance of any one quality requisite to form a public speaker, than in an exquisite combination of them all; whence resulted an extraordinary power of impression, which was greatly aided by a natural and majestic elocution." In this last expression Mr Hall has disclosed much of the secret of Mr Spencer's popularity and usefulness; " a natural and majestic elocution;" this setting forth with simple and unaffected earnestness of manner the grand doctrines of evan-

gelical truth, accompanied as it was with a most en-
gaging countenance and form, constituted the charm,
and led to the success, of this most captivating preacher
of modern times. Let the young ministers of this age
read his " Life and Remains," as published by his gifted
successor, Dr. Raffles; and also his posthumous sermons,
which have been since given to the world, and they will
find nothing whatever of extraordinary genius; no
lofty eloquence, in the usual acceptation of that term;
no profound speculation; no splendid imagery or diction, but they will meet at every step with the doctrine
of Christ crucified, set forth with manly vigour, in
plain, perspicuous language; the utterances of a mind
well instructed in the way of salvation, and of a heart
overflowing with benevolence for the good of his fellow-
creatures. To what then shall we attribute, under God,
his success, not only in filling the large town in which
he lived, and the nation at large, with his fame, but
(what was infinitely more important in itself, and far more
eagerly coveted by him,) in bringing so many souls to
Christ? There is but one answer to be given to this,
and that is, it was the fascination of his manner. He
was in earnest. The stream of his simple, elegant,
though by no means profound thought, flowed forth
with a resistless impetuosity that carried away his
hearers before it. There is scarcely any more instructive lesson to be learnt, or any more important inference
to be drawn from the short life of this young minister,
so mysteriously cut off at the very commencement of
his career, than the vast consequence of an animated
manner of preaching the gospel.

I may here advert to another individual, who was
considered to be, in a particular way, one of the most

impressive preachers of his time, the late Mr Toller, of Kettering. He also no doubt owed much of the effect which his sermons produced, to his mode of address; and their effect proves that vehemence, boisterousness, and vociferation, are not essential to earnestness and deep impression; for nothing can be more calm and subdued, though nothing more solemnly commanding, than his whole demeanour in the pulpit. His printed sermons are characterised by strength of thought uttered in language of great perspicuity, though not irradiated by any coruscations of brilliant genius. "A noble simplicity and careless grandeur," says Mr Hall, with whom he lived on terms of most intimate friendship, "were the distinguishing features of his eloquence." There was an irresistible charm in his manner which threw a spell over all his hearers, and fascinated alike the learned and the illiterate; he made the latter to understand, and the former to feel. I never heard him but once, but it was on a memorable occasion, the ordination of Mr Robertson of Stretton, at which Mr Hall delivered the admirable charge afterwards published under the title of "The Difficulties and Encouragements of the Christian Minister." It is impossible ever to forget, and equally so to describe, the effect produced by two such preachers on such an occasion: it was the first time I ever heard either of them, and the last that I ever heard Mr Toller, and it almost seemed as if I had never heard preaching before: both were excited no doubt, and stimulated to do their best, not only by the occasion, but by the presence of each other. The terms employed by Mr. Toller's biographer were the most appropriate that could be selected to describe his style and manner, "simplicity and careless grandeur." It was impossible not to listen; neither eye nor ear played truant for a moment while he was preaching; his delivery was not the rushing torrent of impassioned eloquence which gushed afterwards from the lips of his distinguished fellow-labourer, but the majestic, silent flow of a noble river. "In the power of awakening pathetic emotions," says Mr Hall in his Memoir, "he has excelled any preacher it has been my lot to hear. Often have I seen a whole congregation melted under him like wax before the sun: my own feelings on more than one occasion have approached to an overpowering agitation. The effect was produced apparently with perfect ease. No elaborate preparation, no peculiar vehemence or intensity of tones, no artful accumulation of pathetic images, led the way: the mind was captivated and subdued, it hardly knew how. Though it will not be imagined that this triumph of popular eloquence could be habitual, much less constant, it may be safely affirmed that a large proportion of Mr Toller's discourses afforded some indications of these powers." The following is Mr Hall's description of the effect of two sermons preached in his hearing by this eminent man.

"It was about this period (1796) that my acquaintance with him commenced. I had known him previously, and occasionally heard him; but it was at a season when I was not qualified to form a correct estimate of his talents. At the time referred to, we were engaged to preach a double lecture at Thrapstone, nine miles from Kettering; and never shall I forget the surprise and pleasure with which I listened to an expository discourse, from 1 Peter ii, 1, 3. The richness, the unction, the simple majesty which pervaded his address, produced a sensation which I never felt before: it gave me a new view of the Christian ministry. But the effect, powerful as it was, was not to be compared with that which I experienced on hearing him preach at the half-yearly meeting of the Association, at Bedford.

The text which he selected was peculiarly solemn and impressive : his discourse was founded on 2 Peter i, 13-15, 'Yea, I think it meet, as long as I am in this tabernacle, to stir you up, by putting you in remembrance ; knowing that shortly I must put off this my tabernacle,' etc. The effect of this discourse on the audience was such as I have never witnessed before or since. It was undoubtedly very much aided by the peculiar circumstances of the speaker, who was judged to be far advanced in a decline, and who seemed to speak under the impression of its being the last time he should address his brethren on such an occasion. The aspect of the preacher, pale, emaciated, standing apparently on the verge of eternity, the simplicity and majesty of his sentiments, the sepulchral solemnity of a voice which seemed to issue from the shades, combined with the intrinsic dignity of the subject, perfectly quelled the audience with tenderness and terror, and produced such a scene of audible weeping as was perhaps never surpassed. All other emotions were absorbed in devotional feeling : it seemed to us as though we were permitted for a short space to look into eternity, and every sublunary object vanished before 'the powers of the world to come.' Yet there was no considerable exertion, no vehemence, no splendid imagery, no magnificent description ; it was the simple declaration of truth, of truth indeed of infinite moment, borne in upon the heart by a mind intensely alive to its reality and grandeur. Criticism was disarmed ; the hearer felt himself elevated to a region which it could not penetrate ; all was powerless submission to the master-spirit of the scene. It will be always considered by those who witnessed it as affording as high a specimen as can be easily conceived, of the power of a preacher over his audience, the habitual or even frequent recurrence of which would create an epoch in the religious history of the world." Memoir of Mr. Toller.

This description, even though some allowance should be made for the eloquence of friendship, is replete with instruction to our rising ministers. They may learn the vast importance of the manner in which a sermon is delivered, as well as the matter of which it is composed. Nor is this the only lesson, nor perhaps the most valuable one, to be learnt from this short but precious piece of ministerialbiography ; for we gather what it is that, to minds of the highest order, such as Mr. Hall's, constitutes the nearest approach to perfect pulpit eloquence, and to which even such commanding intellects yield themselves up with willing submission; not the artificial elaboration of men intent upon producing a great sermon; not the magniloquent diction and splendid imagery sought with ambitious eagerness by those who aim to shine; not the cold, abstract, philosophical reasoning of a metaphysical dialectician, but the simplicity and earnestness which aim to instruct the judgment, to awaken the conscience, and to affect the heart. All great minds love simplicity and detest affectation. This was especially the case with Mr. Hall. His censure of the mental quality most opposed to earnestness amounted sometimes to eloquent extravagance and burlesque, and his sarcasms were not unfrequently tinged with uncharitable bitterness; as his admiration of simplicity was occasionally expressed in somewhat exaggerated panegyric. The ambition of a preacher whose aim is usefulness might well be gratified by a remark which he once made after hearing a sermon, " I should not wonder if a hundred souls were converted to night ? " *

These are only a few out of innumerable instances which could be adduced to prove the vast importance which attaches to an effective delivery. Far greater numbers of our preachers fail for want of this, than from any other cause; and the fact is so notorious as to need no proof beyond common observation, and so impressive as to demand the attention, not only of the professors, but the committees, of all our colleges. It is too generally the case that adequate culture is not bestowed

* The editor may be permitted to notice that this sermon was by the author; as some who would be glad to know what preacher was alluded to, might not gather this from the text.

upon the speaking powers of our students, from the beginning to the end of their course of study. There is great assiduity manifested in securing them fulness of matter, but far too little in giving them impressiveness of manner. Assistance is granted to make them scholars, philosophers, and divines; but as to becoming good speakers, they are, I fear, left pretty much to themselves. Nay, it is not even inculcated upon them, with the emphasis it should be, to try to make themselves such. A complete system of ministerial education naturally includes great attention to elocution; and this should commence as soon as a student enters college, so that by the time he is put upon the preaching list, he may have some aptitude for the management of his voice, and not have his thoughts diverted then from his matter and his object, to his manner. He should by that time have acquired the habit of speaking well, so as to be able to practise it with facility, and without study. The great objection to lectures on elocution is, that they are apt to produce a pompous, stiff, and affected manner; but this is an abuse of the art; its object should be to cure the vices of a bad, and to supply the wants of a defective enunciation, and to form an easy, natural, and impressive delivery. When will preachers learn that preaching is but talking in a louder tone, and with a little more emphasis of manner? Why affect a preaching or a praying tone, a method of speaking peculiar to the pulpit? A conversational manner, occasionally elevated animated and energetic, as impassioned passages and feeling may require, is what we want. There are some men who are good talkers out of the pulpit, yet bad speakers in it. How much more acceptable would they be, if they would carry their easy, natural manner of conversation with them into the sacred desk !

I entirely concur therefore with Dr. Vaughan, in his important and impressive remark, "that let our students fail in the matter of a good elocution, and so far as regards their ministry among Protestant Dissenters, it will matter little in what else they may succeed." This is sustained by a reference to the great number we observe, who, though soundly orthodox in sentiment, possessed of large acquirements in scholarship and philosophy, partaking of undoubted piety, and desirous of doing good, yet make no way, can with difficulty procure a charge, and are filled perhaps with wonder, that men very much their inferiors in natural talent and literary acquirement, are every where followed, while they are every where neglected. The problem is easily solved, the mystery soon explained ; these inferior men, by their earnest, animated manner, make their more slender abilities tell more upon the popular mind, heart, and conscience, than do the heartless dissertations and elaborate essays of dull scholars, frigid philosophers, and bad speakers, though possessed of useless stores of knowledge.

It should, however, be remarked, that there is nothing more likely to be mistaken than animation in the pulpit. There are many young ministers, who, being aware of the importance of a graceful and effective elocution, take no small pains to acquire it, by studying and practising the most approved rules of the art. But it is not this alone for which we contend ; for as the lessons of the dancing master produce only stiff and formal action, where there is no natural ease and elegance, so the

teacher of elocution can do little to form an earnest and
energetic speaker, where there is no living source of
animation in the soul. It is not a pompous, swelling,
ore rotundo style of speaking that constitutes the excellence of an orator; not "the start and stare theatric;"
not modulations of the voice that sound as if the speaker
were regulating tones and cadences by the fugleman
motions of a teacher standing before him; but the
impassioned vivacity of one who feels intensely his subject, and speaks under the influence of strong emotion,
as one determined to make others feel. The secret of
animation, and the source of earnestness, lie, as I have
said, in an intense feeling of the subject of discourse;
in a mind deeply impressed, and a heart warmed, with
the theme discussed. All men are in earnest when they
feel. Hence the anecdote of the pleader, who was so
disgusted with a client's cold manner of stating her case,
as to tell her that he did not credit her tale. Stung by
this reflection upon her veracity, and this disbelief of
her grievance, she rose into strong emotion, and affirmed
with expressive vehemence the truth of the story.
" Now," said he, " I believe you."

The hacknied but valuable precept of the old poet remains, and ever will remain, as true as when first uttered,
" Weep yourself, if you wish me to weep." Sympathy is
the speaker's most powerful auxiliary : there is nothing
so contagious as strong emotion. We have most of us,
perhaps, seen a large portion of a congregation brought to
tears by the pathetic and faltering tones, the tremulous
lips, and suffused eyes of the preacher. But then it
must be sincere, and not simulated emotion, must be excited by a subject worthy of it, and must be shewn when
the people's minds are prepared to sympathise with it. It

is well said there is only a step between the sublime and the ridiculous; and the same remark may be applied to the pathetic, it may degenerate into mere puking. Genuine emotion is the charm of all speaking upon moral and religious subjects, and in the absence of it, the most measured and stately elocution, whatever pleasure it may impart to the ear, will have little power to affect the heart. We have sometimes listened to lofty and well composed music, to an overture for instance, which we could not but admire; but it was still cold admiration, for the whole piece had not a note of passion from beginning to end; but some simple melody followed it, which by the pathos of its notes or the power of its associations touched every chord in our hearts, and raised in us a tumult of emotion. Thus it is with different preachers, we listen to one, whose excellent composition, and sonorous, perhaps even musical voice, command our admiration; but not a passion stirs, all within is cold, quiet, and without emotion, his speaking is good, but it does not move us: while another has perhaps less talent, indeed less oratory in one sense, but has tones, looks, and manner all full of earnest feeling, and every word of his coming from his heart, awakens by sympathy a correspondent state of feeling in our hearts. Who is likely to be moved by hearing a man discuss the most awful realities of eternal truth, such as the danger and doom of impenitent sinners, the glories of heaven, and the torments of hell, with as much coolness, and with as little emotion as a lecturer on science would exhibit when dwelling on the facts of natural history? Is it probable there can be any earnestness in the hearers, when there is none in the preacher? "How is

it," said a minister to an actor, "that your per-
formances, which are but pictures of the imagination,
produce so much more effect than our sermons, which
are all realities?" "Because," said the actor, "we represent fictions as though they were realities, and you
preach realities as though they were fictions." It is
difficult to believe that a dull, cold, statue-like preacher,
whose passionless monotony is a mental opiate for his
hearers, can himself credit the message he is delivering.
What, that man who never elevates or depresses his
voice from one given pitch of soporific dulness, whose
tone never falters, whose eye never glistens, whose hand
never moves, who speaks as if he was afraid of awakening the slumberers whom his "drowsy tinklings" have
lulled to sleep, he feel the weight of souls; he in
earnest for their salvation; he endeavouring to pluck
them as brands from the burning! Who will credit it?
It is true he may have no great compass of voice, and a
naturally phlegmatic mind, with great deficiency in
the natural powers of oratory; but place him by the
side of a river where he has seen a fellow-creature fall
into the water, and let him throw a plank or a rope to aid
the drowning man to escape, will he not have power of
voice, and of animated tones, and of persuasive earnestness then, as he directs the object of his solicitude to
the means of deliverance? Will he not rise out of his
monotony there? Will he not make himself heard and
felt there?

By an earnest manner, then, is meant, the method
of delivery produced by a deep and feeling sense of
the importance of our message. We are to persuade,
to entreat, to beseech; and these modes of speech have
an utterance of their own. What must Paul's manner

have been, how impassioned and impressive, when he made Felix tremble, and Festus exclaim, "Thou art beside thyself, much learning doth make thee mad!" But even the sublime and awful truths of revelation, if they do not press upon the heart of the preacher, and command and possess it, will be but coldly handled and feebly discussed. It is only when the love of Christ constrains us, and bears us away as with the force of a torrent, that we shall speak with a manner befitting our great theme. If we are not intensely real, we shall be but indifferent preachers.

This shows us the vast moment of our living under the powerful impression of the truths we preach. We cannot, like the actor, have a stage dress and character to put on for the occasion, and to put off when the curtain drops. There may indeed be a factitious earnestness excited by the sound of our own voice, and by the solemnities of public worship; but this will usually be fitful, feeble, assumed, and very different from that burning ardour which is the result of eminent piety, and which imparts its own intensity of emotion to the words and tones of the speaker. It was the patriotism of Demosthenes that communicated the fire to his eloquence: he loved his country, and trembling for the ruin that Philip was bringing upon the liberties of Greece, he poured forth his lightning-words in tones of thunder. His philippics were a torrent of the strongest emotion, bursting from his heart, though guided in its course by the established rules of eloquence. He could never have spoken as he did, had not the designs of the Macedonian and the dangers of Greece, wrung his soul with anguish. So must it be with us, our animation must be the earnestness.

not of rhetoric, but of religion: not of art, but of
renewed nature; and designed not to astound, but to
convince and move; a manner studied and intended
not to attract a crowd, and to excite applause, but to
save the souls of men from death. For this purpose
whatever means we employ and whatever rules we lay
down, to cure the vices of a bad elocution, and to
acquire the advantages of a graceful one, (and such an
aim is quite lawful,) we must ever remember that the
basis of a powerful and effective pulpit oratory will be
deep and fervent piety; and in the absence of that, the
most commanding gift of public speaking will be but as
"sounding brass or a tinkling cymbal."

Dr. Cotton Mather, in his invaluable work, now
nearly forgotten, entitled, "The Student and Preacher,"
in speaking on this subject, remarks:

"It is a pity but a well prepared sermon should be a well pro-
nounced one. Wherefore avoid for ever all inanes sine mente sonos,
and all indecencies; everything that is ridiculous. Be sure to speak
deliberately. Strike the accent always upon the word in the sentence
it properly belongs unto. A tone that shall have no regard to this is
very injudicious, and will make you talk too much in the clouds. Do
not begin too high. Ever conclude with vigour. If you must have
your notes before you in your preaching, and it be needful for you,
De scripto dicere, which even some of the most famous orators, both
among the Grecians and the Romans, did; yet let there be with you
a distinction between the neat using of notes, and the dull reading of
them. Keep up the air and life of speaking, and put not off your
hearers with a heavy reading to them. How can you demand of
them to remember much of what you bring to them, when you remember nothing of it yourself? Besides by reading all you say, you
will so cramp and stunt all ability for speaking, that you will be
unable to make a handsome speech on any occasion. What I therefore advise you to is, let your notes be little more than a guide, on
which you may cast your eye now and then, to see what arrow is to
be next fetched from thence; and then with your eye as much as may
be on them whom you speak to, let it be shot away with a vivacity

becoming one in earnest for to have the truths well entertained by the auditory. Finally let your perorations be lively expostulations with the conscience of the hearer; appeals made and questions put unto the conscience, and consignments of the work over into the hands of that flaming preacher in the bosom of the hearer. In such flames you may do wondrously."

Pity that Dr. Mather had not gone a little farther than this, and affectionately advised his younger brethren in the ministry to begin their career without any notes at all in the pulpit; advice still more necessary in this day, as there seems a rising inclination to adopt the practice of reading. Nothing can be conceived of more likely to repress earnestness, and to hinder our usefulness, than this method becoming general. True it is that some preachers may rise up, who, like a few living examples, may, in despite of this practice, attain to eminence, honour, and usefulness, such as rarely fall to the lot of ministers in any denomination; but this will not be the case with the greater number, who not having commanding intellect to lift them above the disadvantage of this habit, will find few churches willing to accept their dulness, for the sake of the accuracy with which it is expressed. And who can tell us how much greater our greatest men would be, if they delivered their sermons without their notes? Think of Whitfield, Hall, Parsons, reading their sermons. What a restraint upon their noble intellects and their gushing hearts! Where is reading tolerated but in the pulpit? Not on the stage, nor at the bar, nor in the senate. It is conceded that we lose something of precision and accuracy by spoken discourses, as compared with those that are read, but is not this more than made up by what we gain in ease and impression? The aid borrowed from the expressions of the countenance and graceful action is lost by him who slavishly reads; the link of sympathy between his soul and those of his audience is weakened; the lightnings of his eloquence flash less vividly, and its thunders roll less grandly through this obstruction. Perhaps even those who do read are aware of the disadvantages of the habit, and would say to their younger brethren, whose habits are not yet formed, avoid if you can, the practice of reading your discourses. There are however occasions, when from the nature and extent of the subject, this practice is not only allowable, but necessary.

In connexion with the subject of preaching, I may consider, with propriety, the matter and manner of prayer. There is a close and obvious connexion between the two, for earnest sermons should ever be associated with earnest prayers; and it cannot be doubted that a pious, faithful, and devoted minister is scarcely less useful, at any rate in keeping up the spirit of devotion in his congregation, by the latter, than by the former. His chastened fervour, like a breeze from heaven, comes over the languid souls of his hearers, and fans the spark of piety in their hearts to a flame: while on the contrary, the dulness and coldness of some public prayers are enough to freeze what little devotion there may be in the assembled people. We have thought too little of this, and have too much neglected to cultivate the gift, and to seek the grace, of supplication. If entreating and beseeching importunity be proper in dealing with sinners for God, can it be less so in dealing with God for sinners? Our flocks should be the witnesses of both these acts on our part, and hear not only how we speak to them, but how we plead with God for them; they should be the auditors of our

agonizing intercession on their behalf; and be convinced how true is our declaration that we have them
in our hearts. How such petitions, so full of intense
affection and deep solicitude, would tend to soften their
minds, and to prepare them for the sermon which was
to follow! Who has not beheld the solemnizing and
subduing effect upon a congregation of such holy
wrestling with God? The audience seemed to feel as
if God had indeed come down among them in power
and glory during the prayer, and was preparing to do
some work of grace in their midst. The rudest and
most turbulent spirits have sometimes been awed, and
the most trifling and frivolous minds made serious, by
this holy exercise. We who practise extempore prayer
have advantages in this respect, of which we should not
be slow to avail ourselves. Not being confined by the
forms of a liturgy, but left to our own choice, we can
give harmony to all the various parts of the service,
and make the scripture we read, and the hymns we
sing, as well as the prayers we present, all bear upon
the subject of the sermon, and thus give unity of design,
and concentration of effect, to the solemn engagements
of the sanctuary. This should be an object with every
minister, in order that the thoughts of the people may
flow pretty much in one channel, and towards one point,
without being divided or diverted. Moral, as well as
mechanical effect depends upon the combination of
many seemingly small causes. But more especially
should the prayers be in harmony with the sermon, and
every preacher knows what the sermon is to be. If he
is about to address himself in a strain of beseeching
importunity to the impenitent and unbelieving, how
much would it tend to prepare them for his appeal, if

his heart were previously, in their hearing, to pour forth a strain of fervent pleading with God on their behalf. They would thus be awed and subdued into a state of mind likely to render the forthcoming sermon effectual, by the blessing of God, for their conversion. Such a prayer would be the most appropriate introduction he could give to his discourse. But then especial care should be taken that the hymn, and even the tune, interposed between the prayer and the sermon, should not be of a kind to divert the current of thought, much less to efface the solemn impressions already produced, and hinder the effect of the discourse about to be delivered. I remember to have heard a preacher, who was going to preach a very solemn sermon, breathe out one of the most impressive strains of intercession for the impenitent I ever listened to, as if anxious to begin by his prayer the work of conversion, which he hoped to finish by his sermon. The people sat down in solemn awe, when as if by the prompting of the wicked One, who catches away the seed of the word out of the heart, the clerk gave out a most inappropriate hymn, and the choir* with a band of musical instruments, sang a tune more inappropriate still. As may be easily imagined, the seriousness produced by the preacher was instantly dissipated, and the preparation for the sermon entirely destroyed. How true is it, that the singing-seat is often hostile to the usefulness of the pulpit, and the

* Perhaps, after all the attempts to improve our congregational singing by organs and choirs, there is nothing more devotional and effective than the plan of a thoroughly good precentor, as he is called in Scotland, or clerk in England, especially if the congregation be trained as well as exhorted to join in this sublime part of worship. This would shut out the evils which not unfrequently occur where there is a choir.

choir in opposition to the efforts of the preacher! Finney, in his book on Revivals, descends to so minute a specification of the circumstances to be attended to in preparing for a revival, as to expose him to the ridicule of many of his readers, and no attempt is made here to defend him, or to recommend his volume; but still there is true philosophy in the spirit of his directions, which amounts to this; that the effect of sermons, as indeed of all public speaking, depends often upon very little things. Trifles have great power to divert the current of thought, to break the chain of reflection, and to disturb the process of emotion. Every thing connected with public worship should be still, orderly, and solemn, as befits a service conducted in the presence of God, and with reference to him.

Returning to the subject of prayer, it becomes every minister to take especial care that this shall be conducted with propriety, not only on account of its nature and design, as addressed to God, and as the medium of obtaining blessings at his hand, but because of its moral effect upon the people. We object to pre-composed forms, (and we think on sufficient grounds,) as wanting in adaptation to the ever changing circumstances of the congregation, to the events of the time, and to the services of the minister, and as tending to produce formalism; but we are bound to take care that all these benefits are secured by our free prayers, and that they are in every respect adapted to edification. But is there not room for much improvement in our public devotional exercises? In some cases there is too much elaboration and appearance of study; though in far more, a want of richness and and fulness of unction aud importunity. The prayers are often too excursive and

vague, a mere string of petitions which have no connexion with each other, and are without unity of
design, or definiteness of object. There are some admirable remarks on the subject of extempore prayer in
Foster's sketch of Mr Hall's character as a preacher,
which go to prove that more concentration of thought
on particular topics would produce a greater effect than
that unrestrained discursiveness which characterizes too
many of our devotional exercises. We pass too rapidly
from one subject to another, and thus as it were surprise our hearers, by their being brought to a new topic,
before they are aware that they had left the preceding
one; and it may be safely affirmed that it is very
difficult to join in prayers which do not detain the
thoughts on certain things for a few moments. " Things
noted so transiently do not admit of deliberate attention,
and seem as if they did not claim it." With the liberty
of unrestricted variety which we possess, why should
it be thought necessary to go always over the same
ground, and to bring in the same topics, in the same
exact order, in much the same length, and in almost
the same words? Why may we not sometimes drop
every thing else, and break out into a continued strain
in reference to one continued object? How deeply
the audience would be convinced of the importance
which we at any rate feel to belong to it, and how
likely would such a method be to engage them in deep
sympathy with us, in reference to it! We should also
be careful to avoid all personalities which would excite
curiosity or disturb devotion, and especially all lauda-
tory epithets on the one hand, and criminatory ones on
the other. In using our freedom, let us take care not
to abuse it, and endeavour that the end and object of

our preaching may be helped, and not hindered, by the method of our praying. If pre-composed forms of prayer have their disadvantages, so also has free prayer; and while we consider the balance of advantage vastly in favour of the latter, let us recollect that our brethren of the Establishment are of the same opinion respecting their liturgy; it becomes us therefore while we charitably bear with each other, each to make the best possible use of the method we prefer.

The manner of prayer, as well as its matter, demands also our serious attention. While the very nature of the exercise forbids every thing showy or elaborately ingenious; every thing quaint, familiar, and irreverent, and enjoins the utmost simplicity and spirituality, it no less prohibits all flippancy, carelessness, and pompous oratory. The most serious, reverent, and devotional manner is required, not only on our own account, but on account of the audience. There are some men whose very tones are enough to extinguish all devotional feeling at once, and render it almost impossible to conceive that we hear a sinful mortal addressing himself to the Holy, Holy, Holy Lord God, before whom the seraphim veil their faces. While on the contrary there are others whose deeply devotional air, subdued manner, and awe-stricken demeanour, remind us that they are indeed speaking to the Almighty. It is not necessary to suppose that earnestness requires boisterousness; a mistake too commonly made by many who work themselves up into vociferation and contortion of features. Such vehemence, like a violent blast of wind, puts out the flame of devotion if languid, when a gentler breeze would fan it to intensity. It is well also to avoid that sing-song tone which we too often hear in those who lead the public devotions. But above all there must be earnestness; the earnestness of deep feeling, of lively devotion, of a heart intent upon its own salvation, and upon the salvation of those who are then waiting to hear the word of life.

Our pleading, though in the highest degree reverential, should be that of men who are standing between the living and the dead, subdued and chastened, yet importunate intercession, such as it might be supposed we should use in addressing an earthly monarch, when interceding for the lives of some for whom we were anxious to obtain the interposition of royal mercy.

CHAPTER VII.

EARNESTNESS MANIFESTED IN THE PASTORATE.

THIS must by no means be omitted. The pulpit is
the chief, but not the only, sphere of ministerial solicitude and action : just as preaching is God's first, but
not his exclusive, means of saving souls. Many ministers
have fallen into one or other of two opposite mistakes ;
one class have thought to do every thing in the pulpit as
preachers, while they have neglected the duties of the
pastor ; the others have purposed to do every thing as
pastors, but have neglected the diligent preparation
of their sermons. Of the two errors the latter is the
more mischievous, inasmuch as no pastoral devotedness,
however intense, will long keep together a congregation
among Protestant Dissenters, much less collect one,
when the preaching is indifferent and unattractive ;
while on the other hand, good preaching will of itself do
much even in the absence of pastoral attentions to keep
the flock from being scattered. But why should not
both extremes be avoided ? Good preaching and good
shepherding are quite compatible with each other, and
he who is in earnest will combine both. He will be a
watchman for souls every where, and seek if by any and
by all means he can save some. He can never entirely
lay aside his anxiety for the objects of his regard, and
is ever ready to manifest it on all suitable occasions.

His sermons are composed and delivered for this object, and he is afterwards inquisitive for the effect they have produced, and watches and prays for the result. His anxious eye is searching the congregation, even while preaching, to see, not who is delighted, but who is seriously impressed. He will not, cannot, be content to go on, without ascertaining whether or not his sermons are successful. Like a good physician, who is watchful for the effect of his medicines upon his patients individually, according to their specific varieties of disease, he will endeavour to ascertain the impression which his sermons have produced on particular persons. He will aim to attract to him the anxious inquirers after salvation, and for this purpose will have special meetings for them, will invite and encourage their attendance, will cause them to feel that they are most welcome, and by his tender, faithful, and appropriate treatment of their cases, will make them sensible that they are as truly the objects of deep interest to him as lambs are to the good shepherd. And though he will very naturally wish not to be too frequently broken in upon in his private studies by those to whom he has appointed set times for meeting him, yet a poor burdened trembling penitent will never find him engaged too deeply or delightfully in study, to heal his broken heart, and to bind up his wounds. It is really distressing to know how little time some ministers are willing to give up from their favourite pursuits, even for relieving the solicitudes of an anxious mind. They read much, and perhaps as the result, preach well-composed, though possibly not very awakening, sermons; but as for any skill, or even taste, for dealing with convinced sinners, wounded consciences, and perplexed minds, they are as destitute of them as if they were no part of their duty. They resemble lecturers on medicine, rather than practitioners; or they are like physicians who would assemble all their patients able to attend, in the same room, and then give general directions about health and sickness to all alike, but would not inquire into their several ailments, or visit them at their own abodes, or adapt the treatment to their individual and specific disease. It is admitted that some men have less tact, and a still greater destitution of taste, than others, for this department of pastoral action; but some skill in it, and some attention to it, are the duty of every minister, and may be acquired by all: and no man can be in earnest without it. He who can only generalise in the pulpit, but has no ability to individualise out of it; who cannot in some measure meet the varieties of religious perplexity, and deal with the various modifications of awakened solicitude; who finds himself disinclined or disabled to guide the troubled conscience through the labyrinths which sometimes meet the sinner in the first stage of his pilgrimage to the skies, may be a popular preacher, but he is little fitted to be the pastor of a Christian church. One half-hour's conversation with a convinced but perplexed person may do more to correct mistakes, to convey instruction, to relieve solicitude, and to settle the wavering in faith and peace than ten sermons. True it requires much love for souls, much devotedness to their salvation, and much anxiety for the success of our ministry, to devote that half-hour to one solitary inquirer after life eternal; but surely no really earnest minister will think his time ill bestowed in guiding that single inquirer into the way of peace.

This individualising labour is more easily carried on and is indeed more important to ministerial success in some situations than in others. In small congregations, for instance, especially when they are found in our lesser towns or villages, the objects of such special attention come more under the notice of a pastor, are more accessible, and can have more time given to them, than in large congregations in more considerable towns. To these smaller churches, individuals, though not of more importance or value in themselves, since the soul and its salvation are of equal worth every where, are of more consequence to the comfort of the minister, and the prosperity of the cause, than they are where a crowd is gathered. Pastors of large churches are much more occupied, both with the concerns of their own flock, and with public business, than their brethren in more retired situations, and are often so much engaged and hurried as to have too little leisure for the individual attentions now recommended; and they are perhaps apt, through having to do with large congregations, to think too little of the units. Still some excuse may be made for them, of which others cannot avail themselves. The accession even occasionally of only a single member to our smaller churches is felt to be of more importance, and produces a more reviving and cheering effect, than the addition of several to the larger ones. We have all something to learn even from the Scribes and Pharisees of ancient times, who compassed sea and land to make one proselyte; and also from the Papists of modern times, who pursue a like course: or to change the example, we want more of the benevolent disposition of angels, who rejoice over one sinner that repents. No efforts would be more likely to be successful, none would more amply reward those who would make them, than selection of the most hopeful individuals in the congregation, and following them up with all the assiduities of special, affectionate, and judicious attention. Such a course of pastoral labour, though it would not altogether be a substitute for pulpit attractiveness, and should never be allowed to supersede the most diligent pulpit preparation, would enable many a minister, not gifted with large abilities, to retain a strong hold upon his flock. This is a line in which almost any one may carry on a career of earnestness.

Another object of pastoral obligation may be mentioned, attention to the young : and they may be divided into two classes, those belonging to the congregation, and those belonging to the Sunday-schools. With regard to the former, it is a matter of congratulation, that the modern plan of Bible-classes is not infrequent nor unsuccessful : but even at this time, it is rather the exception than the rule. It may be feared that there are some who from the beginning to the end of the year, aye, and of their ministry also, take no interest in the youth of their congregations; they have no catechetical classes, no Bible-classes, and even rarely preach to the young. Who can wonder that such men have to complain that their young people go off to other denominations, or what is far worse, to the world? What have they ever done to attach them to themselves, or to their place of worship? Let no man be surprised that his congregation, diminished by death and removals, continually declines, if he neglects to call around him the youth of his flock. Whence does the shepherd look for his future flock, but from the lambs? And who are to constitute our future congregations and churches, but our young people!

I am an advocate also for the catechetical instruction of the younger children, and am sorry that this admirable method of imparting religious truth has fallen into such general desuetude. Even the Bible class, however accommodated to the capacity of the junior members of our congregation, is not altogether a substitute for the practice of catechising, but should be regarded only as an addition to it. There is still a great desideratum for our denomination, and their thanks would be pre-eminently due to the man who should supply it; I mean a set of well-composed catechisms, which might be introduced into all our families and institute a uniform system of religious instruction throughout the body. I say which might be introduced into all our families; for it is by no means my wish or my intention to obtrude the pastor between the parent and child, and take the religious instruction from natural guardians and teachers, to devolve it upon the pastor. It is to parents that the injunction is delivered, "thou shalt teach these words to thy children diligently, and shalt talk of them when thou sittest in thy house," and, "bring them up in the nurture and admonition of the Lord." No pastoral attention should be intended, nor can be adapted, to supersede or interfere with this solemn parental obligation. But the pastor should labour to the uttermost to urge and keep the parents of his flock up to the right discharge of their duty. There are few of us who are not sorrowfully convinced that little is to be expected from our sermons in the pulpit, or our instructions in the class-room, while all our endeavours are so miserably counteracted by the neglect of domestic instruction, and the want of parental solicitude. It is not intended to justify pastoral neglect by advancing the obligations of parental duty, for perhaps we all have been, and are, guilty of a criminal defect of duty, in not giving more of our time and attention to the children of our congregations; but even the time and attention we do give, is likely to be lost, through the low state of religion in the homes of some of our people.

We might very naturally expect that our churches would be chiefly built up from the families of our members; whereas the greater number of accessions are from those who were once the people of the world. There is a great mistake on this subject, into which both parents and ministers have fallen; and that is, that the conversion of the children of the professor is to be looked for more from the sermons of the minister, than from the instructions of the parent; whereas the contrary is the true order of things; and if domestic piety and teaching were what they ought to be, it is the order which would be found to exist. There is unquestionable truth in the proverb, "Train up a child in the way he should go, and when he is old he will not depart from it." Were the nature and design of the domestic constitution thoroughly understood, and its religious duties early, judiciously, affectionately, and perseveringly discharged, the greater number of our young people would be converted to God at home. Were all religious professors who are parents, real and eminent Christians; were they, from the time they became parents, to set their hearts upon being the instruments of their children's conversion; were they to do all that prayer, instruction, discipline, and example could do, for the

formation of the religious character of their offspring;
and were they carefully to abstain from every thing
which would obstruct that end, it might be confidently
expected that it would be within the hallowed precincts
of such homes, and not in the sanctuary, that the
children of the godly would usually become godly
themselves. It should then be, and will be, an
object with every truly earnest pastor, to bring up the
parents in his church to a right sense and faithful
discharge of their functions. He will labour to impress
upon them the solemn obligations under which they
live, to train up their children for God. It will be a
matter of prayer and solicitude with him to excite them
to their duty, and to keep them in it. For this purpose
he will not only bring his pulpit ministrations to bear
much upon parental obligations, but he will make a
point of visiting the families connected with his church,
to pray with them, and to hold up the hands of the
parents in this godly duty. Deeply is it to be regretted
that this part of pastoral occupation, as well as catechising, has disappeared amidst the bustle and engrossing power of trade, and the public business of modern
religious institutions. How little do the families of
our people know of us in the character and hallowed
familiarity of the pastor! When are we seen amidst
the domestic circle as the respected and beloved minister of that lovely and interesting group, labouring, by
our affectionate, serious, and solemn discourse, and by
prayer as serious, solemn, and affectionate, to entwine
ourselves round the young hearts which there look up
to us with reverent regard? Why, why do we neglect
such important scenes of labour, such hopeful efforts
for usefulness? What power would this give to our

sermons, and what efficacy to our ministrations ! These
young ones would grow up to love us, and it would not
be a light or little thing which would break them off
from our ministry when we had produced in them such
a personal attachment to ourselves. But then we must
take especial care that our conduct in the houses of our
people should be such as to give weight and influence
to their religious instruction of the family, and to ours
in the sanctuary. We must be known there as the
servants of God, the ministers of Christ, the watchmen
for souls ; and not merely as the table-guests, the parlour jesters, the gossiping story-tellers, the debating
politicians, the stormy polemics, the bitter sectarians ;
much less as the lovers of wine.* Would to God that

* When will the ministers and members of our churches begin
generally to inquire, whether it is not expedient for them, if not for
their own sakes, yet for the sake of the community, to discontinue
altogether the use of intoxicating liquors! When it is considered
that one-half of the insanity, two-thirds of the abject poverty, and
three-fourths of the crime, of our country, are to be traced up to
drunkenness; that more than £60,000,000 are annually expended in
destructive beverages; that myriads annually die the drunkard's
death and descend still lower than the drunkard's grave ; that
thousands of church members are every year cut off from Christian
fellowship for inebriety; that every minister of the gospel has to
complain of the hindrance to his usefulness from this cause ; and that
more ministers are disgraced by this than by any other habit; that,
in short, more misery and more crime flow over society from this
source than from any other, war and slavery not excepted; and that
by the highest medical authorities these intoxicating drinks are
reduced, as diet from the rank of necessaries to luxuries ; it surely
does become every professor of religion to ask whether it is not
incumbent upon him, both for his own safety and for the good of his
fellow creatures, to abstain from this pernicious indulgence. On the
authority of Mr Sheriff Alison, it is stated that in the year 1840, there
were in Glasgow of about 30,000 inhabited houses no fewer than
3010 appropriated to the sale of intoxicating drinks. The same gen-

those of my brethren who have acquired the habit of
smoking, if they will not leave it off, would abstain
from the practice in the houses of their friends, and
confine it to their own : and not permit the inquisitive eyes of the junior members of the families
which they visit, to see the pipe brought out as
their necessary adjunct. Did they know the regrets
of their best friends, and consider the power of
their example, they would, at any rate, so far abstain
as to wait till they had reached their own habitation,
before they indulged themselves in their accustomed
gratification. Still, it is freely conceded, without jus-
tifying this habit, there are some who are addicted to it,
so grave serious and dignified in other respects, as to
furnish by their general demeanour an antidote against
their example in this particular. But what antidote can
be found to neutralize the mischief inflicted by the
levity and frivolity of the parlour-buffoon, whose
highest object in going to the houses of his friends,
seems to be to tell a merry story, and to excite a
hearty laugh? In his hands and lips the pages of
"Punch" are far more in place, as they are, perhaps, far

---

tleman declared that the yearly consumption of ardent spirits in that
city amounted to 1,800,000 gallons of the value of £1,350,000. No
fewer than 30,000 persons there go to bed drunk every Saturday
night : 25,000 commitments are annually made on account of drunkenness, 10,000 of which are of females. Is Glasgow worse than many
other places? Professors of religion, ponder this : and will you not
by abstaining from a luxury lend the aid of your example to discoun-
tenance this monster crime and monster misery? It is in the power,
and therefore is it not the duty, of the Christian church to do thus much
to stop this evil, which sends more persons to the mad-house, the jail,
the hulks, and the gallows, more bodies to the grave, and more souls
to perdition, than any other that can be mentioned? Can the church
be in earnest till it is prepared to make this sacrifice?

more frequently seen, than those of David, Isaiah, or Paul. Happily we have very few that go to this extreme of lightness and frivolity,·but we have far too many, (as is the case with all denominations, and with ours not more than others,) whose hilarity is destructive at once of their dignity, their seriousness, and their usefulness, as ministers of Christ. Not that I contend for affected demureness, and solemn grimace, or even perpetual sermonizing conversation ; as if a pastor could not talk, without violating official decorum, upon any topic but religion, and were letting down his dignity, or desecrating his sanctity, if he joined in ordinary conversation, and partook of, or even helped, the cheerfulness of the circle. By no means : he is not to appear like a spectre that has escaped from the cloister, to haunt the parlour, striking every face with paleness, and every tongue with silence. He is a man, a citizen, and a friend, as well as a minister ; and has a stake and an interest in the great questions which occupy human minds, and engage their conversation : and provided he do not forget what is due to his ministerial character, he need not throw off what belongs to him in common with others. Nay, his very cheerfulness may be made a part of his earnestness, by being taken up and employed as a means to conciliate the affections of all around him. The man who is seriously cheerful, who engages in general conversation, and accommodates himself to the innocent habits of those with whom he associates, and does this in order really to do them spiritual good, and aid him in the great work of saving their souls, will find in the sublimity and sanctity of his end, a sufficient protection from abusing the means. This is widely different from the unchecked levity and unrestrained frivolity in which some indulge, and which make it difficult to imagine how they can feel the value of souls, or the obligation of attempting their salvation. Howard at a masquerade, or Clarkson at a fancy ball, would not have been more out of place: a physician who has just come from the ravages of the plague, and was immediately going back to them, would not be more out of character, if he was seen wasting his time and amusing himself with the tricks of a merry andrew, than is a messenger of God's mercy, and a preacher of Christ's gospel, in the circles of folly and vanity, and he himself the Momus of the party.

But I now advert for a few moments to the field for a pastor's earnestness which is presented by the children of the Sunday-school. By a most fatal error, too many of our ministers deem those institutions as either beyond their duties, or below their notice. A pastor is, or ought to be, the head and chief of each department of religious instruction established in the congregation under his care. He is the teacher, the superintendent, and the party responsible for the religious knowledge, of all the flock, and the Sunday-school is a part of it. A wrong state of things has grown up among some of us Dissenters, for two three or four hundred rational minds and immortal souls are brought every Sabbath-day to our Sunday-schools, and to our places of worship, for the very purpose of receiving religious instruction; and yet all is carried on without its being once thought by the pastor that he has any obligation to attend to it; or by the congregation or the teachers, that he has by virtue of his office a right and a reason to interfere in it. In most cases the pastor has given the matter out of his hand, and has thus raised up, or been accessory to there being raised up, a body of young instructors in matters of religion, who act independently of him, and who, in some instances, are confederated against him. This is not as it should be. The teachers are, or ought to be, a pastor's special care; to qualify them for their office, and to assist them in its duties, should be thought by him no inconsiderable part of his functions. Nor should even the children themselves be viewed as persons with whom he has nothing to do. There are always among them some whose minds have been brought to serious reflection, who are inquiring with solicitude after salvation, and whom he should take under his own special teaching and care, and aim to guide into the way of faith, peace, and holiness: and he should not neglect to give frequent, affectionate, and solemn addresses to the rest. In a Sunday-school of two or three hundred children there are as many immortal souls, exposed by their situation in life to peculiar dangers, yet all capable of eternal blessedness, and all brought weekly under the eye of the pastor: and yet by how many of our pastors are these hopeful objects of religious zeal and benevolence shut out of the sphere of their ministerial solicitude, and handed over to the Sunday-school teachers, as if there were no hope of a minister's saving the soul of a poor boy, nor any reward for his saving the soul of a poor girl! This obligation of attending to the souls of Sunday-scholars, while it is incumbent upon all ministers, is especially so upon those who are labouring amidst much discouragement in small congregations. Many of these men are continually uttering complaints as to the fewness of their hearers, and the inefficiency of their labours; and yet perhaps have never thought of turning their attention to the two or three hundred youthful minds which are every Sabbath-day before their eyes, and under the sound of their voice. No one who ever threw his mind and heart into his Sunday-schools had to complain that he laboured in vain, and spent his strength for nought. No part of ministerial labour yields a quicker or a larger reward. By some it is made the main pivot on which their whole system of religious instruction turns, and flourishing congregations have risen up under its potency. I have myself been the astonished and delighted witness of this, especially in one well-known instance,* and am so deeply impressed with its importance, that I conjure my brethren not to neglect this means of usefulness, or to throw away the golden opportunity which the circumstances of our country still hold out.

Nor is it Sunday-school instruction alone which claims our attention, but daily education. In this we must be in earnest also. It is one of the great subjects of the day: and belongs to us, as much as to any one. We must not allow the minds of the poor to be wholly withdrawn from our influence, but must exert ourselves according to our ability and opportunity to train them up for society and God. Others know and feel the importance of this, if we do not. The Roman Catholic priests are aware of it, so are the clergy of the Established Church, and so are the Methodist ministers: and shall Dissenting ministers be behind the most zealous and devoted friends of education? I trust not.

But there are other departments of the pastorate in which earnestness will manifest itself: there is visiting

* Mr Gunn of Christchurch Hampshire. ED.

the sick, especially those whose disease is chronic, and leaves their minds at liberty for conversation; and there is also the difficult but incumbent duty of rebuke, warning, and ecclesiastical discipline. A devoted servant of Christ will never neglect the state of his church, but will be solicitous to maintain such order there, as shall be pleasing to him to whom the church belongs. Like a good shepherd he will look after his flock, and will endeavour to avoid the denunciations of God delivered by the prophet Ezekiel: " Woe be to the shepherds of Israel that do feed themselves! Should not the shepherds feed the flocks? The diseased have ye not strengthened; neither have ye healed that which was sick; neither have ye bound up that which was broken; neither have ye brought again that which was driven away; neither have ye sought that which was lost." Impressive description of our duty! May we be found so discharging it as to avoid this fearful woe!

I may appropriately introduce here the words of the Bishop of Calcutta, when vicar of Islington, in his admirable and heart-searching introduction to the edition of " Baxter's Reformed Pastor," published by Collins, in his series of " Select Authors."

"What have we been doing as ministers? Lamentably as we have failed in a general estimate of the vast importance of our office, we have failed as lamentably in all those parts of it which relate to personal inspection and vigilance over our flocks. We have confined ourselves to preaching, to ecclesiastical duties, to occasional visits to the sick, to the administration of the sacraments, to the external and secular relation in which we stand to our parishes; but what we done in personal care and direction, in affectionate catechetical conferences, in going from house to house, in visiting every family and individual in our districts, in becoming acquainted with the characters, the wants, the state of the heart, the habits, the attendance upon public worship, the observance of the Sabbath, the instruction of children and servants, the family devotions, of each house? Have we looked after each individual sheep with an eager solicitude? Have we denied ourselves our own ease, and pleasure, and indulgence, in order to 'go after Christ's sheep, scattered in this wicked world, that they may be saved for ever?' What do the streets and lanes of our cities testify concerning us? What do the highways and hedges of our country parishes say as to our fidelity and love to souls? What do the houses and cottages and sick chambers of our congregations and neighbourhoods speak? Where have we been? What have we been doing? Has Christ our Master seen us follow his footsteps, and going about doing good? Brethren, we are verily faulty concerning this. We have been content with public discourses, and have not urged each soul to the concerns of salvation. Blessed Jesus! thou knowest the guilt of thy ministers in this respect, above all others! We have been divines, we have been scholars, we have been disputants, we have been students; we have been every thing but the holy, self-denying, laborious, consistent, ministers of thy gospel."

It has long appeared probable to me, that we, as Dissenting ministers, have something to learn in reference to this part of our duty from the clergy of the Church of England, and even from the priests of the Church of Rome. We do not perhaps sufficiently enter into the meaning and functions implied in that very expressive phrase, "the cure of souls;" a phrase which comprehends far more than the preaching of sermons, and the duties of the Sabbath and the sanctuary, however well performed. There is a definiteness, an explicitness, in this beautiful expression, into which we have need more deeply to enter. It is true we have our word "pastor," which in the impressive Saxon term "shepherd," implies a great deal; but it is neither so specific nor so solemn as the description conveyed by "the cure of souls." Nor do I think we have all the functions which this phrase implies, so much within the range of our habitual contemplation as those by whom it is employed. In leaving college, and entering upon the sphere of our ministerial labour, our attention is perhaps often chiefly fixed upon the pulpit, without taking sufficiently into consideration the various private duties of which this is but the centre: while the clergy, though not altogether neglecting the work of preaching, enter upon their parishes with a wider range of view, as regards the duties of their office. The visitation of the sick, the catechising of children, and an attention to private exposition of the Scriptures and individual cases, enter more into their plans of clerical activity than into ours. There seems to be with them more sense and admission of the claims which their flocks as individuals have upon their time and attention, than with us. Our sphere is felt to be the pulpit, and our relation to be to the congregation as a whole. It is not unlikely we take more pains in the preparation of our sermons; for as our discourses are usually much longer than those of the clergy of the Establishment, we must of course spend more time in composing them. It will also be said that the parochial system of the Church of England gives to its ministers, by its restriction to localities, advantages which we, whose flocks are scattered all over the expanse of a large town, do not possess. There is something in this, but not so much as appears at first sight, inasmuch as attachment to favourite preachers is as strongly felt in the Establishment as it is with us, and overleaps all distinctions of streets. It is also affirmed that it is more a part of the system of the Church of England to inculcate on their parishioners this looking up to their clergy in all spiritual matters out of the pulpit, as well as to his sermons in it. If it be so, it must be confessed that it is an excellence; and if we have it not, the sooner we obtain it the better. There seems to be in our system as much room for it, as in that from which we have separated, perhaps more; since the voluntary choice of their pastor by the people themselves is a more solemn surrender into his hands of the oversight of their spiritual affairs, than the compulsory acceptance of the minister who has been appointed by a patron, without asking the consent or approbation of the congregation. But the fact is, we have too much contented ourselves with the functions of the preacher, to the neglect of those of the pastor, and have thus taught our people to regard us too exclusively in the light of the former. What we need, therefore, is more earnestness in the pastorate, as well as in the pulpit, for it is in this we are brought into most powerful competition with the clergy at this day. Let us then take up the phrase, as descriptive of the duties of our office, and consider ourselves as called by the Holy Ghost, chosen by the people, and ordained by the laying on of the hands of the presbytery, to "the cure of souls:" a cure which we are to carry out by all the beseeching entreating of the pulpit, and all the endless and ceaseless assiduities of the pastorate.

Such, then, is a view, and but an imperfect one too, of an earnest ministry.

I would have made it more comprehensive and impressive if I could: for the reality can never be overdrawn nor exaggerated. Let any one consider what that object must be which occupied the mind of Deity from eternity; which is the end of all the divine dispensations of creation, providence, and grace, in our world; which is the purpose for which the Son of God expired upon the cross; which forms the substance of revealed truth, and employed the lives and pens of apostles; to which martyrs set the seal of their blood; in short, let him recollect that the end of the Christian ministry is the salvation of immortal souls, through the mediation of our Lord Jesus Christ, and then say if any thing less than an earnest ministry, is befitting such an object, or if earnestness can comprehend less than has been set forth in these chapters.

CHAPTER VIII.

EXAMPLES OF EARNESTNESS IN THE MINISTRY.

THE power of example is proverbial. We are constituted to be moved, as well as directed, by it. It
teaches us how to act, and impels us to action. Hence
the excellence of Scripture; it is a book of models as
well as of maxims. Towering above all the rest, standing out in bold relief beyond all the others, is the
character of Christ. He is an example of all excellence, and an example to all persons. To the
ministers of the gospel his beautiful and perfect em-
bodiment of all that is holy and lovely commends itself
with peculiar energy. He was himself a minister of
the gospel, sent by the Father in the same manner as
he has sent others. He is the great model, the Divine
archetype as a preacher and a teacher, which they
are to copy. He is to be imitated in the manner as
well as in the matter of his preaching; he is to be
closely and constantly followed in his liveliness, his
tenderness, his fidelity, his solemnity. We of all men
are under the most solemn obligations to tread in his steps
and do as he did. But I now select from all his qualities, his earnestness. In this, as well as in every
thing else, he surpassingly excelled all his most devoted servants. When he came into the world, he said,
"Lo, I come, in the volume of the book it is written

of me, I delight to do thy will, O God." When he emerged from his obscurity at Nazareth, and entered on his public ministry, he commenced a career of increasing and untiring activity. His eye, his heart, his tongue, embraced one object, and one only, the salvation of souls. We see him always in action, never in repose. Follow him where we will, we find him always working, preaching, praying, or weeping, but never loitering. He gathered up the very fragments of his time, when waiting in the house of Martha for his food, and when waiting at the well of Samaria while his disciples had gone into the city to purchase provisions, and employed those brief intervals in doing good. He was the compassionate Saviour, and not the cold and heartless philosopher. His preaching was the breathing of a soul replete with love, his discourse was the overflowing of mercy. He was not a mere personification of reason, but an incarnation of love; and sent forth not the moon-beams of a cold and clear intellectuality, but the sun-rays of a fervid and fructifying benevolence. To save souls he scrupled not to go, where but for this object we should have never seen him, to feasts and weddings, as well as funerals. From the hour when he thus addressed his mother, "Wist ye not I must be about my Father's business," his meat and his drink were to do the will of his Father. He denied himself all that was of an indulgent and self-gratifying nature; his only relaxation was devotion, which, after labouring all day in the city, he sought by prayer upon the mountains, and in the midnight air. As a scene of earnestness, never surpassed till he ascended the hill of Calvary, behold him bathed in tears over the guilty city, and choked in his utter-

ance by the sobs with which the foresight of the
approaching destruction of Jerusalem convulsed his
bosom! O, that was a spectacle which was enough to
draw into a sympathy of grief the moral universe!
What a heart that must have been, which on such a
spot, and at such a time, could find relief for its intense
emotions only in tears! Truly has it been said, that
melting scene is inferior in pathos, in tender and solemn
grandeur, only to Calvary itself. But this was only a
prelude to what followed. In prospect of the hour of
the solemn and mysterious scenes of Gethsemane and
Golgotha, he exclaimed, "I have a baptism to be baptised with, and how am I straitened till it is accomplished." His eagerness for man's salvation was such
that the guilty heart of the traitor was too slow in its
purpose for his love, and he quickened the movements
of Judas by those memorable words, "What thou doest,
do quickly." He made haste to the cross. He was
almost impatient for the hour of sacrifice. He could
brook no delay in love's redeeming work.

Here, ministers of the gospel, here is your pattern.
This earnestness is your model. You are to be something like this. The work of Christ in saving souls is
to be regarded in a double aspect by you, both as the
means of your personal salvation, and the example for
your official character. We have too much forgotten
the latter. Even though as Christians we may have
looked on his conduct as our exemplar, we have too
much neglected to do so as ministers. As servants we
have not kept our eyes fixed as we ought to have done,
upon our Great Master. Shame upon us, that we have
been so little careful to catch the fire of intense and ardent
devotedness from this glowing and Divine example.

We have seen the sun, let us now turn to the stars: we have beheld the Master, let us now contemplate the servants. Perhaps the former is so high above you that you are discouraged by its loftiness and perfection: well, look now at some nearer your own level. First of all, observe the apostle Paul; and where shall we find any thing so nearly approaching to the earnestness of his Divine Lord, as the conduct of that wondrous man! From the moment of his conversion on his way to Damascus, he had but one object in existence, and that was the glory of God in the salvation of souls; and but one way of seeking it, and that was the preaching of the cross. Wherever he went, whatever he did, to whomsoever he addressed himself, he was ever watching for souls. Whether reasoning with the Jews in their synagogues; or discoursing with the philosophers on Mars' Hill; or preaching to the voluptuous inhabitants of Corinth; or appealing to the Ephesian elders at Miletus; or pleading in chains the cause of Christianity before the tribunal of Festus, in the presence of Agrippa; or writing letters from prison to the churches he had planted, we find him every where and always the earnest minister of Jesus Christ. There is one expression in his address to the Ephesian elders which reveals in a short compass the whole spirit and marrow of his preaching; "Remember that by the space of three years, I ceased not to warn every one of you, night and day, with tears." The terrors of the Roman government could not extract from his firmness a single groan, but the sight of an immortal soul perishing in iniquity, and amidst fatal delusions, altogether unmanned him, and suffused his face with tears, which in other cases would have been the sign of weakness. O those tears, those tears, how they reprove us for our insensibility, and how they prove to us our deficiencies! Every view we can take of this illustrious servant of the cross fills us with astonishment and admiration. His conversion and history seem designed to teach us how much energy may be compressed into one human heart, to be developed in one single life; what sufferings may be endured, what power exerted, what results produced, by one man who is constrained by the love of Christ, and filled with all the fulness of God; and what God can accomplish in fulfilling the purposes of his wisdom and love, by the instrumentality of an individual of our species. There is a short sentence in his epistle to the Philippians, which in a few words sums up his whole life and labours, "For me to live is Christ." What profundity of meaning, what developement of soul, what comprehension of purpose and plan, do those few monosyllables convey! "Christ is my life: apart from him and his work I have no separate existence. I have grown into that one object, and it absorbs me."

This is earnestness: and what obligation to cultivate it rested on Paul which does not rest on us? What was Christ to him, which he ought not to be to us? Why should he thus labour for souls, and not we? Is there a single reason which governed him, that ought not to constrain us? Ministers of Christ, read this great man's life with a view to know what you ought to be, and how you ought to live and labour. In view of what this blessed apostle was, and how he laboured, will you be satisfied with cold intellectuality, flowery orations, subtle metaphysics; with thinking you have answered the end of your calling when you have composed two sermons a week, and kept your people tolerably well satisfied with your labours? Will you think it enough to be a close student, a hard reader, a good writer, though all this while souls are not converted to God, nor the cause of religion advanced in the world? Talk you of your hard labour, severe trials, scanty incomes, ungrateful congregations, and fickle friends? Listen to his tale, and be silent. "In labours more abundant, in stripes above measure, in prisons more frequent, in deaths oft. Of the Jews five times received I forty stripes, save one. Thrice was I beaten with rods, once was I stoned, thrice I suffered shipwreck, a night and a day have I been in the deep; in journeyings often, in perils of waters, in perils of robbers, in perils by mine own countrymen, in perils by the heathen, in perils in the city, in perils in the wilderness, in perils in the sea, in perils among false brethren; in weariness and painfulness, in watchings often, in hunger and thirst, in fastings often, in cold and nakedness. Beside those things that are without, that which cometh upon me daily, the care of all the churches. Who is weak, and I am not weak? who is offended, and I burn not?" Is there to be found in human composition or history such a passage as this? In reading it who can help asking, "what have I done or suffered for Christ, that can give me a title to be ranked as a minister of Christ after this?"

But perhaps this also is too lofty an example to have much weight with you; then take an instance next from the Nonconformist's Memorial. It appears from the diary of that eminent servant of Christ, Oliver Heywood, that in one year, besides his stated work on the Lord's-day, he preached one hundred and fifty times, kept fifty days of fasting and prayer, and nine of thanksgiving, and travelled fourteen hundred miles, in the service of Christ and immortal souls. And when we consider that these journeys must have been either on foot or on horseback, this distance was more than ten thousand miles by our modern railways. And then think of Baxter, that wondrous man, who though hunted and imprisoned by the demon of persecution, and tortured with the stone, was always preaching and writing, till he had composed and published those hundred and twenty volumes, the very writing of which, as to the mechanical labour alone, seemed enough to occupy a whole life, and as to which the celebrated Dr. Barrow said, that "his practical works were never mended, nor his controversial ones ever confuted."

Now turn to those extraordinary men, Wesley and Whitfield; and who can read the account of their amazing labours, and equally amazing success; without something of a self-reproachful and desponding feeling, as if we were living almost in vain? When we see them dividing their whole lives between the pulpit, the closet, and the class room; sacrificing all domestic enjoyment and personal ease; encountering savage mobs, and addressing congregated thousands; travelling backward and forward the whole length of the kingdom, and crossing the ocean many times; moving the populations of cities, and filling nations with the fame and the fruit of their evangelical labours; breathing little else than the atmosphere of crowded chapels and preaching rooms, except when they lifted up their voice under the canopy of heaven; regaling themselves, not with the dainties of the table, nor the repose of the soft luxurious couch, but with the tears of the penitent, and the songs of the rejoicing believer; making it their one and only business to seek the salvation of souls, and their one and only happiness to rejoice in the number of their conversions; indifferent alike to the savage fury of their persecutors, and the fond flatteries of their followers; sometimes rising from a bed of sickness to address the multitude in circumstances which rendered it probable they would exchange the pulpit for the tomb; to sum up all in one short sentence wearing out life in labour so great that it looked as if they were in haste to die: when we see this, how can we endure to think of the way in which we are living, or how can we imagine we are living at all? How can we read their lives, and not blush for ourselves? How can we witness their earnestness, and not feel as if we knew nothing of the passion for saving souls?

And what shall be said of Brainerd, the first missionary of Christ amongst the Indians of North America? See him harassed by nervous and gloomy dejection, and wearing down by slow consumption; yet for the love of souls dwelling amidst savages, helping to build his own comfortless and ill-furnished hut; living at times on parched corn; when travelling and benighted in the woods, sleeping, if sleep he could, wet and cold in a tree; throwing himself down on his return to his own solitary dwelling on his hard bed, with none to comfort him; and amidst such privations, long tried and harassed by the want of success in his apostolical labours; and all this for the love of souls, and the glory of Christ? Where, O where, even among modern missionaries, to say nothing of ministers at home, do we find this rigorous self-denial, this self-sacrificing disposition, this intense desire after the salvation of souls ?

I may profitably refer to one more instance of devotedness, and that shall be of a pastor, Dr. Payson of America, whose biography should be read by every Christian minister. Many have read it, and I should hope with no small advantage. During his ministry his solicitude for the salvation of souls was so earnest, that he impaired his health by the frequency of his fastings and the importunity of his prayers. His whole life was spent in one constant series of efforts to produce revivals of religion; and the anguish of his mind, when his labours failed, was so acute as to bring on bodily disease. It was said of him by his biographer, that his language, his conversation, and his whole deportment were such as brought home and fastened to the minds of his hearers the conviction, that he believed, and therefore spoke. So important did he regard such a conviction in the attendants on his ministry, that he made it the topic of one of his addresses to his clerical brethren, which he entitled, "The importance of convincing our hearers that we believe what we preach." In the course of this address he remarks, that a minister who acted thus,

"in delivering his message as an ambassador of Christ, would show that he felt deeply penetrated with a conviction of its truth and infinite importance. He would speak like one whose whole soul was filled with his subject. He would speak of Christ and his salvation, as a grateful, admiring people would speak of a great and generous deliverer, who had devoted his life for the welfare of his country. He would speak of eternity, as one whose eye had been wearied by attempting to penetrate its unfathomable recesses, and describe its awful realities, like a man who stood on the verge of time, and had lifted the veil which conceals them from the view of mortals. Thoughts that glow and words that burn would compose his public addresses, and while a sense of the dignity of his official character, and the infinite importance of his subject, would lead him to speak as one having authority, with indescribable solemnity, weight, and energy, a full recollection that he was by nature a child of wrath, and that he was addressing fellow men and fellow sinners, mingled with compassion for their wretched state, and ardent desire after their salvation, would spread an air of tenderness over his discourses, and invest him with that affectionate, melting, persuasive earnestness of manner, which is best calculated to affect and penetrate the heart. To say all in one word, he would speak like an ambassador of Him who spake as never man spake, and we would say, 'we speak that we do know, and testify that we have seen.'"

When disabled by increasing disease from preaching, Dr. Payson carried with him into his sick chamber all his undiminished earnestness for the salvation of souls. Having come from, on one occasion, the administration of the Lord's Supper, he rose, and thus addressed his flock :

"Ever since I became a minister, it has been my earnest wish that I might die from disease which would allow me to preach a farewell sermon to my people; but as it is not probable I shall ever be able to do this, I will attempt to say a few words now: it may be the last time I shall ever address you. This is not merely a presentiment: it is an opinion founded on facts, and maintained by physicians who know my case, that I shall never behold another spring.

"And now, standing on the borders of the eternal world, I look back upon my past ministry, and on the manner on which I have performed its duties; and oh, my hearers, if you have not performed your duties better than I have done, woe! woe! be to you, unless you have an Advocate and an Intercessor in heaven. We have lived together twenty years, and have spent more than a thousand Sabbaths together, and I have given you at least two thousand warnings. I am now going to give an account how they were given; and you, my hearers, will soon have to give an account how they were received. One more warning I will give you. Once more your shepherd, who will be yours no longer, entreats you to flee from the wrath to come. Oh, let me have the happiness of seeing my dear people attend to their eternal interests, that I may not have reason to say, 'I have laboured in vain, I have spent my strength for nought.'"

After this he entered his chapel but once more. Confined now to his house and to his room, he still carried out his intense desires to be useful in saving souls, by dictating letters and addresses to individuals and bodies of men. Persons under anxious concern for their salvation, young converts entering on the Christian life, ministers just commencing the arduous duties of their office, and various bodies and classes of individuals, were sent for to visit him in his sick chamber, and receive his dying counsels and admonitions. What messages also went forth from that scene of agony and of glory to ministers and friends! His "ruling passion was strong in death." His love for preaching was as invincible as that of the miser, who dies grasping his treasure. Dr. Payson directed a label to be attached to his breast when dead, with the words, "Remember the words which I have spoken unto you, while I was yet present with you;" that they might be read by all who came to look at his corpse, and by them, he being dead, yet spake. The same words at the request of his people, were engraven on the plate of his coffin, and read by thousands on the day of his interment.

Here was a beautiful instance of ministerial earnestness; and if I have dwelt longer on this than on some of the still more illustrious ones which have preceded it, the reason may be found in the fact, that it is the example of a minister of our own times, and placed in nearly the same circumstances as ourselves; and also in the wish that many who have not read that most instructive piece of ministerial biography, may be induced by these extracts to peruse the volume. That man's heart must be in a bad state indeed, both as a Christian and a minister, who is not made the holier and more earnest by contemplating that bright and lovely example.

Leaving the ministry, and turning towards the laity, for some rare examples of unquenchable earnestness, I find two deserving above most of honourable mention, and assiduous imitation, Lady Huntingdon, and the late Thomas Wilson of Highbury. In the former we see a peeress, related of course to many noble families, to whom the honours of the court and the elegances of fashion were accessible, relinquishing from the hour of her conversion to God, all those pomps and gaieties of the world, and consecrating her rank, her influence, and her wealth, to His glory and the salvation of souls; quitting the saloons of the gay for the conventicles of the pious, and the society of nobles, statesmen, orators and wits, to hold converse with itinerant preachers; selling her jewels to enable her to purchase chapels; opening her drawing room for religious worship; and undiverted and unmoved by the wonder, reproach, and sneers of a proud and scoffing aristocracy, pursuing with an intensity which they could comprehend as little as they could the objects to which it was directed, the spread of evangelical truth, and the salvation of immortal souls, both among the rich and the poor. In this one object her whole life was bound up, apart from it she had neither occupation nor enjoyment.

Pretty much the same in substance may be said of the late Treasurer of Highbury College. We needed not the very valuable and interesting memoir of this inestimable man, with which his son has favoured the world, to convince us of this; much as the conviction is deepened, and the impression perpetuated, by the

complete view of his life and character there presented
to our view : those who knew Mr Wilson, (and who
of every party in the religious world did not know him ?)
always considered him as a person of extraordinary
zeal and great benevolence, and a most useful specimen
of an earnest man. This character will be assigned
to him even by those who differed from him in some
views of the object on which he lavished the energies
of his active mind, and the resources of his ample fortune. But now that the whole outward career of this
indefatigable man is laid before us, and the mechanism
of his heart, as the spring of his energy, is disclosed
to us in this seasonable and instructive biography,
we learn the important lesson, how much one man,
whose heart is given to the work, may accomplish in
the way of evangelising our dark and wretched world.
Perhaps modern times have produced and presented few
more striking instances of that quality of character
which it is the design of this volume to illustrate and
to enforce. He selected his one object of life, and that
was the support and spread of evangelical religion by
building chapels, and educating and supporting ministers, in connexion with the denomination to which
he belonged. For this he retired from business, and
consecrated to it his time, his fortune, his influence,
and his piety. His journeys from home, and his
occupation at home, were in a great measure devoted to this. He had his office, his clerk, his house
of business, his correspondence, all in reference to this,
just as the merchant has for his commercial affairs.
To this were directed his conversation in company, and
his musing and letters when alone. The consummation
of one scheme of usefulness in his line of effort was

but the commencement of another. While others
talked, he worked. We knew where to find him, and
how he was employed. If a voice from heaven had
commanded him to build chapels and educate ministers,
he could not have pursued that object with more fixedness of aim, unity of action, and steadiness of perseverance, than he manifested. He knew his object, and
therefore needed no counsel ; he loved it, and suffered
nothing to divert his mind from it : he saw its practica-
bility and hearkened to no objections. If others would
act with him, well ; if not, he would go alone. It was
not brilliant talents, nor a princely fortune, nor a commanding eloquence; though he had good abilities, a
handsome income, and an easy utterance ; but it was
earnestness that made him what he was, and enabled
him to do what he did. Yes, Thomas Wilson was an
earnest man : and would to God that all whom he
helped to introduce into the ministry, partook, in the
still more sacred duties of their calling, of his intensity
of action.

CHAPTER IX.

MOTIVES TO EARNESTNESS.

I. EARNESTNESS is demanded of the Christian minister alike by his theme and his object.

When Pilate proposed to his illustrious prisoner the question, "What is truth?" he brought before him the most momentous subject which can engage the attention of a rational creature; and if Christ refused to give an answer, his silence is to be accounted for by the captious or trifling spirit of the querist, and not by any insignificance in the question. Truth is the most valuable thing in the universe, next to holiness; and truth, even that truth which by way of eminence and distinction is called the truth, is the theme of our ministry. Take any branch of general science, be it what it may, and however valuable and important it may be considered, its most enthusiastic student and admirer cannot claim for it that supremacy which is implied in the expression, the truth. Who shall adjust the claims to this distinction of the various physical and moral sciences, and declare, in opposition to the false pretensions of usurpers, which is the rightful possessor of the throne? Who? The God of truth himself; and He has done it: He has placed the Bible on the seat of majesty in the temple of truth, and has called upon all systems of philosophy whatever to fall down and do it

homage. This is our subject: eternal, immutable truth.
Truth given pure from its Divine Source, and bearing
with it the evidence and impress of its own Omniscient
Author. O what, compared with the truths of revelation,
are the loftiest and noblest of the sciences: chemistry,
with its beautiful combinations and affinities; or astro-
nomy, with its astounding numbers, magnitudes, dis-
tances, and revolutions, of worlds; or geology, with its
marvellous and incalculable dates of bygone millions
of ages? What is matter, inert or organized, however
diversified, classified, or combined with its laws of
necessity, compared with minds and souls, and the
laws of moral truth by which their free actions are
regulated? What is nature, to the God of nature?
What the heavens and the earth, to the glorious mind
that looks out upon them through the organ of vision,
as from a window commanding the grand and boundless
prospect? What the fleeting term of man's existence
upon earth, with its little cycles of care, sorrow, and
labour, compared with the eternal ages through which
the soul holds on her course of deathless existence?
The works of creation are a dim and twilight manifestation of God's nature, compared with the grandeur and
more perfect medium of redemption. The person of the
Lord Jesus Christ is itself a wonder and a mystery to
which all other displays of Deity are darkness; this is
the shekinah in the holy of holies of the temple of God's
creation, towards which all orders of created spirits,
from the most distant parts of the universe, reverently
turn and do homage to the great God our Saviour.
This, this, is our theme, the truth of God concerning
himself; the truth of an incarnate Deity; the truth
of man's redemption by the cross; the truth of the

moral law, the eternal standard of rectitude, the tree of knowledge of good and evil; the truth of the gospel, the tree of life in the midst of the paradise of God; the truth of immortality, of heaven, and of hell : the truth couched under the symbols of the Levitical law, and the visions of the Jewish prophets, and fully exhibited in the gospels of the evangelists, and the inspired letters of the apostles. Again I ask, exultingly and rapturously, what are the discoveries of Newton, or of Davy; or the inventions of Watt, or of Arkwright, compared with these themes? Viewing man in relation to immortality, as sinful and accountable, what is art or science, compared with revealed truth? And shall we, can we, be otherwise than earnest in the promulgation of this truth? Shall we touch such themes with a careless hand and a drowsy mind? Shall we slumber over truths which keep in wakeful and energetic activity all other orders of created intelligences, and which are at once the object and the rest of the Uncreated Mind? Let us look at the earnestness with which the sons of science pursue their studies. With what enthusiasm they delve into the earth, or gaze through the telescope at the heavens, or hang over the fire; with what prolonged and patient research they carry on their experiments, and pursue their analyses; how unwearied in toil, and how enduring in disappointment, they are; and how rapturously they hold up to the world's gazing and wondering eye some new particle of truth, which they have found out after all this peering and prying into nature's secrets! Ministers of the gospel, is it thus with the men who have to find out the truths of nature, and shall we who have the volume of inspired revealed truth opened before us, drone, loiter, and trifle over its momentous realities? Shall the example of earnestness be taken from him who analyses man's lifeless flesh, to tell us by the laws of organic chemistry its component parts, rather than from him who has to do with the truths that relate to the immortal soul? Shall he whose discoveries and lessons have no higher object than our material globe, and no longer date than its existence, be more intensely in earnest than we who have to do with the truth that relates to God and the whole moral universe, and is to last throughout eternity? What deep shame should cover us for our want of ardour and enthusiasm in such a service as this!

And then what is the purpose for which this truth, so grand, so awful, so sublime, is revealed by God, and is to be preached by us? Not simply to gratify curiosity; not merely to conduct the mind seeking for knowledge to the fountain where it may slake its thirst; no, but to save the immortal soul from sin, death, and hell, and conduct it to the abodes of glorious immortality. The man who can handle such topics, and for such a purpose, in an unimpassioned careless manner, and with an icy heart, is the most astounding instance of guilty luke-warmness in the universe: to his self contradiction no parallel can be found, and he remains a fearful instance how far it is possible for the human mind to go in the most obvious, palpable, and guilty inconsistency. A want of earnestness in the execution of that com-mission, which is designed to save immortal souls from eternal ruin, and to raise them to everlasting life, is a spectacle which, if it were not so common, would fill us with amazement, indignation, and contempt. We have read the speeches of the great masters of eloquence, both of ancient and modern times: and have sympathised with the intense anxiety, and untiring effort, with which they gave utterance to the mighty words that flashed from their burning souls; and do we condemn as an enthusiast the Athenian orator who so agonized to save his country from the yoke of Philip; the majestic Roman who roused the indignation of the republic against the treason of Cataline; or our own Wilberforce, who for twenty years lifted his voice in appeals to the justice and mercy of a British Parliament against the atrocities of the slave trade? On the contrary, we deem no eulogy sufficient to express our admiration of their noble enthusiasm. But our praise of them, is the condemnation of ourselves; for how far short of them do we fall in earnestness, though the salvation of a single soul, out of all the multitudes that come under the influence of our ministrations, is an event, which is inconceivably more momentous in its consequences, because enduring through eternity, than all the objects collectively for which those men exhausted the energies of their intellects and lives. Do we really believe that we are either a savour of life unto life, or of death unto death, to them that hear us? Or is this mere official phraseology, never intended to be understood in the ordinary import of the words? Is it a matter of fact, or only the solemn garnish of a sermon, the trickery and puffing of pulpit vanity, that souls are perpetually rising from beneath our ministry into the felicities and honours of the skies, or dropping from around our pulpits into the bottomless pit? Are companies of immortal spirits continually summoned from our congregations to inhabit eternity, and people heaven or hell, to swell the numbers of the redeemed, or to add to the multitude of the lost? If this be true, (and we are gross deceivers, mere pulpit actors, reverend hypocrites, if we do not believe in its truth) then where is the earnestness that alone can give consistency to our profession, and is appropriate to our situation, and adequate to our convictions? Have we really become so carelessly, so criminally familiar with such topics as salvation and damnation, that we can descant upon them with the same calmness, coolness, not to say indifference, with which a public lecturer will discuss a branch of natural philosophy? O where is our reason, our religion, our consistency?

II. Earnestness is imperatively demanded by the state of the human mind, viewed in relation to the truths and objects just set forth.

This was glanced at in an earlier part of the work, but must be now resumed and amplified. The entreating and beseeching importunity which was employed by the apostle, and which is found to be no less necessary for us, presupposes on the part of its objects, a reluctance to come into a state of reconciliation with God, which must be assailed by the force of vehement persuasion. Although we have to treat with a revolted world, a world engaged in mad conflict with Omnipotence, yet if the guilty rebels were weary of their hostilities, and in utter hopelessness of success, were prepared on the first offer of mercy to throw down their arms, and in the spirit of contrition sue for pardon, ours would be an easy mission, and we might spare ourselves the trouble of earnestness and expostulation. But the very reverse is the case. "The carnal mind is enmity against God, and is not subject to the law of God, neither indeed can be." The hearts of men are fully set in them to do evil. We find them taken up, occupied, influenced, governed, by the palpable and visible things of the present life; and our business is to engage them in constant resistance to the undue influence of things seen and temporal, by a vigorous faith in the things that are unseen and eternal: our aim and labour are, by the power of the unseen world to come, to deliver them from the spell of the present state, with whose pageantry they are enamoured, and under whose fascination they are well pleased to continue. And all the while they are so occupied by the pursuits of business, so engrossed by the cares, comforts, and trials of life; and are in such breathless haste to pursue, such distracting bustle to possess, and such ardent hope to enjoy, the various objects of their earthly desires, that when we call their attention to serious religion, as the one thing needful, we are deemed intrusive, impertinent, and obstructive, as one who would stop another in a race, to offer him an object foreign to that for which he is contending.

But the difficulty stops not here; if this were all, we should have only a very small share of the opposition which now calls forth our energy and requires our most strenuous efforts; for when we have succeeded in gaining a hearing and arresting attention, we have to contend not only with an indisposition to receive the truth, but a determined hostility against it. We have, as our first business, to fasten a charge of guilt upon men naturally disposed to think well of themselves: to produce a sense of utter worthlessness and depravity in those who, at the utmost length to which their concession will go, admit only some few imperfections and infirmities; to displace a feeling of complacency by one

of self-condemnation and abhorrence; and to substitute
for a general and unhumbled dependence upon Divine
mercy, such a conviction of exposure to the curse of
God's violated law, as makes it difficult for the trembling penitent to see how his pardon can be harmonised
with the claims of justice: to offer salvation upon terms
which leave not the smallest room for self-gratulation,
or the operation of pride; indeed to carry such a
message as frequently excites disgust, calls forth the
bitterest enmity of the human heart, and arouses all its
self-love in determined hostility. And then the salvation exhibited in the gospel is not only opposed to the
pride, but to the passions, of fallen man. It requires
the excision of sins dear as our right hand, the surrender of objects which have enamoured our whole soul,
the breaking up of habits which have grown with our
growth, and strengthened with our strength.

Sometimes we have, in addition to all this, to summon our hearers to a war without, as well as to a
conflict within, and to verify the words of Christ, that
he came to send a sword instead of peace, and to set
parents against children, and children against parents.
What minister has not sometimes felt his courage
ready to quail, and his steadfastness in danger of faltering, when called to lead on some persecuted convert to brave the cruel mockings, reproaches, frowns,
threats, and violence, of his nearest and dearest earthly
connexions? I agonize as I write, to think what I,
among others, have witnessed of this kind. Verily
it is through tribulation that some, even in these
peaceful times, are called to enter into the kingdom
of heaven. And then, following on the difficulties
of the christian ministry, to prevent the first impres-

sions of divine truth from vanishing like the cloud, or
exhaling like the dew ; to drive the inquirer from finding repose any where but at the cross of Christ ; to
guard the feeble, and to inspire the timid with
courage ; to detect the deceit of the heart, and to aid
the novice in breaking off from besetting sins ; to
inspire a resolution of crucifying the flesh, and to
stimulate the soul to an ever onward progress in sanctification ; to meet the epidemic malady of our nature,
which assumes so many shapes, and appears under such
a variety of symptoms, with a proportionate and well
adapted variety of treatment ; to help the believer to
beat down his foes under his feet, and amidst all his
various trials, temptations, and difficulties, to continue
steadfast, immoveable, and always abounding in the
work of the Lord, notwithstanding the counteracting
influence of much unremoved corruption in his heart ;
this, all this, must require in him who has to do it,
earnestness of the most collected and concentrated
kind.

To carry on the ministry of reconciliation in this
revolted world, with the intention and desire of recovering its inhabitants from sin and Satan unto God, when
the opposition to be overcome is considered, must
appear to every reflecting mind the most hopeless of all
human undertakings, apart from the aid of the Holy
Spirit. It is this alone that can induce us to continue
in the ministry another hour. Without this agency,
we must retire in utter despair. But this is not to be
conceived of, much less expected, apart from human
instrumentality ; and man's earnestness is the very
species of instrumentality which the Divine Agent
employs. It is not the feeble ministrations of the luke-

warm and the negligent that God blesses for the
conversion of souls, but the heart-breathed, fervent
wrestlings of the ardent and the diligent. He maketh
the winds his messengers, and flames of fire his ministers. There is then a double argument for earnestness,
in the difficulties which are to be subdued in the accomplishment of our object, and the necessity of the co-
operating agency of the Spirit of God. The former
shows the indispensable necessity of such earnestness,
and the latter encourages us to put it forth. Without
it, we cannot look for the aid of the Spirit; and without
the aid of the Spirit, it would be exerted in vain. May
we be able to take a right view both of our obstacles
and our resources!

III. Consider the aspect of the times, as affecting
the human mind, and the objects of our ministry.

The view which has been just given of the difficulties that lie in the way of the faithful minister, applies
to all countries and to all times, inasmuch as the depravity of human nature is co-extensive with the race
of man. But still there may, and do, exist circumstances to give greater force to these difficulties, in one
age and country, which are not found, at any rate to
the same amount, in others. The features of our own
age are strikingly impressive, and in no small degree
hostile to the success of the gospel, and the prevalence
of evangelical piety.

The sphere of human pursuits, whether we consider
the active or speculative departments, is filled with
unusual energy and excitement. Earnestness is the
characteristic of the age. If we turn our attention to
trade, we see men throwing their whole soul into its
busy occupations, and labouring as if their salvation in

another world depended upon their success on earth. What ardour of competition; what rage for specula-tion; what looking about for novel schemes, and what eagerness to embrace them when offered; what hazard-ous and reckless gambling do we see all around us; leaving out the impetus to all this which the railway system has introduced, and saying nothing of the multi-tudes, who, instead of plodding onward in the beaten path of regular trade, endeavour, by watching the share market, to make one bound to wealth: how engrossing are the pursuits of secular business, in these days of large returns and small profits! Think of the consumption of time, and the absorption of soul, which are necessary to maintain credit and respectability; and also the strength of religious principle which is indispensable to follow the things that are just, true, honourable, and of good report. How many professors are in danger of being carried away, how many are carried away, by the tricks, artifices, and all but actual dishon-esties, of modern trade: and what but a powerful and energetic ministry can be expected to rouse and help God's professing people to bear up against, and to keep in check, much more to subdue, this sordid and selfish spirit? What can be sufficient but an intense devoted-ness on the part of ministers to make things unseen and eternal bear down the usurping power of things seen and temporal? Who but the man that knows how to deal with invisible realities, and to wield the powers of the world to come, can pluck the worldling from the whirlpool of earthly mindedness, which sucks down so many, or prevent the professing Christian from being drawn into it? If our own minds are not much im-pressed with the awful glories and terrors of eternity, we cannot speak of these things in such a manner as is likely to rescue our hearers from the ruinous fascinations of Mammon. How we seem to want a Baxter and a Doolittle; an Edwards and a Howe; a Whitfield and a Wesley, to break in with their thunder upon the money-loving, money-grasping spirit of this grossly utilitarian age !

Then think of the engrossing power of politics. What a spell has come over the popular mind from this source, since the tremendous outburst of the French revolution : for more than half a century the potency of this subject has been perpetually augmenting, till the rustic in the village, as well as the merchant in the city ; the recluse student of the cloister, no less than the man of the exchange, have alike yielded themselves up to the influence of the newspaper, now accommodated, not only to every party in politics, but to every creed in religion, and at the same time cheapened down almost to the poorest member of society. This is matter neither of surprise, nor provided it do not thrust out of consideration other and still more important matters, of regret. It is but the constitution of our country developing the energies of its popular element. The people are claiming their share of power and influence ; may they prepare themselves by knowledge and piety to exercise it rightly ! The stream and tendency of opinion in Europe at large, as well as in our own country, are evidently democratic : but without education and religion the nations will daily become desirous of more liberty, and at the same time less capable of enjoying and preserving it. The less they feel of outward force and of the compulsion of secular power, the more they need the control of moral principles. At such a time, when the elements of good government are, so to speak, in a state of projection, and amidst much repulsion and attraction amongst themselves, are crystallizing into their proper figures, there will be such an unusual degree of interest felt in this great matter, as to throw into the shade matters of still deeper moment.

While all this is obvious in the state of modern society, will any one deny that we want an earnest ministry to break in some degree the spell, and leave the soul at liberty for the affairs of the kingdom which is not of this world? When politics have come upon the minds, hearts, and imaginations of the people, for six days out of the seven, invested with the charms of eloquence, and decked with the colours of party; when the orator and the writer have both thrown the witchery of genius over the soul; how can it be expected that tame, spiritless, vapid common-places from the pulpit, sermons coming neither from the head nor the heart, having neither weight of matter, nor grace of manner; neither genius to compensate for the want of taste, nor taste to compensate for the want of genius; and what is still worse, having no unction of evangelical truth, no impress of eternity, no radiance from heaven, no terror from hell; in short, no adaptation to awaken reflection, to produce conviction, or to save the soul; how can it be expected, I say, that such sermons can be useful to accomplish the purposes for which the gospel is to be preached? What chance have such preachers, amidst the tumult, to be heard or felt, or what hold have they upon public attention, amidst the high excitement of the times in which we live? Their hearers too often feel, that listening to their sermons on the Sabbath, after what they have heard or read during the week, is as if they were turning from brilliant gas-light, to the dim and smoking spark of tallow and a rush.

Another characteristic of our age is an ever-growing taste for elegance, refinement, and luxurious gratification. I cannot wonder at this, nor, if it be kept within proper bounds, greatly regret it. It is next to impossible that the progress of art, and the increase of wealth, should not add to the embellishments of life, and multiply the sources of tasteful enjoyment. But just in proportion as we multiply the attractions of earth, is the danger of our making it our all, and leaving heaven out of sight, and learning to do without it. This is now affecting the church, and the hardy and self-denying spirit of our practical Christianity is in danger of being emasculated, and of degenerating into a soft and sickly effeminacy. Elegance and extravagance, luxurious entertainments and expensive feasts, are beginning to corrupt the simplicity that is in Christ: and amidst sumptuous buildings, gorgeous furniture, costly dress, and gay equipages, professors of religion are setting their affections too much upon things upon earth, and turning away from the glory of the cross, to the glory of the world. Who is to call them off from this pageantry, and make them by God's grace feel how vain are all these things? Who can set up a breakwater against the billows of this ocean of worldly-mindedness, and guard the piety of the church from being entirely swept away by a flood of ungodliness? Who but a pastor that can speak in power and demonstration of the Spirit, a man who shall rise Sabbath after Sabbath in the pulpit, clothed with a potency to throw into shadow, by his vivid representations of heaven and eternity, all these painted nothings, on which his hearers are in danger of squandering their immortal souls ?

Akin to this is a continually augmenting desire after amusement, for the supply of which hosts of ingenious and accomplished persons are in constant requisition. A love for pleasure, diversion, and recreation, is an appetite evidently increasing; and there are those who are ever ingenious and ever busy to supply its demands. Religion is no enemy to rational enjoyment, even though it be not strictly scriptural; and those who supplant the low and vulgar sensualities on which the multitude have fed, by pleasures more refined and elevated, are doing service to their country and to their species. But still, a taste for amusement, both mental and bodily, may be carried too far, and many foreseeing and deeply reflective minds are of opinion that it is prevailing too far now.

There cannot be a thoughtful mind, if it looks upon our sojourn in this world as a probation for eternity, but must reflect with serious alarm and grief upon the endless devices which are suggested by the wisdom that comes from beneath, to hide from men their duty and their destiny as immortal creatures. It seems as if by common consent, men were striving who should be most successful, by inventing new kinds of diversions, to blot from the mind all considerations of eternity. Pleasure-taking is the taste of the day, a taste which has been increased into an appetite by the facilities for travelling afforded by railways. Before its desolating influence, the sanctity of the Sabbath, and with it of course the prevalence of religion, are likely to be destroyed. It may be said that any thing is better than the ale-house and the gin-shop. This is freely admitted, but it may be questioned whether some of the modern stimulants to pleasure do not lead to, and not from, those scenes of iniquity. The people, it is affirmed, must have recreation. Be it so, but let it be of a healthful kind, and let the great aim of all who have any influence upon the public mind be to endeavour to implant a taste for the recreations afforded by cheap and wholesome literature, by quiet home enjoyments, and, above all, by the sacred delights of true piety.

In connection with this may be mentioned, as one particular species of amusement, the taste for works of humour, which has much increased in this country within the last ten years. There is no sin in mirth; man is made to enjoy it, and there is a time to laugh as well as to weep. And he must be a very misanthrope, a vampire which in the dark night of sorrow would suck the last drop of happiness from the human sufferer, who would forbid the smiles of gladness, and every thing which ministers to the gratification of the laughter-loving heart. But it is a different thing from this, to wish to keep this propensity within due bounds, to prevent it from becoming the staple of life, and to remind men that they have other things to do in this world than to laugh and be merry. Dr. Vaughan says,

"We are not certain that some of our wise men do wisely, who are going abroad just now with their cap and bells, in the hope of securing better attention to their lessons from the foolish. A fondness for grotesque jokes and everlasting caricature, bears as little resemblance to manly feeling, as the ecstacies of a young lady over the last new novel. Truth is a grave matter, and can owe little ultimately to the services of a buffoon. It loses half its dignity, if often presented in association with the ridiculous. Those who find their chief pleasure in broad farce, are rarely capable of a due exercise of earnest and reverential feeling. Your great wits do not spare their best friends, and your votaries of fun are generally persons prepared to sacrifice any thing to their god. The mind which is wont to pay much homage to the laughers, too often forgets to pay a real homage to any thing higher. In such a service, the fine edge of moral feeling is almost of necessity worn away. Not that we should send a man to the bow-string because he has indulged a laugh. On the contrary, the man who cannot so indulge is not a man to our liking. There is something wrong in him, physically, mentally, and morally. All truly healthful men, in the spiritual as well as in the natural sense, know how to enjoy their laugh. But your great laughers are generally slow workers. To make a merriment of folly is not to displace it by wisdom. Our proper business here is neither to grin nor to whine, but to be men. We say not that good may never be done by means of ridicule, but we are convinced that its general effect is such as we have ventured to indicate. It is an instrument, moreover, which has two edges; use it, and you have no right to complain of its being used." British Quarterly Review, No. vi, p. 254.

These are wise and true sayings, as seasonable as they are important, and called for by the excessive taste for that species of composition which now prevails. If any thing need be added in corroboration of these arguments it is the fact stated by the justly lamented Dr. Arnold, that since the publication of periodical works of humour, he had perceived a visible declension of manly sentiment and serious thoughtfulness among the elder boys of his school. This is strong and decisive testimony as to the influence of a continued indulgence in broad farce. Is there not precisely the same effect produced on the minds of our young men? Nothing can be more opposed to the serious spirit which true religion requires, or more destructive of it, than this constant supply of new materials for laughter. Nor does the mischief stop with the young and the worldly, it is infecting the professors of religion. It is hard to conceive how earnestness and spirituality can be maintained by those whose tables are covered, and whose leisure time is consumed, by the bewitching inspirations of the god of laughter. There is little hope of our arresting the evil, except we make it our great business to raise up a ministry who shall not themselves be carried away with the torrent; who shall be grave, without being gloomy; serious, without being melancholy; and who, on the other hand, shall be cheerful without being frivolous, and whose chastened mirthfulness shall check, or at any rate reprove, the excesses of their companions. What a demand does this state of things prefer for the most intense earnestness in our Sabbath-day exercises, both our prayers and our sermons! In this modern taste we have a new obstacle to our usefulness of a most formidable kind, which can be subdued only by God's blessing upon our fidelity and zeal. Men are wanted, who shall by their learning, science, and general knowledge, give weight to their opinions, and influence to their advice, in their private intercourse with their flocks; and shall, by their powerful and evangelical preaching, control this taste, and counteract it by a better.

Nor must I omit to notice, and to notice with peculiar emphasis, the impetus that is now given to the human understanding through all its gradations, from the highest order of intellect down to the humblest classes of the labouring population. I have already alluded to this subject, but on account of its importance must here refer to it again, and a little more at length. As regards the labouring classes, education is advancing among them with rapid strides, as far at least as the counteracting tendency of the manufacturing system will allow. The poor must, and will, be instructed. The change of opinion on this subject that has come over a large portion of the community within the last quarter

of a century, is indeed marvellous; and instead of tirades
upon the danger of educating the people, we now hear
from the same persons descants upon the evils of ignorance.   This is a happy change, and its results will
be auspicious, but they will not be without some tempo-
rary admixture of evil.   It is really refreshing to read
the schemes which are now put forth for the education
of the working classes, by all parties in religion and
politics.   And improvement in education is not confined,
and cannot be confined, to the lower classes.   The
universal mind is awakened, and in motion onwards : it
is in a state of intense excitement and irrepressible
activity.   Discoveries in science, and inventions in art,
come so fast upon us, that we have scarcely recovered
from the surprise produced by one, before another calls
upon us to indulge in new wonder.   Feats of human
skill, especially in the department of engineering, are
performed or projected, which make man in the pride
of his intellect feel as if nothing was impossible to
him.   As might be expected, knowledge is flowing, by
the thousand rills of the press and cheap books, through
every department of society.   The annual expenditure
of millions of pounds in cheap literature shows to what
extent information on all subjects is reaching all classes
from workmen upwards.   Knowledge is the great idol
around which the multitudes are gathering to pay their
homage and record their vows.   Is there any thing in
such a state of things at which the friends of religion
should take alarm?   Quite the contrary.   Christianity
began her career, as every tyro in history well knows,
in the most enlightened age, and amongst the most
polished nations, of antiquity ; and has never from that
moment to the present, shrunk from the day-light of

learning and science, to skulk in the darkness and gloom of barbaric ignorance; and its ministers should ever be foremost as the patrons of knowledge. But it is evident that such a state of things requires their indomitable earnestness in the sacred duties of their calling, to secure for religion its due pre-eminence amidst all the various claimants upon the public attention. Allowing to general knowledge all the importance that is claimed for it, it is not, apart from religion, a sovereign remedy, a grand catholicon, which can heal the disorders, and restore the moral health of diseased humanity. There are some, and indeed not a few, in our own country, as well as upon the continent of Europe, who dream (and all history proves it to be but a dream), of regenerating the world by the principles of reason and the aid of secular education. They think they can regulate society without religion, and renew the heart of man without God. We might ask them what philosophy did for such purposes in Egypt its cradle, or in Greece its temple? They forget that by the permission of Providence a grand experiment was made in the latter country, during the five centuries next preceding the Christian era, by the sages of its schools, to see what knowledge, apart from Divine revelation, could do to reform the moral world, and make it virtuous and happy. We venture to call for the result, and if the advocates of reason refuse to give it, an apostle shall supply the answer: "The world by wisdom knew not God." Still more in point is his testimony in Rom. i, 28, 31. It would seem as if, not satisfied with a single demonstration, our modern philosophers were hazarding a second trial. Again with still greater advantages, and with still greater confidence, they are

flocking to the ordeal. Education is to be improved
and extended; the press is pouring forth its cheap literature; science is broken down to such fragments, and
measured out in such drops as even children's minds
can receive and digest; and every appliance is to be
furnished to give effect to the knowledge thus communicated; lecturers on all subjects are travelling through
the country, and pouring forth streams of information
in every direction; while rational and invigorating
amusements are to come in to aid the general improvement. Those who believe in the sufficiency of knowledge alone to improve the taste and raise the morals
of the nation, indulge in the largest expectations that
society will be regenerated by these laborious efforts;
but, without a prophet's eye, we may predict they are
doomed to certain and bitter disappointment. We may
confidently anticipate that the second experiment will
have the same result as the first, and prove not only
that the world by wisdom will never know God, but
that nothing less than the foolishness of preaching will
achieve its moral reformation. The state of our popular
literature, as moulded to a considerable extent by these
men, proves that the experiment of teaching mankind
to do without religion, is going on. In much of what is
read by the masses, there is unconcealed hostility to
Christianity. Infidelity of the boldest and most daring
kind is availing itself of many of the cheap publications
of the day, with an energy and a success that would
astound as well as alarm those who are not in the
secret. But still many guides of the popular mind,
perhaps most of them, would not patronize this open
assault upon the foundations of our faith : they go
a more insidious, though scarcely a less injurious way

to work; they act upon the principle that the best way to attack religion, and the least likely to shock prejudice and excite alarm, is to say nothing about it, to treat the whole subject as a negation, a nonentity, a thing to be forgotten, with which it is no part of their business to concern themselves, and which may be left to float quietly to the gulph of oblivion. In many cases false principles on the subject of revealed religion, are worked into the staple of scientific books, and many readers are made infidels almost before they are aware of the dreadful perversion. All that it is thought necessary to provide for the million in the way of reading, is amusement and general knowledge : and to a very great extent the object is accomplished. The labouring classes, with increasing knowledge, are more and more alienated from religion. The masses are not won to Christianity, but sullenly stand aloof from it, doubting whether it deserves their attention.

In such a state of things, what kind of ministry is it that is wanted? The answer is easy, men of earnestness; of earnest intellects, earnest hearts, earnest preaching, and earnest faith. Men whose understanding shall command respect, whose manner shall conciliate affection, and whose ministrations shall attract by their beauty, and command by their power. The accessibility of the labouring classes gives us an advantage in approaching them; neither prejudice nor fashion bars us out from them. We have neither to scale the walls of bigotry, nor to silence or evade the dogs of angry intolerance : the door is open, and we may walk in. But we must be men of the age, men who understand it; and who know how to avail ourselves of its advantages, and to surmount its difficulties. But I cannot do better here than refer to an admirable article in the Eclectic Review, on the Modern Pulpit, the following extract from which is to the point.

"What is good preaching? Alas, how many answers would be given to this question! And yet is not the true answer, the preaching by which souls are saved? Then, the best preaching must be that by which the greatest number of souls are saved. In order to that end, however, men must be brought within the sphere of the pulpit; and to bring the greatest number of men within that sphere is the design of Dr. Vaughan in his treatise (on the Modern Pulpit), and it is ours. In one word, what we specifically want in the modern pulpit is, adaptation. Now we have read a good deal in our time, not more than enough, of the necessity of adapting the efforts of the pulpit to the constitution of the human mind, to man's moral nature, to his actual condition as fallen, guilty, wretched, and exposed to future punishment. And not seldom have we read most seasonable injunctions, addressed to our young ministers, on the personal adaptation of their discourses to the condition of individual men. All this we regard as of equal importance at all times, and in all conceivable circumstances. But at present our aim is to excite as much attention as we can to the truth, that along with these general and fixed adaptations, there is required a constantly varying adaptation to the constantly progressive changes of society."

The writer then goes on to explain what he means by this varying adaptation of the pulpit to the advancement in society, in reference to one portion of it, the working classes.

"Education is raising these great masses of the community into higher degrees of intellectual culture. New powers are at work. Incredible facilities are multiplied for diffusing knowledge, spreading opinions, and increasing the number of thinkers. Now in such an age, to say nothing of other views of society, it is obviously the duty of evangelical preachers to adapt themselves to the circumstances in which they are placed; not, [as this talented writer would be among the last to suggest,] by withdrawing from the pulpit the great themes of the mediatory system, and substituting for them philosophic truth, or a rationalised gospel; but by such a general line of conduct with reference to the circumstances of a growingly enlightened age, and such a strain of preaching as shall lay hold of the public mind, and bring it under that doctrine, which, and which only, is the power of God unto salvation. Let there be a just estimate formed, and which to be just cannot be a low one, of the mental powers of the common people; a judicious and hearty sympathy with their real wants and reasonable wishes; a studious consideration of the means by which the multitude shall be brought back to the sanctuaries of religion, which they have to a considerable extent deserted; an assiduous endeavour to connect the functions of the pastor with the literary cultivation of the people. For these purposes let there be correct information of their state of intellect, their prevailing habits, their peculiar temptations, their literary tendencies and aspirations as to the books they read; let there be all this, but then let it be only as so much power put forth to bring these masses under the influence of the gospel. Oh, it were a noble triumph of the modern pulpit, to see men of strong principle, and self-controlling wisdom, gathering round them the most boisterous elements of our social atmosphere, conducting the lightnings with which its darkest thunder-clouds are charged, and showing to the nation they have saved, that the preaching of the cross is still the 'Power of God.' "

Of course such an enterprise of home-evangelisation will require that our ministers shall be men of action. Adaptation, then, there may be, and should be, in the sermons and the general habits of the ministry, to the age in which they live, in the way of laying hold of public attention, widening the sphere of their action, and adding to their influence as preachers of the cross. Stronger intelligence, profounder thinking, more logical argumentation, more varied illustration, more chastened composition, more refined sentiment, more genuine philosophy, may be required in this, than in some preceding ages; but all must be in harmony with the simplicity that is in Christ, and must appear only so much added to the height or ornaments of a pedestal which is to exalt the Saviour, and not to exhibit an idol, however beautiful, in his place.

Having referred to the state of public opinion and

feeling with reference to religion among the lower classes, it may not be amiss to glance at the higher and more educated portions of the community. Many of these are moving in two lines, or in a stream that divides into two channels; and flows in two diverging directions; the devout and imaginative going off to Puseyism, and a large part of the rest to philosophical infidelity. Many of our men of letters have adopted a loose, unsystematised theism, which is in some cases a new edition of the opinions of our English deists of the last century; and in another, and a still more numerous class, bears a strong affinity to the pantheistic or mystic theory of the German philosophy. Of the disposition of modern science, in the persons of some of its more illustrious votaries, to retire from revealed religion, as if ashamed to be seen in its company, we have an affecting instance in the great octogenarian naturalist of Prussia. It is indeed a melancholy spectacle to witness such a man as Humboldt, whose eye has seen so much of the visible universe, and whose pen has recorded so ably the researches of his vast genius; whose intellect seemed formed by the Creator, not only to study his works but to proclaim his glories, send forth such a work as "Kosmos," and in that work declare it was no part of his business to trace the wonders he describes to their still more wondrous Author! How deeply painful to see this high priest of nature officiating with such zeal and devotion at the shrine of matter, and yet never throwing one grain of incense on the altar of the Infinite Mind which made the worlds! Yet this is only a specimen of other similar cases. Alas, alas, that such a mind should be so warped by the modes of thinking prevalent among his countrymen, and should have sent forth perhaps his last gift to the lovers of science, with the Hegelian pantheism too obviously interwoven in it !

In such a view of the state and tendency of educated minds in this age, I see an additional argument for an earnest, and at the same time intelligent and educated ministry. We want men, and we are not without them already, who can enter the lists and do battle with the seductive and dangerous forms of error that have done such mischief on the continent of Europe, and are likely, without great vigilance and stout resistance, to repeat the mischief here also. The spirit of mental philosophy which was called up by Locke, and has since been sustained in different schools by Reid and Kant and those who have descended from them, is at the present moment widely diffusing itself through the English and American mind. Education will no longer be confined to literature and natural science. A disposition and determination are formed to explore the world of mind, as well as that of matter, and to give to subjective studies a place, and that a very high one, perhaps above the objective ones. Psychology is now the favorite pursuit of great multitudes of reflective intellects, and will be still more so. The mind of Germany is operating with power and success upon the mind of England, to an extent which is surprising, and in some views of the case alarming. It is, one should think, impossible to trace the progress of transcendentalism from the time of Kant to that of Hegel, and to see how, as it diverged more and more widely from the metaphysics of our own land, it has associated itself with rationalism in theology, and led on to pantheism in philosophy, and not feel some apprehension for the result of its introduction to this country. Perhaps the practical character of the English understanding will be one of our safeguards against a system which to the great multitude must ever remain a matter of mere scientific speculation. It may, however be feared that some of our young ministers, and our students in theology, especially those of speculative habits, captivated by the daring boldness, the intellectual vigour, and the theoretic attractions of the great German philosophers, may too adventurously launch forth on this dangerous ocean, and make shipwreck of their doctrinal simplicity, and practical usefulness. Let them be assured that neither the transcendentalism of Kant, nor the eclecticism of Cousin, is a safe guide for men who would be useful in saving souls. The warning voice has already been lifted up in high places on the other side of the Atlantic, where German philosophy was likely at one time to be received with avidity; and there will not be wanting voices to utter words of warning in this country also. It would not only be useless, but unwise to treat this, or any other system of philosophy, as the tree of knowledge of good and evil, which the command of God, and the flaming sword of the cherubim forbid us to approach : this, as well as every other object of human inquiry, may be studied, and by a cautious and discriminating mind, may be studied with advantage. I would by no means contend that there is nothing in the industry of German investigation, in its method of analysis, in its habit of considering everything subjectively; or even in the systems which are the fruits of its researches, which may not be borrowed with advantage by ourselves; but I must raise my voice in emphatic protest against what I see manifested by some in this country, the willing and entire surrender of the understanding to a school, the masters of which have left us no gospel but a fable, and no God but Nature.

A work has lately made its appearance, which is likely to be extensively circulated among those who have any taste for philosophical studies, or any wish to become acquainted with German literature, and which cannot fail to command attention, and will certainly secure for its accomplished author the admiration and respect of his readers; I mean the "History of Modern Philosophy," by the Rev. J. D. Morell. It is impossible to deny that this gentleman unites to fidelity as an historian, the impartiality and candour of a true philosopher, and great ability as a writer. It is on some accounts a happy circumstance that such a subject has fallen into his hands, since Mr. Morell's attachment to evangelical truth, will qualify him, I trust, to be a safe pilot for the English mind through the perilous seas he has undertaken to navigate. It may be hoped that his own attachment to the subjective system of philosophy will not lead his ardent readers and admirers to go further in that direction than his own discriminating and well-balanced mind would wish or approve; and I am quite sure that he would join with many, who are perhaps more apprehensive than he is of the influence of German philosophy, in the opinion, that no more direct way can be taken by our young ministers to hinder their usefulness, than to allow such studies to obscure the simplicity of their matter, or to deaden the energy of their manner, as preachers of the gospel;

and I hope that he would also most emphatically say, "Beware lest any man spoil you (as preachers) through philosophy and vain deceit."

From a very able and complimentary critique on Mr Morell's work, contained in the twelfth number of the "North British Review," obviously by the late Dr. Chalmers, the following passage may with advantage be introduced here. Speaking of Carlyle, the reviewer says,

"They are not creeds, but men, who are the objects of his idolatry, which under the name of hero-worship, he renders alike to those of most opposite opinions, as to Luther, and Knox, and Cromwell, on the one hand, so with equal veneration to the lofty poets and transcendentalists of Germany, upon the other. He is a lover of earnestness, more than a lover of truth: and it would not be our counteractive at least to urge that he should be a lover of truth, more than a lover of earnestness. We should rather say that both are best; and would our island only not be frightened from its propriety by the high-sounding philosophy of the continent, neither overborne by its pretensions, nor overawed by its cabalistic nomenclature, would our savans and theologians but keep unmoved on the ground of common sense, and by their paramount demand for evidence at every step, lay resolute arrest on the pruriences of wanton speculation, then, while they rejected all that was unsubstantial and unsound in the dogmata of the transcendental school, it were well that they imported the earnest and lofty enthusiasm of its disciples into the phlegmatic universities, and no less phlegmatic churches of our land. We do not need to take down the frame-work of our existing orthodoxy, whether in theology or in science. All that we require is that it shall become an animated framework, by the breath of a new life being infused into it. Ours has been most truly denounced as an age of formalism: but to mend this, we do not need to exchange our formulas, only to quicken them; nor to quit the ground of our common sense for baseless speculations; nor to substitute the Divine Idea of Fichte for a personal and living God; nor to adopt for our Saviour a mere embodied and allegorised perfection, and give up the actual and historical Jesus Christ of the New Testament; nor finally, to go in quest of a chimerical ontology in upper regions far out of mortal ken; and for visions of merest fancy there, to renounce either the certainties of our own palpable and peopled world, or the truths which He who dwelleth in the heavens brought down from heaven, because no man can ascend into heaven, or tell the mysteries and glories of a place which he never entered. What we want is, that the very system of doctrine which we now have, shall come to us not in word only, but in power. As things stand at present, our creeds and confessions have become effete, and the Bible a dead letter: and that orthodoxy which was at one time the glory, by withering into the inert and lifeless, is now the shame and the reproach of all our churches. If there have been the revival of a more spiritual philosophy in France, or elsewhere, it might well humble us; but this is not exactly the quarter from which we should expect our revival to come. Prayer could bring it down from above; and it is only thus that all which is good in Puritanism: its earnestness without its extravagance; its faith, without its contempt for philosophy; its high and heavenly-mindedness, without the baser admixture of its worldly politics and passions; it is only thus the Augustan age of Christianity in England, an age which Mr Carlyle has done so much to vindicate and bring to light, will again come back, to reform our State, and bless our families."

From this article it is perfectly evident that if England should have a tendency to go wrong, Scotland will do something to put us right, and that the followers of Reid, improving on their master, will do much to keep the disciples of Kant in check, and hold the balance even between the Scotch and German philosophies. Surely nothing more need be said to shew and prove what kind of men are wanted for such an age, and to indicate that for times of such excitement, we must have ministers of strong intelligence, simple faith, and entire devotedness. It is, in every view we can take of it, an earnest age, and earnest men alone can at such a time do anything anywhere, and least of all in the pulpit. Events, with trumpet-call, summon us to our post, with every faculty awake, and every energy engaged. Amidst the din of business, of politics, of science, and of fashion; amidst the jeṣts of laughers, the eloquence of orators, and the clamour of parties, the voice of the preacher will not be heard, unless he speak loudly, nor be listened to unless he speak earnestly and intelligently; we shall gain no heed for our holy religion, unless we put forth all our strength; it will be pushed aside, overborne, trampled down in the jostling crowd, if we do not exert our mightiest energies to bear it up, and to make way for it through the throng and the strife of earnest secularities.

Let us not deceive ourselves by substituting any thing else for this. It may be all very well and proper in its place to keep pace with the times in which we live as regards other matters; in classical, mathematical, and philosophical literature, in academic degrees, in tasteful architecture; but these things, in the absence of a living power of intense devotedness, will be but as flowers to shed their fragrance upon our grave, or as sculpture to decorate our tomb.

IV. We may next contemplate the earnestness displayed by some other religious bodies, with which, it may be truly said, we have to compete, and in some instances to contend.

And first of all let us look at the activity of the Church of Rome. What a change has of late years come over that wonderful and dreadful system, so far as its external circumstances are concerned! Many are disposed to think lightly of its present condition, efforts, prospects, and hopes: and it will be acknowledged it is unwise and impolitic for Protestants to lend their aid in magnifying the power and swelling the pride and expectations of the Man of Sin. But it is no less unwise and impolitic on the other hand to miscalculate his forces, to shut our eyes to his efforts, and to deny his victories. What we need is just as much of alarm as shall rouse us to action, without producing panic; enough of fear to lead us to buckle on our armour, and yet not so much as to paralyse our energy. Look at the condition and prospects of Popery now, as compared with what they were soon after the French revolution. Weakened by the withering scorn of an infidel philosophy, to which its own corruption had given rise, it was ill-prepared to sustain the shock of that awful outbreak of human passion, and fell an apparently lifeless corpse before it. The Gallican church was subverted; its priests banished; its property confiscated; its places of worship closed. A French army was in possession of Rome, and the Pope a prisoner in France, while his adherents were trembling and dispersed in all parts of the world. The opponents of Romanism exulted in the confidence that its days were numbered, and its end was come. They exulted too soon. The lifeless corpse which then lay prostrate in Europe, has since then shown signs of returning animation, its wounds have been healed, it has risen from the earth, and recovering its full health, is going forth at this time with giant strength to contend with Protestantism for the mastery of the world. Popery has gained political power in England. It is renewing its old fight in France for the education of the people; its chapels, its priests, its bishops, its monks, its missions, are everywhere multiplying; its ancient craft and cruelty are again called into activity, as Tahiti can witness; it is drawing hundreds, if we include both clergy and laity, of influential persons from the Church of England, and tainting with its spirit hundreds more

who remain behind to diffuse the corruption still more
widely; it has done much to blot from the memory
of statesmen its past history, and to hide from their
eyes its hideous form; and with an ardour kindling to
an intense flame, and a hope flushed into a stronger
confidence by these victories, it is still going on from
conquering to conquer. Rome has however to set off
against these bright signs portents as fearful and appall-
ing, the confiscation of ecclesiastical property and the
dissolution of monasteries in Spain; the rapid defection
going on in Germany, under Rongé and Czerski; the
conversion to Protestantism of whole congregations and
parishes in the south of France; the rising spirit of
free enquiry even in Italy; and the growth of knowledge and the advance of education everywhere. The
great battle of the Reformation has to be fought over
again, we are in the field of action, the forces are
mustered and the conflict going on; and we are unworthy of the position and false to our vows if we do
not give our best and noblest energies to the cause.
Let us take pattern from our foes, and imitate their
intensity of action. They are in earnest, if we are not.
Were it possible for us to see a perfect disclosure, in
one bird's-eye view, of all that is going on in the
Vatican, that most astounding instance of centralisation
out of the bottomless pit; could we see the gigantic
intellects, burning hearts, and busy hands, that are
working in that focus of all daring and mischievous
attacks upon the world's intellectual and spiritual welfare, we should feel that we are safe from the tyranny
of that audacious system, only under the vigilance of
the Omniscient eye, and the protection of the Omnipotent arm. But that help and that vigilance are not to

be looked for by the supine and lukewarm, and can be expected only by zealous activity and confiding prayer.*

But this is not the only instance of earnestness which we should contemplate, and from which we should gain a stimulus for our own activity. The Church of England also is in earnest. Many of us can recollect the time when it was not so. A pervading secularity characterised her clergy; a drowsy indifference her people; if the former got their tithes, and ate, drank, and were merry; and the latter got christening, confirmation, and the sacrament when they died, it was all they cared for. The only thing that moved either of them to a pang of zeal, was the coming of the Methodists into the parish; and when they were mobbed away, they relapsed again into their former apathy. Exceptions there were, bright and blessed, but they were only exceptions. Thank God it is not so now. A vivifying wind has swept over the valley of dry bones, and an army not only of living, but of life-giving, men has sprung up. Venn, Berridge, and Romaine; Newton, Cecil, and Simeon, have lived and have awakened a new spirit in the church to which they belonged. Look at that church as she is now to be seen, full of energy and earnestness: divided it is true into parties, as to theological opinion; to a considerable extent Romanised in her spirit, and aggressive in her designs; but how instinct with life, and a great deal of it life of the best kind!

* Since these pages were written, what wondrous convulsions have shaken all, and revolutionized some, of the nations by which the Papacy is upheld. While I write, the seat of the Beast, the throne of Antichrist, is tottering. The Pope is a fugitive, Rome is in the hands of the people, and Italy itself likely to become the domain of liberty! What shall the end of these things be?

Even the Orthodox and the Puseyite clergy are all now active, preaching, catechising, visiting the sick, instituting and superintending schools. The day is happily gone by when the taunt of fox-hunting, play-going, ball-frequenting parsons, could be with justice thrown at the clergy of the State-church: they are now no longer to be found in those scenes of folly and vanity, but at the bed-side of the sick man, or in the cottage of the poor one. We must rejoice in their labours and in their success, except when their object and their aim are to crush Dissenters. There are very many among them of the true apostolic succession in doctrine, spirit, and devotedness: many whose piety and zeal we should do well to emulate: many to be united with whom in the bonds of private friendship and public co-operation, is among the felicities of my life. Sincerely and cordially attached to their church, they are labouring in season and out of season, to promote its interests. Who can blame them? Instead of this, let us imitate them. Their zeal and devotedness are worthy of it. I know their labonrs, and am astonished at them. Think of a clergyman, and multitudes of such there are, who, besides his other labours, spends four or five hours every day in going from house to house, visiting the sick, instructing the ignorant, comforting the distressed. Can we wonder that such men should lay hold on the public mind? Is it not in the natural course of things that it should be so? It is admitted that the clergyman of a parish has advantages for this species of ministerial occupation which we have not: he considers all the people within a certain topographical limit as belonging to him, as being in fact his cure; and most, if not all, of them, except such as by profession belong to other denominations, look upon him in the light of their minister. This ever active assiduity, in addition to the Lord's-day exercises, is admonitory to us. Can we see this new sight, the whole Church establishment, from the Archbishop of Canterbury down to the curate of the smallest village, with all their comprehensive agency of Pastoral Aid Societies, Ladies' District Visiting Societies, Scripture Readers, Church of England Tract Societies, and other means of influence and power, in busy commotion, dotting the land all over with churches and schools, and by all these efforts labouring so entirely to occupy the nation, as to leave no room for, and to prove there is no need of, any other body of Christians, can we have all this constantly before our eyes, and not see our need of an earnest ministry, not only if we would maintain our ground, but make any advance? Not that I mean to assert that the evangelical clergy would altogether wish to push us off the ground. I believe there are many who unfeignedly rejoice in the existence, operations, and success, both of the Methodists and Dissenters, and who would consider it a deep calamity for the nation if they were arrested in their career of evangelical ministration. The spirit of the Evangelical Alliance is diffusing itself abroad. Sectarianism is, I hope, beginning to wither at the root; and Christian charity is grappling with the demon of bigotry. But still we are at present not prepared for the fusion and amalgamation of all parties into one, and till then we may learn from each other; and with the most entire good will towards my brethren in the Church of England, without envy or jealousy, I call upon my other brethren, those within my own denomination, to imitate the zeal among the clergy of the Establishment, of which they are witnesses. I am a Dissenter from conviction, as well as by education, and know not the lure which would induce me, or the suffering which would terrify me, to abandon my principles. I believe as I ever have believed, since I reflected upon the subject, that the Establishment of religion by the enactments of secular legislation, has no sanction from the New Testament, is a corruption of Christianity, and is injurious to its spirit; and I believe the time will come, when the same views will be entertained by all the genuine followers of Christ; hence I am, and ought to be, anxious, while I cultivate a spirit of brotherly love towards those who differ from me, to uphold, though without wrath malice or any uncharitableness, the denomination by which my conscientious opinions are embodied and expressed. Dissenters of England, and especially Dissenting ministers, I say therefore unto you, be in earnest; first of all, and chief of all, in attachment to the doctrines of evangelism, to the creed of Protestantism, to the great principles which God has employed in every age and country where true religion has had existence, to vitalise the dead, and purify the corrupt, world. Be it your prayer, your endeavour, your hallowed ambition, to possess a ministry of competent learning, and especially of soundly evangelical sentiment; a ministry which as regards their pulpit ministrations, shall be the power of God to the salvation of souls; a ministry which in the simplicity of their discourses and the intensity of their zeal, the fervour of their piety, and the all-comprehending extent of their labours, shall vie with the best specimens of the clergy of the Church of England. There is earnestness among them, and if we would not be swallowed up in the rising tide of their zeal, let us meet it with a corresponding intensity. Let each minister, in his own separate and individual sphere of action, set himself to work, and put forth all his energies, without waiting for combination with others. Not that I speak against combination. We have far too little of it, and this is our weakness. In polity we are too independent, and should be vastly improved as regards our internal condition and our external influence, if we were more compact. But as to ministerial earnestness, we need not wait for others: each man can do what he wills, and may do much, though no other man did any thing. Ministerial activity, like Christian piety, is a matter of individual obligation, and no one is so dependent upon his neighbours, that he needs to halt till they are ready to march with him.

Nor is it necessary nor proper, advocate though I be of the Evangelical Alliance, that we should be silent as to our views of the spirituality of Christ's kingdom. As we are not to sacrifice love for truth, so neither are we to sacrifice truth for love, nor to throw away a smaller diamond of truth out of regard to a larger one. All truth must be held, as well as all love. I differ from some of my brethren in my views of certain confederations for the maintenance and spread of our Nonconformity, because I believe that whatever good they may do in one way, they do more harm in others; but I do not differ from them in my conviction that our principles ought, as a part of the New Testament, to be taught, and to be taught with earnestness. If true, they must be important, and if important at all, very important: subordinate I know, immeasurably so, to the doctrines whereby men are saved; but still of consequence. Provided the gross misrepresentation, the exaggerated statement, the studied caricature, the un-charitable imputation, the withering sarcasm, the bitter irony, and the malevolent ridicule, be expunged from controversy, and there be as much of the delicacy of love, as there is of the firmness of truth, there can be no harm, but must be much good, not only in stating our own opinions, but in answering those who differ from us. All systems of church-polity derive their value and importance from their subserviency to the cause of evan-gelism. Church-of-Englandism or Dissent apart from this, is but as the pole without the healing serpent which it was erected to exhibit; and to be zealous about either, except as viewed in reference to the truth as it is in Jesus, is but like contending about the wood of the cross, to the neglect of the Saviour who was crucified upon it. How, then, are we to meet that abounding zeal which we ourselves perhaps have been in no small degree the occasion of awakening, but by a corresponding vigour of action? We cannot advance, nay we cannot keep our ground, without it. We have to contend against an energy which is astounding and all but overwhelming; and if this cannot move us to earnestness, nothing will.

V. This state of mind and action is within the reach of every minister of Christ.

Some men, from natural energy of character, may be more prone to, and better qualified for, this fervid and devoted zeal, than some others. They are of a more mercurial temperament than their phleg-matic brethren, who creep while they fly, and who require more stimulus to rouse them into activity than is necessary to keep the others at their full speed. This is constitutional to a very considerable extent; but it is after all, more of a moral than a natural inability in many; and the sinners whom they address and call to repentance, and to whom they declare that the only hindrance they have to true religion is an impotence of will, are just as excusable for their want of penitence and faith, as any minister under heaven is for a want of earnestness. He may never be able to be a scholar, or a philosopher, or a mathematician, though he may acquire more of all these attainments than he supposes is within his reach, if he will but give himself to early rising, make a good apportionment of his time, and adopt a well-arranged plan of study. His situation and engagements may be such, however, that he may not hope to rise to eminence in these pursuits; but nothing forbids his activity, zeal, and entire devotedness to the great work of preaching the gospel, and caring for men's souls. He may not be a consummate orator, for perhaps he has not voice for this; but he may, if he pleases, use what voice he has with good effect; he may not have the ability required for finished composition; but he can, if he gives time and labour, produce sermons full of spiritual power: he may not be able to attract around him the rich, the literary, or the great; but he can interest the poor, and engage the children of the Sunday-school, and perhaps, their parents; he may not have ten talents, but he need not wrap up his one in a napkin and bury it in the earth. Every man has one talent at least, with which he can busily trade and acquire profit for his employer and reward for himself. If the pride of some men over-estimate the number of their talents, the modesty, or in some cases the indolence, of others, leads them to make too low a calculation of theirs. There is a source of latent energy in most men, which they have been so far from exhausting, that they have scarcely opened it; they have in many cases to break up virgin soil. I knew a minister of Christ, and loved him well, who was in a situation where he had done little, and feared he never should do more. Every thing was dull around him, and he was dull with it. It pleased God to remove him to a new situation, and then he became a new man. He revived from his torpor, and every thing revived around him. He now evinced an activity and energy which surprised himself and those who knew him. He formed a new congregation, instituted a variety of religious organizations of a useful kind, and was one of the most earnest men I knew. All this energy was not a new creation, but a resurrection. So it might be with many other ministers. Principles of activity are within them, only waiting for the influence of circumstances, or their own will, to give them life, motion, and vigour. Away then with the excuses of indolence, the fears of timidity, the objections of modesty, and the opiates of conscience; for it is these which prevent a man from being zealously affected in a good thing. Every minister can be an earnest minister if he so wills: he is earnest when any thing in which he has a deep interest is at stake. Let his house be on fire, or his health or life be in danger, or his wife or child be in peril, or some means of greatly augmenting his property be thrown in his way, and what intensity of emotion and vehemence of action will be excited in him! He needs but the pressure upon his conscience of the interests of immortal souls; he needs but a heart so constrained by the love of Christ, as to be borne away by the force and impetuosity of that hallowed passion; he needs but a longing desire to be wise in winning men to Jesus; he needs, in fine, but a heart fully set to accomplish the ends and objects of his office, to possess that high and noble quality of soul which it is the object of this work to recommend. There are the same constitutional varieties in tradesmen as in ministers, and yet we never hearken to the former, when in justification of their failure for want of energy, they tell us they have no physical capacity for, or tendency to, activity. Our reply to them is, that what is deficient in them by nature, must be made up by reason and resolution. I say the same to the preacher of the gospel, and while by the representation I would constrain his conscience by a sense of obligation, I would equally aim to interest his heart by awakening his hope. He may never with his measure of talent be able to reach the success of some more gifted and more favoured brethren; but he may have a measure of his own, far more than enough to recompense any labour he may bestow; and instead therefore of spending his time in envying others, or sitting down in despair and doing nothing, because he cannot do as much as they, let him rise up, and have the blessed consciousness and reward of doing what he could.

Young ministers of the gospel, and students preparing for the ministry, who may read these pages, you can possess and exhibit real earnestness; all its delightful excitement, all its blessed results, and all its eternal consequences, are within your reach. There is no lion in the street, except such as your own imagination sees there, and your own sloth has placed there. Make the effort, it is worth the making: try, you can but fail, and it is better to fail, than not to make the attempt. Think what a result may issue from new devotedness.

We have never yet any of us adequately estimated the immense importance and momentous consequences of our work. How can we? They are eternal, and who can duly estimate eternity? Do we believe what we preach, that the conversion of a soul is of more consequence than the creation of a world? Is this sober truth, or mere rhetoric? Is this fact, or the mere garniture of a sermon; only a dash of eloquence, an artifice of oratory? If true, and we know it is so, how momentous it is! A soul, weigh it in the balances of the sanctuary, and settle its worth; appraise its value. Salvation! wondrous word, and more wondrous thing. One word only, but containing millions of ideas; uttered in a moment, but requiring everlasting ages, and all the amplitude of heaven, for the unfolding of its meaning. Archbishop Williams, who was also Lord Keeper in the time of Charles the First, once uttered this memorable speech: "I have passed through many places of honour and trust both in Church and State, more than any one of my order for seventy years before; but were I assured, that by my preaching I had converted one soul to God, I should therein take more comfort than in all the honours and offices that have ever been bestowed upon me." What a confession from an archbishop, that he did not know he had been the instrument of converting a single soul to God; what importance does the confession stamp upon the work of saving souls; and what a stimulus should it supply to us who are engaged in this divine employment!

How vain and worthless a thing is the popular applause which some receive for their eloquence, compared with the proofs of usefulness in the conversion of immortal souls? What are the flatteries of the foolish or even the eulogiums of the wise; what the honeyed compliments, or golden opinions of the most distinguished circle of admirers, weighed against the testimony of one redeemed sinner whom we have been the instrument of saving from death, but as the small dust in the balance! How have some men, pre-eminent for their intellectual might, and accustomed to fascinate the spell-bound multitude by the power of their eloquence, yearned amidst all their popularity for some more substantial, satisfying, and abiding reward of their labour, than that admiration of their talents, which they were accustomed to receive! They were not unsusceptible to the emotions of vanity, nor un-gratified by the expressions of applause, at the time: but when they found that this was all the result of their labours, they sickened at the incense and the honey, and exclaimed in the bitterness of disappointment, and the anguish of self-reproach, " Is this all my reward? Oh, where are the souls I have converted from the error of their ways? " We have a striking proof of this in the late Dr. McAll, whom it was my privilege to call my friend. It was impossible for this extraordinary man to be ignorant either of his great powers, of the estimate in which they were held, or of the effect they produced on others by his pulpit exercises. Nor was he by any means unsusceptible of the influence of applause. But how empty did this appear to him as compared with the abiding results of real usefulness; which if he had not enjoyed in such large measures as some others, it was not for want of any anxiety to obtain it. " Deeply affected was he often," says Dr. Leifchild, " by the fear of not being useful in his ministry." " I have admiration enough," he would say, " but I want

to see conversion and edification." He spoke of some
other neighbouring ministers, whose churches he said
resembled a garden which the Lord had blessed, or
whose spots of verdure were more vivid than his own;
but added, that his emotions in making the comparison,
partook of a character that absorbed or overwhelmed him
with sorrow for himself. I remember on one occasion
after a brilliant speech from himself he listened to a
much plainer and less oratorical brother, whose address,
however, seemed to be penetrating the minds of the
audience, and produced on their countenances an appearance of being deeply affected. At that moment,
the speaker hearing a loud sobbing behind him, turned
round; it was McAll. "Ah," he said afterwards, " I
would give the world to be able to produce that effect
in such a legitimate way." Though the desire thus
ardently breathed, was elicited on the platform, it extended to every description of ministerial address.
"Oh," said he to Mr. Griffin, again and again, " I care
nothing what the people may think or say of my abilities
if I may but be useful to souls !" and once with a kind
of swelling indignation, "God knows, I do not want their
applause, I want their salvation." This is eminently
instructive and impressive, and is one of the most convincing instances which the history of the pulpit can
furnish of the worthlessness, compared with the salvation of immortal souls, of every object of ministerial
pursuit, and every other reward of ministerial labour.
This was not the confession and lamentation of one
whose envy led him to depreciate the value of that
which he had no hope of obtaining, but of one who
was the admiration of every circle into which he entered, and whose surprising talents commanded the

plaudits of all who heard him. How much of the power of that vast intellect, of that splendid eloquence, and of the admiration and eulogium which they drew upon him, would Dr. McAll have given up for a portion of the usefulness, which he saw was granted to the humbler but more effective talents of some of his far less gifted brethren. Let the men who are but too apt to envy such displays of genius, and who, when they see the spell-bound multitude listening in breathless silence, or dispersing with audible applause, fret because they cannot do as much with their enchantments, study the scene before us: let them follow Dr. McAll home from the crowded, fascinated, admiring congregation, leaving behind him the atmosphere perfumed and vocal with the delight of his hearers, to commune with God and his own heart in his closet, and there hear him exclaiming with a burst of agony, "Lord, who hath believed our report, and to whom has thine arm been revealed?" Let them mark all this, and learn that, in the estimation of the most gifted minds, there is no object of pursuit so sublime, and no reward for ministerial labour so rich, as the salvation of immortal souls.

VI. We may next direct our attention to the fact that earnestness has usually been successful in the accomplishment of its object, and that little has ever been achieved without it.

I admit, and in the conclusion of this work shall more emphatically state, the necessity of a Divine influence to convert the soul; but still the Spirit works by means, and by means best adapted to accomplish the proposed end. We do not look for the Spirit to convert souls without the truth; it is by the presenta-

tion of this to the judgment, and by the co-working
of Divine grace upon the heart, that the great change
of regeneration is effected. It is evident, however,
that this blessed result can take place only in those
cases where the truth is really contemplated. The
attention must be fixed upon it, or no result can take
place. Attention, and to a certain extent abstraction
of mind, may be said to be essentially necessary to the
work of conversion. Hence those preachers are not
only likely to be most useful, but are most useful, who
have the greatest power of fixing their own attention
upon the truth, and holding the mind abstracted
from all other topics. When the attention is by their
manner of preaching withdrawn from foreign matters,
and fixed upon the truth then presented, the Spirit in a
way of sovereign mercy gives forth his influence to
change the evil bias of the heart towards the truth thus
exhibited. We perceive in different preachers very various
kinds of power to engage the attention : some do it by
their commanding eloquence ; others by their impressive
delivery; others by their burning ardour; others by their
melting affection ; and some even by their eccentricity ;
but amidst all these specific varieties of manner, we shall
find power to arrest and fix the attention. A preacher
may be immeasurably inferior to many others in the
vigour of his intellect and richness of his imagination,
and yet may be very far their superior in seizing and
holding the minds of his hearers. We cannot hope to
do good if we do not succeed in gaining the attention
of our hearers, and our expectations of accomplishing
the objects of our ministry may be indulged with much
confidence, if we can so preach as to compel our hearers
to listen to us. There is a striking incident mentioned

in the "Life and Remains" of Mr Cecil, of St. John's Chapel, Bedford Row, that master of pulpit eloquence. He was once invited to preach in a village, where the joyful sound of evangelical truth was rarely heard in the parish church, and where he thought it probable he should have no other opportunity to proclaim it. To his mortification, when he got half way through the sermon, he perceived that he had not succeeded in gaining that close attention of the people which he deemed essential to the success of his sermon. The time was going by, the case seemed desperate, and it occurred to him that something must be done, or the opportunity was lost; and pausing for a moment where the subject admitted of his trying his experiment, he said with some degree of that impressiveness which pertained to him, "Last Monday morning a man was hanged at Tyburn," and then went on to make the recent execution bear upon the subject of discourse. The expedient of course succeeded, the wandering eyes of the congregation were fixed upon the preacher, and their truant minds upon the sermon. He gained their attention, and it was rivetted to him throughout the remainder of the discourse. Such self-possession is a noble qualification for a public speaker: and the lesson taught by the anecdote is, that we must have the attention of our congregations, or we can do them no good; and that the more we command this, so as to lead them to think of the truth, the more likely we are to do them good. The history of all successful preachers will prove that amidst a vast variety of means of gaining attention, they each had the power of doing so, and in that power lay the secret of their success.

Let any one who is at all in doubt whether the importance of earnestness is overstated in this work, consider who among departed ministers have been, and who among living ones are, the most distinguished as successful preachers of the word of God. If he apply this to the fathers and founders of Nonconformity, he will find that in the first rank stand Baxter, Bunyan, Doolittle, Clarkson, Flavel, Heywood, and Howe: and when he has read their glowing, pungent, and powerful appeals to the hearts and consciences of their hearers, he will not wonder that such sermons effected the high purpose for which all sermons should be preached, that is, the conversion of sinners. Coming on to latter times, it is unnecessary, after what has been said, to mention Whitfield and Wesley, except to reiterate that in addition to other high and nobler qualities, earnestness was the great means of their extensive success. They lived and laboured for scarcely any thing else than the salvation of immortal souls. As a proof of the intensity of their zeal, reference may be made to the race of men into whom they breathed the fervour of their own souls, and whom they raised up to carry on their own great work. With here and there an exception, the present race of Methodist and Dissenting ministers are stiff, formal, cold-hearted men, compared with not only the leaders, but the immediate followers of those illustrious instruments of the modern revival of evangelical religion. How few of us are worthy to be mentioned with Coke and Fletcher, Rowland Hill, Berridge, and Grimshaw; with Cecil, Newton, and Romaine. What men were raised up in Wales by the Whitfield movement, Daniel Rowland, Jones of Llangan, Howell Harris, and their successors, John Elias, Christmas Evans, and Williams of the Wern; men who caused the mountains of their romantic country to echo to their mighty voices, and who filled its vallies with the fruits of their impassioned oratory ! If we look across the Atlantic, what a wonderful man do we discover in Jonathan Edwards, whose printed sermons, which were only in accordance with his ordinary ministry, are full of such earnestness as he exhibited in the specimen given earlier in this work, and whose ministry was so full of its successful results. Call to recollection Stoddard, Bellamy, Dwight, Davies, who in the land of the pilgrim fathers diffused abroad by their unreserved devotedness the savour of that Name which is above every name. In Scotland there have been the Erskines, the McLaurins, the Walkers, the Dicksons, and others of bygone days, whose remains tell us how they handled the word of God, and whose memoirs inform us of their success. In these venerated men we see the secret of all ministerial power; desire amounting to fervour for the conversion of sinners, and adaptation in their preaching to accomplish it.

If the illustrious company of reformers, who next to the apostles, present the most august examples of burning zeal, be not referred to, if the majestic and mighty Luther, the profound Calvin, the heroic Zuingle, the intrepid Knox, the elegant and classic Melancthon, are passed over, it is not only because they are too well-known to need a mention, but also because they may be thought too high above the ordinary sphere of ministerial activity to be imitated : and yet if the pattern of the great Master himself is placed before us for contemplation and imitation, surely that of the most renowned of his servants need not be withheld. What singleness of aim, unity of purpose, and concentration of energy,

were there in those rare and extraordinary men, and
what less could have carried them on and through
their noble career !

Descending to others, what men have been with us
in the recollection of the present generation; the horizon
has scarcely even yet ceased to glow with their radiance;
the original and striking Fuller, the mighty Hall, the
seraphic Pearce, and the lion-hearted Knibb; the intellectual Watson, and the masculine Bogue; the
eccentric yet generous Wilks, the judicious Roby, the
mild yet persuasive Burder, the pathetic Waugh, the
wise and tender Griffin, the captivating and lovely
Spencer, and the eloquent McAll. Honoured be their
names, fragrant their memories, and precious the recollection of their example ! May we who survive
cherish the recollection of their life and labours, and
never forget that their greatness and their usefulness
arose not more from their talents, than from their devoted earnestness in the cause of evangelical truth.

But coming to other and living examples, more upon
the ordinary level, it may be well to look around upon
those by whom in our own day, and before our own
eyes, the ends of the Christian ministry and the object
of evangelical preaching are most extensively accomplished, and to inquire by what order of means this
has been done. It would be invidious to mention the
names of living men, and to select from among the
multitude those who are pre-eminent above their fellows in usefulness, in popularity, and in the constant
exhibition of evangelical truth. Two names, however,
may here obtain a place, honoured by us all, and an
honour to us; the names of men widely differing, yet
of equally conspicuous and acknowledged excellences,

who are too far above us to excite our envy, and whose celebrity will defend this willing, affectionate, and admiring testimony, from the charge of invidious selection or fulsome adulation; and who, each in his own sphere, one in the northern and the other in the southern hemisphere, is shedding the lustre of an evening star, and reflecting upon the church the glory of that great Sun of Righteousness, in whose attraction it has been his delight through a long, and holy, and useful life, to revolve: who yet live, and long may they live, that our younger ministry may learn in the holy labours of Chalmers * and Jay, how beautiful and how useful is human genius when sanctified by grace, and devoted to an earnest preaching of the gospel of salvation.

But we are not considering now what may be done, and is done, by the gifted few, who by their rare

---

* Alas, that so soon after this paragraph was penned, one of these venerated names should be expunged from the record of living men, and added to the list of the illustrious dead! Yes, the mighty Chalmers is gone; and to quote the apostrophe of Hebrew poetry, selected by Mr Jay as his funeral text for Rowland Hill, we may utter the wail and exclaim, "Howl, fir tree, the cedar has fallen!" The very glory and pride of Lebanon has fallen, and every one who surveys the gap which his removal has made in the forest, feels that there is no source of consolation under such a bereavement, but that which is supplied by the consideration that the Lord lives. It is beyond my ability to describe or to eulogise this wonderful man, whose death has clothed the whole church of God in mourning; I would therefore only say that ever since his vast intellect was irradiated by the light of truth, and his noble heart was brought by faith under the constraint of love to Christ, he has exhibited one of the finest specimens of the character I have attempted to delineate in this volume; so that every student of divinity in our colleges, and every minister of every denomination, may be directed to Dr. Chalmers, as one of the most beautiful types and models of an Earnest Minister. Dr. W. Lindsay Alexander's funeral sermon, which contains an admirable analysis of his mind and character, will well repay perusal.

endowments are fitted, and designed, to enrich our theological literature by their valuable works, or to gather around our pulpits the literary or philosophical spirits of the place in which they dwell; they are the exceptions in all denominations to the general rule of preachers, even as those who listen to them are the exceptions to the general rule of hearers. Our remarks apply to the men who move the masses, who operate upon the popular mind as it is most commonly found; and what are they? not men of high scholarship, profound philosophy, or elegant composition; but men of energy and earnestness, men laying themselves out for usefulness, men of business and of tact in the management of their fellow-men, men of heart, of feeling, and perseverance. Where is a large congregation, a flourishing, well-compacted church to be found? There is an earnest man. Where, in what country, or in what denomination, does one such man labour without considerable success? Where has the faithful, devoted, energetic preacher of evangelical truth, to use in a figurative sense the words of the Lord's forerunner, had to say, "I am the voice of one crying in the wilderness?" Where do we find small congregations, dissatisfied or declining churches, and empty chapels? Where do the ways of Zion mourn, and her gates languish, because none come to her solemn feasts? Certainly not where the ministers are as flames of fire. No matter where, or under what discouraging circumstances, one of these sacred flames may commence his labours, he will soon draw around him a deeply interested and attentive congregation ; no matter what may be the denomination with which he may be associated, he will not only excite the indifference, or subdue the prejudice, by which he is surrounded, but will awaken interest and conciliate regard. Under the magic power of his devotedness, blessed as it will be by God the Spirit, the verdure and beauty of spring will succeed to the gloom, desolation, and sterility of winter, and the wilderness and the solitary place shall be glad for him, and the desert rejoice and blossom as the rose. In some cases the change has been as sudden and as complete as in Russia, from frosts and snows to flowers and fragrance: churches that seemed only the repositories of the dead, and places for monuments and epitaphs, have become crowded with living and listening hearers of the joyful sound : and chapels once far too large for the last remains of a former congregation, have been soon found too small for the new one that has filled up its place.

It would be no unprofitable exercise for any one to look round upon some of our most successful ministers, and after surveying the extent of their usefulness, to say to himself, "How has that man done this? What have been the means by which, under God, he has accomplished so much?" Unhappily there are a few, perhaps, who are so enamoured of what is literary, intellectual, or philosophical, that even in great ministerial success, they see little to admire or to covet, if it be not associated with scholarship and science. This is a bad state of mind, indicates a worse state of heart, and proves that the man who is the subject of it, has totally mistaken the end of the ministerial office. Some of our most useful preachers are far more conscious of their deficiencies in literature and philosophy than these supercilious scholars may imagine, and would purchase, at almost any cost, if they could be obtained, by money, the attainments which their limited education never enabled them to acquire; but at the same time they would not give up their usefulness for all the literature of Greece and Rome, with all mathematics and philosophy in addition: and amidst their deficiencies in all that would give them weight and influence in the world of letters, they feel adoringly thankful for all that other kind of weight and influence which they have acquired in the church. Their labours in the pulpit have gained them an acceptance which is far more surprising to themselves than it can be to others. Peradventure also, they may have launched on the sea of authorship, and have had a prosperous course, where many expected they must soon make shipwreck. None can be more sensible than themselves of defects in their compositions, and often they have been ready to blame their presumption in taking up their pen, and to resolve to lay it down for ever; when perhaps some instance of usefulness has come to their knowledge, as if to reprove their vanity, wounded by a sense of their own deficiencies, and to make them thank God, and take courage. They knew their own department of literary action, and aimed at nothing higher than to be useful; willing to bear the sneer of literary pride, and endure the lash of critical severity, so that they might accomplish the only objects of their ambition, the salvation of immortal souls, and the establishment of believers in their holy faith. Such men there are among us, who owe their success not to a finished education, for it was their misfortune not to enjoy this precious advantage to the extent to which it is now carried; nor to high scholarship, to which they make no pretensions, but to an intense desire to be useful, and to something of earnestness in carrying out the desires of their hearts. In addition to the direct usefulness of their labours, they may be useful in another way, by showing that where great literary acquisitions have been precluded, still simple earnestness without them, may be blessed of God for accomplishing in no inconsiderable extent the great ends of the Christian ministry.

It has been said, in reference to secular matters, that a man who has decision of character enough to make up his mind to be rich; who has a measure of talent to uphold his resolution; and a rigid system of self-denying economy, will ordinarily succeed: and observation seems to support the remark. With far greater certainty may it be said, that he who enters upon his ministry with an intense zeal for God; an ardent passion for the salvation of souls; a well sustained, deep piety, a tolerable share of talents and acquirements; and a fixed purpose in humble dependence upon God's grace, to be a useful minister of Christ, will not fail of his end. The failure of such a man would be a new thing in the earth. I know of no such case, and I do not expect to meet with one. In dealing with sinners and calling them to repentance, we tell each, he may be saved if he will: not intending by such an expression that he can be saved without the Spirit of God; but that he may secure that Divine power if he have faith to receive it: so we may also venture to say to every minister of Christ, it is his own fault if he is not useful; intending by such an assertion, that as the gospel he preaches is God's own truth; as preaching is his own institute; as the minister is his own servant; and as He has promised that his grace shall be added to them, it would seem as if in the case of entire or extensive failure, a minister has himself only to blame.

But we may look at the power of earnestness, as seen in the cause of error as well as in that of truth. It has as often served a bad cause as it has a good one. Islamism owes its existence and its wide dominion to this quality in its extraordinary founder. Mohammed exhibits one of the most wonderful instances of this quality the world ever witnessed; and with what dreadful results was it followed in his case! We may say the same of Popery; that stupendous fabric of delusion, which throws its dark and chilling shadow over so large a portion of Christendom, owes its erection and its continuance to the intense devotedness with which it has inspired its votaries: it is this that upholds a system constantly at war with the dictates of reason, the doctrines of revelation, and the dearest rights and liberties of humanity. It is the mysterious and indomitable earnestness of its priesthood, which has resisted the attacks of logic rhetoric and piety, of divines philosophers and statesmen, of wit humour and ridicule; and which, in this age of learning, science, commerce and liberty, enables it not only to maintain its ground, but to advance and make conquests. The Church of Rome, which would in the hands of a lukewarm priesthood fall by the weight of its own absurdity, or be crushed by the hands of its constant assailants, is still strong in the hearts of its members: because each of them from the Pope down, through all its civil and ecclesiastical gradations, to its most insignificant member, is a type of concentrated and intensely glowing zeal.

The pages of ecclesiastical history furnish us with

extraordinary instances of the power of the pulpit, in the sermons of some Popish preachers. I do not now refer to the court of Louis the Fourteenth, which, with that imperious and licentious monarch at its head, was subdued into a transient frame and season of devoutness, by the sermons of Massillon, but to the preaching of far inferior and less known orators; and to effects less courtly, but not less striking. When Connecte, an Italian, preached, the ladies committed their gay dresses by hundreds to the flames. When Narni in Lent, taught the populace from the pulpits of Rome, half the city went from his sermons, crying along the streets, "Lord have mercy upon us, Christ have mercy upon us!" and in one passion week, two thousand crowns' worth of ropes were sold to make scourges; and when he preached before the Pope, to cardinals and bishops, and painted the crime of non-residence in its true colours, he frightened thirty or forty bishops, who heard him, instantly to their own dioceses. When he preached at Salamanca, he induced eight hundred students to quit all worldly prospects of honour, riches, and pleasure, and to become penitents in divers monasteries; and some of them eventually became martyrs. Such was the power of earnestness; but being devoted in this case to the cause of error, being directed rather to the imagination than to the heart, and intended to correct mere ceremonial irregularities, rather than to lead to repentance towards God, and faith in our Lord Jesus Christ, we are not surprised that the storm of passion soon subsided; that Narni himself was so disgusted with his office, that he renounced preaching and shut himself up in his cell, to mourn over his irreclaimable contemporaries; for bishops went back to court, and rope makers lay idle again. This striking fact is replete with instruction, not only as showing the power of the pulpit, but also the essential feebleness of that religion which does not aim at the renovation of the heart, and the transient nature of that effect which is produced by mere rhetoric, unaccompanied by a sober exhibition of the truth to enlighten the judgment, to warm the affections, and to awaken the conscience.

But it is not only on this grand scale that we see the power and success of ardent zeal, even in a bad cause; for there is no system of opinions, and no course of religious practice, however remote, not only from the truth of revelation but from the dictates of common sense, and even the decorum of society, but if preached and propagated by men of intense ardour, will gain for a while disciples to believe it, and apostles to propagate it. If men are really in earnest in blowing bubbles, some will be found to look at, admire, and follow them. I have already said that earnestness is contagious: a man in this state of mind and action is sure to draw some others under the influence of his own example. If this is the case with a bad cause, how much more may we expect it to be so in a good one! Every thing then combines to prove that our want of success must be traced up rather to our neglect of the right means to obtain it, than to any backwardness on the part of God to give his blessing to intelligent, judicious, and earnest exertions.

Surely, surely, there must be, I repeat, a latent power in the evangelical pulpit, viewed as a moral and well adapted means of impression, which has not, except by Whitfield and a few others, been studied, discovered, and applied. Surely if we had more intense piety, stronger faith, more knowledge of the human heart, more anxiety to obtain an impressive elocution, more ardent longings after the conversion of sinners, we could and should by God's grace move and command the masses. There is, there must be, neglected power somewhere.

VII. The state of our denomination demands immediate and devoted attention to the subject.

In speaking of our own denomination, I find in its general condition much cause for thankfulness and congratulation. In the number of our churches and the competency of a very large number of their pastors; in our colleges and schools; in our missionary and other organizations; in our periodical and other religious literature; in our public spirit and liberality, I see signs of prosperity, and tokens for good: and if we are true to ourselves and to our 'cause, we have nothing to fear. Our opponents cannot do us so much harm as we may do ourselves. With a system of doctrine which we believe is taken from the New Testament, and a system of polity which in all its general principles is derived from the same source, we may not only stand our ground, but advance, if we will present the former in all its fulness, and administer the latter with discretion and charity. Every thing, under God's blessing, depends upon our ministry. This, which is important to every denomination, is especially so to ours. We go forth not only unsupported by the wealth, power, and fashionableness of the Established Church, but without the aid of that elaborately organized combination which is to be found in some sections that separate from it. Our ministers, so to speak, do not contend in regiments formed in rank and file, but single handed, and should

therefore be all picked men, each possessed of courage
and of skill. Let us only take care to send none but
such into the field, and we may hope for a still more
abundant measure of prosperity than we at present
enjoy.

There is room enough for all denominations in the
vast wilderness of our neglected and unchristianized
population, and we have no need to look at each other's
labours with jealousy and envy. Satan is ruining souls
faster than all of us united can save them. It is a mark
of deep malignity of heart, and a proof that it is the
distempered zeal of bigotry, and not pure love to God
and souls, that moves us, when we see with uneasiness
the success of other denominations of evangelical Christians, and rejoice over their failure. To seize with
avidity any acknowledgments of, and lamentations over,
a want of usefulness, and then tearing them from their
connexion and exaggerating their statements, to hold
them up exultingly to the world, and tauntingly to the
denomination from which in frankness and in sorrow
they have come, may suit well with the strategy of
polemical warfare, and serve the cause of a party, but ill
accords with the spirit of divine charity, and cannot
promote the interests of our common Christianity. In
many places of worship connected with the Establishment, even where the gospel is preached, but preached
with feebleness, we find small congregations, and few
souls converted to God. Do we rejoice over this? On
the contrary, it is a grief and a lamentation. And is
there a heart so envenomed with the gall of bigotry, as
to rejoice in the confession now made, that many of our
congregations are withering away under the effete
ministrations of incompetent men? Such a withering

is indeed going on in many places. The fact cannot be concealed, it is notorious. We have been incautious in the admission, not of bad men, for few of these ever find their way into our pulpits; not of heretical men, for we take care not to receive such; but of incompetent men: not always incompetent in intellect, but in talents for public speaking and the active duties of the pastorate. From this cause, combined with the increased energy and activity of the Church of England, our congregations are diminishing in some places, though multiplying and increasing in others. With the freedom of action we possess, unrestricted by parochial limits and ecclesiastical laws; with the world all before us, and Providence our guide; with a good feeling towards us on the part of the middle and lower classes, we have every ground to hope for success, if we can obtain an adequate number of energetic and earnest preachers; but we have not taken sufficient care to find out and educate the right sort of men, and in some places are certainly losing ground. Considerable towns might be mentioned where congregations once numerous and flourishing, are reduced down to mere skeletons, under the dull and deadening influence of feeble, yet good men. It is more easy to settle an incompetent minister over a church than to remove him. It is true we have advantages for such removal not possessed by the Church of England. The pastorate is not in our churches a freehold; yet it must be confessed that even with us, the difficulty of getting rid of a pastor, except for immorality or heresy, and only on the ground of inefficiency, is not small. That a minister should wish to stay when he has preached away nearly all his congregation, breeds a suspicion of the purity of his motives, and is a reflection upon the integrity of his character. To reduce a congregation and scatter a church, first by inefficiency, and then by obstinacy in retaining the post in opposition to the wishes of the flock, and the advice of friends, is a serious matter to account for to God. Some such men talk of waiting for the leadings of Providence. One is at a loss to find out what rule of interpretation for ascertaining the will of God they have adopted: to every body else but themselves, deserted pews and a dissatisfied as well as a reduced church, are a sufficient indication that Providence is leading to their removal. In such a case one should suppose there needed no voice from heaven to say to the minister, " Arise, and go hence ;" nor any finger to come forth, and write " Ichabod" in flaming characters on the walls. It is sometimes said that the people must suffer the consequences of a hasty choice: and so far as they are concerned, they deserve it; but they suffer not alone, for the denomination suffers with them in its strength, character, and efficiency. The work of conversion, not only in our own denomination, but in the Church of England, and among the Methodists, goes on but slowly, and the spirituality of the great bulk of professors is too low. This is confessed and lamented by the Evangelical clergy, and by the Wesleyan ministers, as well as by ourselves. The Spirit's influence seems in some way and from some cause obstructed: and in the absence of this, our denomination is more likely to feel and manifest the visible results of it than almost any other; and such a consideration should lead us to more serious thoughtfulness and earnest prayer for a revived and intensely devoted ministry.

CHAPTER X.

THE MEANS OF OBTAINING AN EARNEST MINISTRY.

THIS is a most important part of my subject: for however desirable the blessing may be, yet if it cannot be obtained, or if there are no means by which we can obtain it, the discussion and contemplation of it are useless, and even worse, being calculated only to excite a fruitless wish, or what is most injurious of all, a disposition to neglect the means we have. But we are not to entertain so desponding a view. Men there have been, and blessed be God, men there are, and that in no small number, in every section of the Christian church, labouring with intelligence, zeal, and success, both in the metropolis and in the provinces; men of whom their age need not be ashamed, and over whom any age would have rejoiced. Still there are too many of an opposite character; far too many, to render the question impertinent and out of season, " How shall such a ministry be obtained?"

I. It is imperative first of all to have the truth deeply engraven upon all hearts, that the church is the conservator of the christian ministry, and that it is her business, and almost her first and most important business, to see that she discharges well her duty in this momentous affair. She has at the present time, not

only to provide for her own edification, but also to
secure, by all possible vigilance and care, the adminis-
trative transmission of our holy religion through following ages, pure, undefiled, and unimpaired in its
capacity to confer essential and eternal benefits upon
the children of men.   But it is obvious that for such a
function the church must be regarded as a purely
spiritual body.   And it should be deemed a question
of no small moment, bearing as it does upon the controversy about church government, what system of polity
has the most direct tendency and the greatest power
to call out, secure, and perpetuate an evangelical and
effective ministry.   An ecclesiastical system which
of itself has no effectual provision for this, cannot
surely be of Divine origin, and that which has the most
obvious and direct tendency to this, is most in accordance with the Word of God.   A church without
such a conservative principle cannot be the church
of the New Testament, much less that which includes
various and ever active influences against it.   Nothing
but a spiritual church can provide a spiritual ministry,
and any spiritual ministry which a worldly church may
have cannot be so much the result of the system, as
of something extraneous to it.   Even in spiritual
churches, if discipline be relaxed, and worldly-minded
persons be admitted, the conservative principle, the vital
piety of the members, is impaired ; and if at the same
time there be neglect of discipline, it will be altogether
lost, and heretical men come in to fill the places of those
who were the preachers of the truth as it is in Jesus.
It is well, therefore, for all our churches to bear in constant recollection, this their high and sacred function
as conservators of an evangelical ministry; and to

maintain that vital godliness, and that wholesome discipline, in which alone this power of conservation resides. Let the churches consider their high, their glorious commission: let them remember they must be such, that the Christian truth, both as to doctrine and practice, and the calling out and supporting fit men to uphold and preach it, may be safely trusted to their vigilance and care. But let them forget this and corrupt their fellowship by the admission of worldly-minded professors, and " the mounds are gone, the fence is broken up, and wolves may enter in, not sparing the flock." " Preserve this spiritual condition of the church, and it is what it was intended it should be, an undying torch, which, while it is the light of the present age, shall safely light successive ages along the only way which leads to happiness and heaven."

II. Let the subject be thoroughly considered, and universally admitted, that this is the ministry we want, and must have. In an age like the present, when so much is said about knowledge, and such high value is attached to it, there is a danger of our being seduced from every other qualification, and taken up with this. The establishment of the London University, and the incorporation of our Colleges with it, have given our students access to academic degrees and honours: and there is some danger in the new condition of our literary Institutions, lest our young men should have their minds in some measure drawn away from much more important matters, by the hope of having their names graced by the marks of a Bachelor's or a Master's degree. It is a foolish clamour that has been raised against all attention to such matters, and it is a vain and barbarous precaution that would fortify the ministerial devotedness of our students, by restraining them altogether from such distinctions. The studies necessary to enable them to attain this object of their ambition, are a part of their professional education; while the vanity likely to be engendered by success will soon be annihilated by the commonness of the acquisition. When these degrees are so common that almost all ministers possess them, they will no longer be a snare to their possessors. Besides, like every other object of human desire, when once they are possessed, much of the charm that dazzled the eye of hope has vanished. Henry Martyn, when he came from the senate-house at Cambridge, where he had been declared Senior Wrangler of his year, and had thus won the richest honour the University had to confer, was struck with the vanity of human wishes, and expressed his surprise at the comparative worthlessness of the bauble he had gained, and the shadow he had grasped. It is not by closing the door against such distinctions that we can hope to raise the tone of devotedness in our ministry, but by fostering in the minds of our young men at College, and in the minds of our congregations, and our ministers in general, the conviction that earnestness is just that one thing, to which all other things must be, and can be, made subservient, and without which all other things which education can impart are as nothing.

Our congregations need perhaps a little instruction on this subject. I am afraid their taste is not quite so pure, correct, and elevated on this matter, as it should be. There is, it is true, a demand for a vivacious and animated manner of preaching, and it is well there should be such; and provided it be intellectual, there is a decided preference for its being evangelical also; but there is reason to fear that in some cases a small modicum of evangelical truth would do, provided there was abundance of talent. Earnestness is demanded, but with some, it is rather the earnestness of the head, than of the heart; the laboured and eloquent effusion of the scholar, philosopher, or poet, rather than the gush of hallowed feeling of him who watches for souls, as one that must give account. Dulness, however learned or profound, will not do, but the heartless declamations of the pulpit orator will do for some, though it have little tendency to do any thing more than please the intellect or captivate the imagination. There is in this day an idolatry of talent running through society; and this man-worship has crept into the church, and corrupted its members. It is painful to perceive how far it is carried in many circles, and to see what homage is paid, and what incense is burnt, to their favourites. It is not religion or holiness that is thus elevated, but genius and knowledge: it is not moral beauty, but intellectual strength, that is lauded to the skies: the loftiest models of goodness receive but scanty offerings at their shrine, compared with the gods of the understanding. It is very evident that in many cases the gospel is loved, if loved at all, for the sake of the talent with which it is preached, and not the talent for the sake of the gospel. Even the village tyro begins to talk about intellectual preachers. The fact however is admonitory, and shows that imbeciles, however holy, will not do, even in rural districts, in these days. There can be no surer mark of man's moral apostacy, his lapse from the innocence which he had when he came from the hands of his Creator perfect and in the moral image of God, than this disposition to exalt genius above piety.

What an inversion is it of the right order of things, since it must be allowed that man's intellect is not the highest part of his nature. It is by his capacity for virtue and religion that he is removed to the greatest distance from the brute creation, is placed in most direct opposition to fallen spirits, makes his nearest approach to the angels of God, and in any degree resembles the Holy and Eternal One. The God of the Bible is not merely a Divine Intellect, though his understanding is infinite; nor is Omniscience his only attribute, though it is one of his glorious perfections; but God is Love; and when the seraphim select for the subject of their anthem that view of his nature which calls forth their loftiest praise, they contemplate him as the Holy, Holy, Holy, Lord God Almighty. Infinite goodness, and not merely infinite greatness, is the Deity we are called by the inspired writers to worship; and the most sublime descriptions of God, not based upon his goodness, are but the inventions of men, and no true copies of God's representations of his own nature. The prevailing disposition, therefore, to do such homage to talent, rather than to moral excellence, is only another species of idolatry, more refined and subtle than the worship of stocks and stones, but scarcely less guilty.

That some respect must be paid to talent, even in the ministry of the word, is admitted; a disposition to prize it is inseparable from human nature, and is a part of the design of God in forming men with varying powers of the understanding: a fine intellect is to be admired as well as an elegant form or a beautiful flower; and so much the more, as that which is mental is superior to that which is corporeal. But when the Christian public is so enamoured of talent, as to admire it more than the message which it is employed to set forth; when no preacher can be heard with pleasure or even endurance, however sound his doctrine, clear his statements, impressive his manner, or earnest his address, unless his discourse is radiant with the light of genius, and gay with the flowers of rhetoric; when truth itself is unpalatable unless it is sweetened with the honey of human eloquence, and even error so sweetened is swallowed for the sake of its luscious accompaniment; when the hearer of a sermon turns from it with disgust, because it fails to regale his fancy by the brilliancy of its images, or to lull his ear by the smoothness and harmony of its periods; when this is the state of the public taste, and it is to be feared that to a great extent it is the state of it now, surely it is time to call the attention of our congregations to something higher and better.

No one who is attentive to the distinguishing features of the age, can doubt that much is now going on which has an obvious, though of course an undesigned, tendency to corrupt in some degree the simplicity of the public taste with reference to preachers and their sermons. The pulpit has some reason to be jealous of the platform, and the sermon of the speech. If the modern practice of endless speechifying had only done something to break down the stiffness and formality of sermonic speaking, and to introduce a more easy, fluent, and energetic method of address on the part of the preacher, and a corresponding taste for a more vivacious method of instruction on the part of the people, it would have conferred a substantial benefit; but with it has come perhaps the opposite evil of making the preacher too oratorical, and the people too fastidious; and of destroying somewhat of the solemnity and spirituality of both. No doubt some degree of earnestness will still be observed, but it may be the earnestness which is anxious to please, rather than that which is desirous to convert; which aims to gratify the fancy rather than to save the soul.

It is in vain then to hope for such a ministry as that which it is the object of this work to describe and to recommend, till our congregations are brought to see its vast importance, and to supplicate that it may be given them. In this case, as in every other, the demand will bring the supply, as well as the supply create the demand. When the churches shall be brought up to that state of piety, that deep solicitude about salvation, that intenseness of pursuit of eternal life, which shall make them anxious to have ministers who will aid them in the momentous business; and when they shall say to the tutors and committees of our colleges, "You must not only send us learned men, but earnest men," then will the minds of our excellent professors be still more fixed on the most essential qualifications of the Christian ministry, and still more anxiously endeavour to meet this demand. And when our destitute congregations shall let it be distinctly known that it is not merely a Master of Arts, nor a merely eloquent speaker, nor even a good divine that they want, but one who shall watch for their souls, and feed the flock of God, then the attention of our young ministers will be still more turned to the end of their ministry, and the qualifications necessary for the just discharge of its functions. Let the church therefore only be rightly instructed on this subject, and fix properly its standard; let it be brought up to the conviction, that only men intent upon saving souls, will be useful, and such men will come at its bidding.

III. There should be much prayer presented to God for a supply of earnest ministers. It must never be forgotten that ministers are called, qualified, and blessed, by the Lord, the Spirit. Hence the promise of God to the Jews, " I will give you pastors according to mine own heart; which shall feed you with knowledge and with understanding." And hence also the language of the apostle, " He gave some pastors and teachers ; for the perfecting of the saints, for the work of the ministry, for the edifying of the body of Christ." It was a special injunction of Christ to his disciples, but intended to apply to his people in every age, to pray to the Lord of the harvest to send forth labourers into the field. From these passages, as well as from the general principle that every good gift is from the Lord, we learn that a faithful ministry is one of God's gifts, and a precious one it is; and were the church in a high spiritual state, it would constitute one of the chief subjects of its prayers. Perhaps we are not brought to feel with sufficient depth of conviction our dependence upon God for this great blessing, for there is little doubt that the church's prayers and the church's possessions would bear in this particular some tolerable proportion to each other. We cannot conceive of any case in which the promise, " Ask, and ye shall receive," would be so abundantly fulfilled, as in reference to this. It has not been enough considered what kind of men are wanted at all times, and especially in these, for the ministry of reconciliation ; that in fact we need men formed exactly and in all respects, except inspiration and the power to work miracles, upon the apostolical model. Much the same work is now to be done as was done by them, and we must have men as full of the power of God, and the grace of the Holy Spirit, to do it. Let it be seen what ministers have to contend with in this day; not indeed the spirit of persecution, not sanguinary laws, not the amphitheatre, the axe, or the stake; but obstacles in some respects more formidable; for the trials I have just mentioned, if they lessened the number of professors, raised those that stood firm into the devotion of seraphs, the courage of heroes, and the constancy of martyrs; but our obstacles are the emasculating influences of ease and prosperity; the insidious snares of wealth, knowledge, and fashion; the engrossing power of trade, politics, and secular ambition; and then let it be considered what kind of preachers and pastors we want for such an age. If we had nothing more to do, and were contented to do no more, than to keep religion up to the low level which it now maintains, ministers of a common stamp might suffice; but to keep in check all the enemies of vital godliness which threaten the devastation of the church; to resist, by the potency of personal example and the energy of the pulpit, the worldly spirit which threatens to eat out the very core of vital piety; to keep up the evangelizing zeal which is awakened, and to blend with it a sanctity and a spirituality which shall make it as effective as it is busy; to do battle with all the forms of error by which our common faith is likely to be assailed; and to do this not only by the force of intellect, but by being strong in the Lord, and in the power of his might; to achieve this we want men of the same spirit as those who under the direct commission of Christ, preached the word of salvation with the Holy Ghost sent down from heaven. Have we many such men in the field? If not, why not? Must not the church of God blame herself, for not having sought such men by all the wrestling power of believing prayer. Had she felt the need of such men, and had she lifted up, not her hands and her voice merely, but all the energies of her renewed nature, in beseeching supplications to Him who is ascended to bestow this very gift, she would have obtained all she asked or wanted. Let the church only set her heart upon such a blessing as this, let her faith be equal to the expectation of it, and her prayer be as her faith, and she will have it. Why should she not expect it? What is there in the nature of the boon that forbids her to look for it? Does it contradict a single promise, or contravene a single arrangement, of her Divine Head? Does it compromise his honour, or require his unwonted interposition? Does it involve any stepping out of his ordinary course of action? Why then should it be thought incredible that she should obtain a more, a far more devoted and successful ministry, than she now possesses? Does the gospel of God's grace, either at home or abroad, prevail as it could be wished and might be expected? Does the work of conversion go forward extensively, and Christ's Kingdom make fresh encroachments on the empire of darkness as might be looked for? Who will venture to answer in the affirmative? Does love to Christ and souls beat in any man's heart, with so feeble a pulsation that he must be satisfied with what is doing, and be contented that things should go on as they do? Is there nothing to be done, no way to accelerate the work of redeeming mercy, no method to pour the principles of spiritual fertility more rapidly and more diffusively through the moral wilderness of our barren world? Yes, one way is yet open, and that is for Zion to awake and bestir herself, and lay hold of God's strength, saying, " Send us more labourers into the field." We have forgotten to pray for ministers of a right stamp. The subject has never occupied, in our private, family, and social devotions, the place which its importance demands. It has been occasionally and coldly alluded to, but has not been lifted up to heaven with importunity by men who felt that they could not do without it.

"Truly if ever there was a period when the whole Christian world should be down upon their faces before the throne of mercy, imploring with all the importunity, and boldness, and perseverance of faith, a race of ministers, each full of the Holy Ghost, as was Barnabas or Paul, that period is passing over us. Not from one place or another, but from all quarters of the earth, testimony multiplies daily that amidst the greatest possible facilities for converting the world, a greatly increased and more devoted ministry is indispensable. This testimony comes to us, not indeed as the Macedonian cry came to the apostle in a supernatural vision; but in a manner not less affecting or decisive as to its purport. It is a real sound which flies round the land and rings in our ears all the day long; 'Send us preachers,' is the universal, ceaseless demand, at home and abroad. It comes from more than a thousand of our destitute churches; it comes from the cities, from the wilderness, from the islands, from the uttermost parts of the sea, from tracts until lately unknown to civilized man. This cry which sounds so loudly and so complainingly in our ears, should by general consent be turned into prayer and sent up to heaven. And shall we longer forbear to do this? Shall we stand and hear that unusual cry and feel no inclination to direct it to the ear of Him from whom help alone can come? Is it not a mysterious species of infatuation to forbear to lift up our cry to the Lord of the harvest? Why do we not, if this be the case, abjure the very religion of Jesus, and abandon ourselves, as well as the heathen, and the whole race of man to despair? Why should not a reform forthwith commence, and the place of prayer have more attractions than the eloquence of any mortal, or any angel's tongue? Why then will not every true

Christian make a covenant with himself to change his life in this particular, and from henceforth make it one of his chief subjects of wrestling supplication, that God would give us a more faithful, earnest, and laborious ministry? Why will we not call to mind how Abraham, and Moses, and Elias, and Daniel, and Paul, and above all how the blessed Jesus laboured in prayer, and resolve in God's strength to pray in the same manner? Oh, what an amount of beneficent power would such prayers exert upon the eternal destinies of our world! What wonders of grace would be witnessed in our churches, what accessions would be made to the sacred ministry, what an impulse would be given to the cause of missions, what brightness would be shed on all the prospects of the church!"*

I echo these beautiful sentiments, and earnestly implore for them the attention they demand. They touch us at the right point, and they speak to us at the proper season. We have multiplied and extended, of late, our collegiate institutions, and greatly improved our systems of ministerial education. We can speak of colleges whose architecture † would not disgrace Oxford or Cambridge, and of professors whose attainments in Biblical literature would not be surpassed by many teachers in national seats of learning; but as if to teach us our dependence upon God, few of them are at the

---

* "Religion of the Bible." A Select Discourse, by Dr. Skinner, of New York.

† The age is past when the taunt could with truth be thrown at Dissenters, that theirs is the religion of barns; and if it were not, this would be no reproach to those whose Lord was born in a stable, and cradled in a manger. [Not to mention that meeting-houses more nearly resemble the basilica than any building in the shape of a cross or with a chancel. Ed.] The danger lies in sacrificing too much to beauty of architecture. Splendid men, as pastors and preachers, will do more for us than splendid buildings; not that they are incompatible, but they are by no means inseparable. Butler, the author of "The Analogy," and Jones, the author of the most learned work on the Canon, both studied within the ochre-coloured, old-fashioned walls of Tewkesbury College: while many a dolt has gone forth from our most magnificent buildings.

present moment filled with students; and as to those who are coming forth from them, how great is our anxiety lest they should not prove such eminent and earnest men as we could wish to see them! The same remark will apply to the evangelical party of the Church of England, and all other denominations. I would be the last man to speak lightly of education, but I would be the first to caution the church of Christ against the sin and the folly of making it our supreme dependence. Tutors can impart a knowledge of Latin, Greek, and philosophy, but God alone can bestow the physical and spiritual gifts which constitute the chief qualifications for the work of the ministry. It is a fact which must have struck every attentive observer, that of those who are employed in the ministry of the word, whether in the Established Church or out of it, comparatively few are very eminent. The brightest flowers of humanity are not laid upon the altar of the Lord in great numbers. The majority of ministers are of a common order of intellect, and, as in the firmament of heaven, only here and there a star attracts attention by its magnitude and brightness. Let it not be said that God chooses the weak things of the world to confound the mighty. This appertained to apostles, who, as they were clothed with the power of God by their gifts and miracles, could dispense with all other potency; but it is not the case with us, who without appropriate qualifications of native talent and education, can never expect the blessing of God.

IV. A revived state of the Church would produce a ministry such as that which has been described in the foregoing pages. In the natural order of things it would seem that the church cannot be revived without a previous revival of the ministry; and yet, as the ministry are the children of the church, they can hardly be expected to rise above the level of the community out of which they spring. There is a kind of average piety of almost every age and every church, and our young men rarely come with more than this to our colleges: and therefore, although we do not dispute the fact that little expectation can be indulged of an increased piety in the churches, without an augmentation of ministerial devotedness, yet at the same time, the latter can almost as little be looked for, without the former. Revivals have sometimes begun with the people, who have drawn the ministry up to their own level. A lively church could not long endure a dull and lukewarm pastor, if he partook not of the prevailing excitement, he would feel himself soon obliged to leave his situation. If, therefore, the ministry cannot revive themselves and each other, it were an unspeakable mercy if they should receive an impulse from the people.

As we have already seen, many things in the present age are of a most auspicious character, and give it a lofty pre-eminence above some that have preceded it. Who can witness its busy activity, its generous liberality, its exhaustless ingenuity for the conversion of the world, without admiration and gratitude: but these are not all the elements of true piety, and it may be apprehended that, in inumerable cases, they are only the substitutes for the essential work of regeneration and sanctification. It may be feared that Satan is taking advantage of them to blind the judgment, and to delude the souls, of many. Men of keen observation, who can penetrate the surface, and see what lies below it, are of opinion that underneath this external covering of liberality and zeal, there lies a want of vital godliness; that much of what we see in our multiplied public institutions is but as flowers blooming in a shallow and sandy soil. They who are best acquainted with the state of our churches, express a doubt whether there is not a deplorable lack of that separation from the world in its spirit and customs, which the Christian profession implies. While this is the case, the ministers who come out from such a state of things are likely to rise no higher than their source. Hence it becomes our churches to consider the urgent necessity of their rising to a higher tone of piety, and joining heartily in any efforts that are made to bring about so desirable a state of things. Even those who have themselves drunk deepest into the spirit of the world, will sometimes lament the want of intenseness and spirituality on the part of their ministers: but do they not remember that their own worldly-mindedness is exerting an influence over their pastor, and producing that very state of mind in him which is the subject of their remark and censure? He was perhaps a more holy and heavenly man, when he came to them from college, young and flexible, and was at first surprised and grieved to witness the prevalence of lukewarmness among them; but after striving, in vain, to produce a better state of things among the members of his church, he was gradually drawn down to that low level from which he found it impracticable to raise them. Thus while I admit there is little hope of a revived church which does not rest on the previous revival of the ministry, I am tempted almost to argue in a circle, and to say there is little hope of the revival of the ministry which does not rest on the previous revival of the church.

Let us then, both ministers and churches, set about in good earnest the revival of religion. We act and re-act upon each other. We help or hinder one another. We both want more religion; let the ministry seek it for the sake of the people, and the people for the sake of the ministry. If the ministers will not lead the people, let the people lead the ministers. If the blessing cannot descend from the pulpit to the pew, let it ascend from the pew to the pulpit. Let the church of the living God arise, put on her robe of righteousness, her garment of salvation, shake off the dust from her apparel, and shine forth in the beauties of holiness. We want a better church to make a better world; and a better church would most assuredly make a better world; and we also want a better ministry to make a better church; but if we cannot have them in the one order, may we have them in the other, and find that a better church is making a better ministry. If the rain of heaven collect not upon the hills to pour down its streams upon the vallies, may the vapour of the vallies rise to revive and refresh the tops of the hills.

V. We should, as pastors of the churches, look round our respective flocks, and see what devoted youths of ardent piety and competent abilities likely to be useful as ministers of Christ we have within our circles, and call them out to the work, without waiting for the first impulses of devotion to it to come from themselves. A radical mistake has been committed through our whole denomination, in supposing it is necessary in all cases for the desire after the sacred office to rise

up first of all, and spontaneously, in the breast of the
aspirant. In consequence of this, many have thrust
themselves forward who were altogether unfit for the
work; while many eminently qualified for it, have been
kept back by modesty. Does it not seem to be the
work of the pastors and the churches, to call out from
among themselves the most gifted and pious of their
members for this object? Is not this the working out
of the principle we have already considered, that the
church is the conservator of an effective ministry? Are
not they the best judges of talent and other prerequi-
sites? Should this matter be left to the inflation of
self-conceit, the prompting of vanity, or the impulse, it
may be of a sincere, but unenlightened zeal? Nothing
can be more erroneous than that this call of the church
would be an officious intermeddling with the work of
the Spirit in calling the ministry; for it may surely be
conceived to be quite as rational a notion to suppose
that the Spirit calls a person through the medium of
the church and its pastor, as to imagine that the commission from above comes direct to the heart of the
individual, especially as the church and the pastor, or
at any rate the latter, is usually applied to, as a judge
of the candidate's fitness for the work; and thus after
all, the power and right of pronouncing a judgment
upon the alleged call of the Divine Agent, are vested
with the pastor and the church. To affirm that an individual cannot be supposed to have a very great fitness
for the office, unless his love of souls has been strong
enough to prompt him to desire the work of the ministry, and that he is not likely to be very earnest in it,
if he be sent, instead of his going of his own accord, is
assuming too much; for in the plan here recommended,

it is supposed that the individual who attracts the attention of the pastor is one who, in addition to true piety and competent abilities, has manifested an active zeal in the way of doing good. It is only on such an one that his eye would light, or to whom he would venture to make the suggestion. In all the official appointments recorded in the New Testament, from an apostle down to a deacon, the people were requested to look out for suitable men, and not to wait till they presented themselves. Let us then give our serious attention to this subject, and look out for the most pious, the most intelligent, and the most ardent of our young men, not forgetting at the same time to ascertain their physical qualifications of voice and constitution. It is not studious youths only that will do for this work, mere book-worms who will devour knowledge and make no repayment for it; but such as will unite a thirst for knowledge with an intense desire to employ every acquisition for saving souls. We must be inquisitive after such; and if they are youths in the more respectable classes of society, young men who have known something of good society, and acquired the manners and habits of gentlemen; who have had something to do with business, and have acquired such a proper degree of self-confidence, as will give them weight and influence of character, all the better. Low men, with coarse vulgar manners, may by the power of great talents rise above their origin, and be of value, as diamonds uncut and unpolished; yet how much would the value of those spiritual diamonds be increased by the removal of all that is coarse in them, and the polishing of all that is rough and dim. When vulgarity is associated with slender talents, it is as flint set in lead. There is nothing in gentlemanly manners that deteriorates piety; and much, very much, that adds not only to the gracefulness, but to the usefulness, of the ministerial character. The graces, when baptized at the font of evangelical piety, arrayed in the robe of righteousness, and wearing the ornament of a meek and quiet spirit, are useful handmaids to the Christian pastor, and procure favour for him in the solemn duties of his office. If we may judge from the specimens left on record in the Acts of the Apostles, Paul united the manners of a courtier with the fidelity of a prophet, and threw over the stern courage of a martyr, the mantle of a gentle courteousness. What could be more polished, yet what more faithful, than his address to Festus and Agrippa? And we can imagine that even his denunciation against the High Priest, who had commanded him to be smitten on the mouth, was all the more terrible because of the dignified severity with which it was uttered. Earnestness, then, is not incompatible with refinement, but is rendered more effective by it, and hence the importance of our sending our better educated youths to the sacred office.

Occasionally we may find in our churches some persons possessed of extraordinary talents for speaking and for active duty, who are too far advanced in manhood to go through a college curriculum, but who, notwithstanding, would make admirable preachers, and attain to considerable usefulness, as well as respectability. A man of natural genius, of strong intelligence, of eminent piety, and of pulpit power, is not to be rejected because he has not passed through the schools. Those who remember William Thorp, and especially that great theologian, Andrew Fuller, will not deny that

He who called his apostles, not from the philosophers of Greece, or from the orators of Rome, or from the Rabbis of Jerusalem, but from the fishermen of Galilee, may sometimes select a servant, even in our days, from those classes which have been debarred the privileges of a classical or a philosophical education. Among the prophets of antiquity was Amos, the herdsman of Tekoa. These, however, are the exceptions, not the rule. Even the bishops of our ecclesiastical establishment are lowering their standard of qualifications, as necessary in all cases, for the ministerial functions, and are accommodating their system to the wants of the people, by ordaining men to the sacred office, whom their predecessors an age or two back would have unquestionably refused.* We must not pretend to more fastidiousness than they, nor be horror-struck at the idea of introducing to the pastorate, men, who, though they are neither scholars nor philosophers, are likely to be powerful and useful preachers of the gospel. A collegiate education must be our general rule, which it may be hoped we shall never abandon; but it is a rule from which we must make exceptions in the case of those strong-minded, warm-hearted, earnest men, whose tough broad-sword will do more execution than many a weapon whose blade has received the highest polish that art can give it, and whose hilt sparkles with diamonds.

VI. This is a subject which demands the close and serious attention of ministers themselves. The whole

---

* Several of them have lately determined to ordain as deacons, men who have had no classical education, provided they have good preaching abilities. Latin and Greek are in such cases to be dispensed with.

present generation of our preachers from the oldest to the youngest must give their attention to the matter. I have known men of a past age, whose names are dear, and whose memory is fragrant, who to the last retained the ardour of their zeal, and whose labours, like the flame of the volcano rising from beneath the snow-covered surface of the mountain top, were carried on in association with their hoary hairs: and some such, though they are very few, still linger amongst us. Even they, and we who come next to them, and are verging on old age, must all do something more and something better than we have done for Christ and souls. Our sun is declining, and our shadows lengthen on the plain, but our day's work is not done; and instead of relaxing our diligence, we must work the harder, because the time of working is nearly over. As long as we have strength to grasp the sickle, or light to bind a sheaf, let us work on. Harvest-home will soon be here, and it is time enough for enjoyment when that arrives, and we shall meet our Master and our fellow-servants. To us the admonition comes with solemn emphasis, "Whatsoever thy hand findeth to do, do it with thy might, for there is no work, nor device, nor knowledge, in the grave whither thou goest." For the sake of our younger brothers, let us be diligent. They look upon us as patterns; and let us therefore set them an example which shall come to them with the correctness of a good model, and the power of an ardent inspiration. Let there be no running from our posts as if we were weary of our service, and were panting for the otium cum dignitate. Let it be seen that the earnestness of our minds imparts vigour to our bodies, keeps off the infirmities of our declining years, and enables us to renew our youth like the eagle's. It is a spectacle which the admirer of military glory loves to witness, to behold the veteran soldier, on whose countenance the suns of innumerable campaigns and the swords of his foes have left their visible marks, outstripping in courage, in feats of arms, and in swiftness of foot, all the younger warriors that fight at his side, and to see him rallying their fainting hearts by the strength of his own. Veterans in the hosts of Emanuel, see then your duty! On you it devolves to train the young recruits, and form their character; let them feel that they are by the side of heroes, and catch the inspiration of your heroism. Cast over them your shadow while you live, and they will then be anxious to find your mantle when your spirit has dropped it in her flight to the skies. Let them see you intent upon the conversion of sinners, given up to your work of saving souls: and let them hear in your conversation how much your heart is set upon this work. Show them by the manner in which you are finishing your course, how they ought to begin and carry forward theirs. Correct their mistakes, elevate their aims and inflame their zeal. Do all you can by your private intercourse with them to form their character aright for the service of the Lord. Talk to them modestly of your own success in the ministry, and how you succeeded in this high and glorious achievement. What manner of men ought you to be, by whom the ardour of others will be kindled or extinguished? May God's grace be sufficient for you!

But of what momentous consequence is it that our younger ministers and students should give to this subject its due attention! You have advantages which some who have gone before you never enjoyed, and

which at times make them almost envy your privileges;
but if this be all you seek; if it be the best and the
highest object you aspire to, you have mistaken your
way in going to the pulpit, and had better, whatever of
literature you may acquire, have drudged out life in one
of the darkest of its recesses, or the humblest of its
occupations, than to have entered the Christian ministry.
Oh, what scenes attract your attention, and ought to
engage your energies! There around you are immortal
souls perishing in their sins, each one of more value
than the whole material universe, each capable of being
saved by your ministrations, and sure to acquire, by
neglecting them, a deeper guilt and a heavier condemnation: there, in sight of your faith, is the Son of
God, bleeding upon the cross for their redemption;
there beneath you is the pit of hell, opening wide its
mouth to receive them if they die in unbelief; there
above you is heaven, throwing back its everlasting
portals to receive them, if they are saved; there before
you is the bar of judgment, at which you must soon
meet them, to account for your ministry in reference to
them; and there, beyond all, is eternity with its ever
rolling ages, which are to be spent by them and you in
rapture or in woe. Is this true? Is it fiction, or is it
fact? If these things are not so, you are found false
witnesses for Christ, for they are the common topics and
the first principles of your discourses; but if they are
all realities, then with what state of mind and heart
should they be handled? Begin your ministry, beloved
young brethren, with a clear understanding of its
nature, and a deep impression of its importance. Do
you covet usefulness? Earnestness is essential to it.
You cannot do good in any extensive degree without it.

Listen to those who have gone before you; their testimony is founded both upon experience and observation. All, all will unite in this exhortation, "Be in earnest;" as well the very men who have had the least, as those who have exhibited the most, of this quality of character, and mode of action. Without this you cannot even be popular, to say nothing of usefulness. The public will hear an earnest minister, and will not hear any other. You may call this, if you will, bad taste, and wonder they will not listen to your highly intellectual and philosophical discourses, and be ready to withdraw in resentment the elaborate preparations they so little value, and retire from the pulpit. Whether they or you are wrong, this is the fact. He is an unwise tradesman, who, because he thinks the public taste is vicious, and ought to be corrected, will exhibit in his window, and place upon his shelves, no other goods than those the public will not buy. In this case the taste of the public may be wrong, and that of the tradesman right: but in the case of preaching, if the people demand an earnest exhibition of gospel truth, and their minister, instead of this, will give them nothing but dull, dry, abstract sermons, it is they who are right, and he is wrong: they, better than he does, know not only what they want, but what he was appointed by God to furnish them! Do not then mistake and determine to try to be useful in some other way than that which the God of nature and of grace has prescribed. Do not resolve to try the experiment of opening a new road to usefulness for yourself; another way than that which apostles, martyrs, and reformers have trod, and which the ministers and missionaries of every age and every country have found to be the power of God unto salvation, even the doctrine of the cross; another way which you may deem more befitting your powers and your scholarship, and the enlightenment of the age. You will inevitably go wrong if you do so, and close your career, lamenting your folly, and confessing that your ministerial life has been a lost adventure; a melancholy confession, and one that is not unfrequently made. God gives man only one life, and affords him no opportunity to live through another term of existence, in which to profit by his own experience; but he gives him abundant opportunity to avail himself of the knowledge gained by his own trials as they go on, and by observation of others. You have known enough and seen enough already of what will, and what will not, answer the end of your office, and save souls. You have only to look back, and to look around, to find evidence to guide you. You cannot mistake your means easily, if you do not mistake your object. Settle with yourselves what the latter is, that it is to save sinners by leading them to repent of sin, to believe on Christ, and to lead a holy life; and then you can scarcely fail to perceive that this never has been accomplished, and ordinarily never can be, but by beseeching them, and praying them, in Christ's stead, to be reconciled to God.

We who are growing grey in the service of Christ, feel somewhat anxious about those who are to succeed us. We see with gratitude and wonder what God has wrought by us; and we know how, as instruments, we have done it. We see how souls have been converted, churches have risen up, and believers have lived and died in the faith, and know full well that it was by the testimony of the gospel, plainly but energetically stated. In looking back, we often feel regret that the activity required by the age took from us the opportunity to make greater attainments in elegant literature and general knowledge; but no regret that we have made the great theme of Christ crucified the subject of our ministry, and the salvation of souls the object of our lives. We feel, amidst the gathering shadows of evening, a calm and sweet satisfaction that in that we made a right choice, mingled with a profound humiliation that we have not followed it with more intensity of devotion. We see many things in the review of the past that we would alter, but we would make no alteration in that; we see much that we could improve, but only in the manner by which we could more successfully accomplish that object; and if it were permitted us to live our existence over again, or to speak more correctly, to spend another term, and set out afresh, it would be our high resolve to get more of what the men of science and of literature admire, only to enable us to preach with greater power the doctrine of the cross, and to be better qualified to seek with more ardour, and with better hopes of success, the end of our ministry. The love of applause, and we have all too much of it, is we hope dying in our hearts, or at any rate it appears to be more and more worthless, and the approval of our great Master more and more intensely to be desired. Whether we look back upon the past, consider our feelings for the present, or look at the prospects and anticipate the disclosures of the future, we know of no arguments cogent enough, no language sufficiently expressive, to enforce upon our younger brethren in the ministry, in reference to the purpose of their lives, the important admonition, "Be in earnest."

VII. Considerable care and caution are requisite, and much more than have been exercised hitherto, in the introduction and reception of young men into our colleges. Incompetent ministers are the burden, as inconsistent ones have been the dishonour, of every section of the church, and the hindrance of the progress of the gospel in the world. In hearing them one is ready to wonder how it ever entered into their hearts to conceive they had been called of God to a work for which they seem to possess scarcely a single qualification beyond their piety; and the wonder is doubled to account for any minister recommending them, or any committee receiving them : without intellect, without heart, and equally without voice, they seem sent into the ministry only to keep out others more competent for the work. How many have been permitted to escape from the pursuits of business, in which they might have done well, to endure the greatest privations, and to submit to the most humiliating mortifications, in an office, for the functions of which they were deplorably unfit! How many of them have passed through life in the misery of being amidst a discontented people, or in wandering from place to place, without remaining with any church long! Such cases have been found in every age, and in every denomination, but they were never so numerous as they now are. A spirit of fastidiousness has crept over churches, and unsettledness over pastors. How great then is the responsibility of recommending a young man to enter the ministry! It is an act drawing after it consequences of a most momentous nature, and should never be done without the utmost care and caution. It would be well if ministers would call in others to bear the burthen with them, and to share the responsibility. It may in some cases expose a pastor to some risk of giving offence, if in the exercise of his fidelity he should discourage the aspirations of an unsuitable candidate; but it is an evil from which he would be sheltered, at least in part, by referring the case to the consideration of two or three of his brethren in his vicinity. It is not, however, pastors only who should be cautioned against recommending unsuitable candidates, but the committees of our colleges should be no less careful about receiving them. It is extremely difficult by a first examination, or even by a probationary term, to judge of eligibility and fitness, as great excellence in some cases lies hidden under a very uncouth and unpromising exterior, and in others is very slow to develope itself; while on the contrary, a showy exterior over a shallow substratum is so deceptive, that not only months, but even years, must roll on, before the necessary qualifications can be determined upon. But a false delicacy has sometimes led our committees to retain young men in the colleges, of whose unfitness there remained no question, rather than put them and their friends to the pain of recommending them to discontinue their studies, and return to trade. And it should be recollected that to carry on the education of a young man without any rational probability that he will ever attain to usefulness of any kind, either as an author, tutor, or preacher, is on the part of the committee a betrayal of their trust, and a misapplication of the funds entrusted to their care. Let there be, then, a far greater degree of care and discrimination exercised in the initiative by our pastors than there has been : ten earnest men are better, and will do more for us, than a hundred incompetent ones. It would be better that churches should remain longer without pastors, than gain unsuitable ones; just as it is a far more endurable evil for a man who wishes for connubial felicity, to endure the privations of celibacy any length of time, than to hurry from them into the miseries of an un-happy marriage. We must be more careful in the selection, the reception, and the retention of our students, than we have been. Since it is so difficult to find an egress for those who are once in the ministry, it is highly incumbent upon us to watch with greater vigilance the door of entrance to it.

VIII. There is no class of men to whom we can look so naturally, or with so much entreaty for their aid, in furnishing us with devoted ministers, as our Professors. If the college be the mould in which the preacher and pastor are cast, the tutor is the man who shapes the mould, and pours the metal into it. How much then depends upon these beloved and honoured brethren ! What a trust is reposed with them, how solemn, how awful, how responsible ! If it be a momentous thing for a pastor to have the care of a single church, how much more so, for a tutor to have the care of twenty or thirty youthful minds, each of which is looking forward to the pastorate ; and to have them replaced by others every five years. Such an occupation is enough to make the stoutest heart tremble under an oppressive sense of its responsibilities. The strength of our churches lies in our ministry ; of our ministry in our colleges ; and of our colleges in their tutors. There is nothing about which we ought to be more anxious than about this part of our system. Happily to whatever department of ministerial education we look, whether to the philological, mathematical, or philosophical; whether to hermeneutical or dogmatical theology, we find in our various academic institutions, professors of whom we are not ashamed. If we need improvement anywhere, it is in the homiletical and pastoral department. We can scarcely wonder that in such an age as this, our professors should be anxious to push forward their alumni as far as possible into the regions of literature and science; or that now that the London University gives Nonconformists an opportunity of obtaining academic degrees and honours, they should feel solicitude to give full proof of their official assiduity by their students obtaining those distinctions; but it is well for them to remember that one popular, earnest, and successful preacher will bring more real credit to their college, and give it more favour with the public, than a dozen Bachelors of Arts, and half-a-dozen Masters to boot. The occasional exhibition, and it can be but occasional, of the letters denoting a degree affixed to a man's name, will not often excite the inquiry, " Where was he educated?" but the constant exhibition and effect of his power as a preacher will be a public and permanent recommendation of the institution where he was trained to such efficiency. It is true that natural preaching talent will grow in almost any soil, and under almost any culture; but it may be carried to a higher degree of perfection in one place, and by one hand, than another. There is also such a thing as colleges gaining a special and permanent character, one for turning out better scholars, a second for teaching philosophy better, and a third for carrying on a superior theological training; but that, in the long run, will be the most useful, and the most deservedly popular, which succeeds in sending forth the greatest number of earnest and successful preachers.

All earnestness has a tinge of enthusiasm about it, and as no man can kindle this in the soul of another who has none of it himself, our tutors should have this mental fire, with judgment to keep it in its proper place, to do its proper work; and however they may value classical, scientific, and philosophical studies, their heart should be set on the formation of popular, powerful, and useful preachers. Those who know how much there is to do even in the way of preliminary training, with many young men that enter our seats of learning, and how much of necessity students' time and attention must be divided among the various objects of study, will confess that it is no easy matter to give that prominence to homiletics which their supreme importance demands. But, notwithstanding this, opportunities will continually present themselves, to an anxious and observant professor, for inculcating upon his students that all that he is teaching them will be useless, if they do not make it subservient to their great business of preaching the gospel and converting sinners. But it is of especial importance that our tutors should be upon the alert when their students begin to preach, that in their first pulpit labours they should select the true object of all preaching, pursue it in a right course, and seek it with due vigour. What a student is in his first public services, that he is likely to be through life; and if he has no earnestness then, he is likely to have little afterwards. It happens that as all excellences are rarely combined in one man, many of our professors, though highly gifted as regards talent and acquirement, are not themselves much distinguished as preachers, and therefore can not present in themselves living models of what pulpit power, as to manner, really is. Still, they who cannot illustrate it by example, can teach it by precept. May they see the importance of the subject, and labour to the utmost to inculcate it upon the youths looking up to them for instruction, and make it their chief aim to kindle in their breasts the ardour of pulpit enthusiasm! We can easily imagine with what delight they must sometimes witness the advance by their pupils in extensive and accurate scholarship, in analytical power, in logical acuteness, in metaphysical subtlety; and that in some rare cases they may felicitate themselves on such results of their labour, though they can foresee they will never be associated with pulpit efficiency; but as a general rule, nothing with reference to their students, should gratify, much less satisfy them, short of adaptation to popular effect. The demand preferred by our country upon the military schools is, "Give us soldiers:" upon our medical colleges, "Give us surgeons and physicians:" upon our Inns of Court, "Give us lawyers." The cry sent up to our colleges is, "Give us powerful preachers, devoted pastors." And it will not do to meet this demand, any more than it would the others just quoted, by replying, "We will send you Bachelors and Masters of Arts." Much less will it do to send men who will feed the churches with a dry and sapless verbal exegesis of German theology, instead of the sweet and succulent expositions of our Scotts, our Henrys, our Wardlaws, and our Barneses. Ministers may study the profoundest criticisms for their own improvement and carry on a course of exegetic exposition in the pulpit; but it must be of a character that shall combine impression with instruction; and let our tutors aim to train preachers, who shall make their sermons expository, their expositions sermonic, and both instinct with life and essentially popular. Let them give us in the men they send into our churches, as much as they can of every thing which can polish the taste, inform, even adorn the intellect, and give weight and influence to the character in general society; the more of all these acquirements the better; but let them never forget that what is always wanted for the momentous subject of religion, and what is especially wanted in these times of intense earnestness, is a race of ministers as earnest as the times in which they live. May God help them to train such ministers for us!

IX. If it be the duty of the churches to call out ministers, it must of course be no less their duty to provide means for their education. Among all the objects of Christian benevolence, there is not one which has a prior or a stronger claim than our collegiate institutions, and yet it is too true that they are the last whose demands are properly regarded. Among Protestant Dissenters especially, the main pivot of their whole system is the ministry; upon this, every thing, under God, must turn. As this is strong, every thing else amongst them will be strong; and as this is weak, everything else will be weak. The springs which supply the reservoirs of our evangelizing societies, both at home and abroad, are to be traced back to our colleges: and yet the churches, if we may judge from their conduct, do not seem to be duly aware of this fact. Colleges are not however to be considered as eleemosynary institutions, where a race of literary paupers are sustained by the alms of the affluent; for it is becoming increasingly the practice for our students to pay for their own board : but beyond this, we have the invaluable services of our professors to reward, and many other expenses to defray. This outlay must be borne by the churches in all cases where there is no endowment, or none adequate to the entire support of the institution. And how can property be better applied ? or what expenditure produces a quicker or more abundant return ? A good education for our ministry is cheaply obtained at any price : and every shilling we expend in this way tells at once and before our eyes upon the object for which it is intended. And yet strange to say, there is no object for which we find it more difficult to maintain a regular and adequate supply of means. Foreign and home missions have an annual collection from almost every church in our denomination, and yet how few are there of our churches who grant an annual collection for any college, and what multitudes who never grant such a collection at all ? The platform is the stage of modern activity, but our colleges can make no exhibition there : we can employ no successon of orators to advocate our cause by speeches in support of resolutions ; can exhibit no foreigners ; can produce no excitement by tales of horror, of pathos, or of adventure ; yet where would the platform be but for the pulpit, and what is the pulpit without the college ? We ought not, it is true, to do less for our other organizations, but we ought to do far more for our educational system. We must bestir ourselves, and not allow this on which every thing depends, to fall into the rear, or be thrown into the shadow of one or two deservedly popular societies. If a larger part of the zeal manifested in arguing for the voluntary principle were employed in a more liberal support of our denominational institutions, they would be in a far better state than they now are, and the power of that principle more clearly seen, and more successfully advocated. With all our ardour in the cause of Nonconformity, it is easier to raise large funds for other objects of benevolence than for this. The London Missionary Society, which is chiefly supported by the Congregational body, has an income of nearly eighty thousand pounds a year; while that same body does not raise by voluntary contributions more perhaps than eight or nine thousand for our seats of learning; and even this is not so economically expended as it might be by a consolidation of our colleges. It is high time the whole system were looked into.

It is however somewhat cheering to know that this subject is beginning to be understood by our churches, and a more just appreciation of the value of an educated ministry, to be made by the intelligence of the age; and as a natural consequence there is springing up a more general disposition to support the expense thereby incurred. Many instances have occurred of late, of the owners of property apportioning a large share of it, either in the way of founding colleges, or establishing scholarships, for the education of young men for the ministry. An individual who founds one of these scholarships, may, if he gives his property at the age of thirty-five, and lives to be seventy, have, during his lifetime, and ever afterwards, six or seven ministers, educated by his means, preaching the gospel at the same time; and when he has reached his heavenly home, may welcome to glory through a long succession of ages souls that have been saved by the labours of those ministers for whose education he had set apart his property. How laudable and how noble an object of honourable ambition does such a proposal present to those who have at once the wish and the means to do good! Let the churches collectively, and their wealthy members individually, well consider then the obligation laid upon them to provide all that may be necessary to ensure the education of a ministry adapted to the circumstances of this extraordinary age!

CHAPTER XI.

THE NECESSITY OF DIVINE INFLUENCE TO MAKE THE MINISTRY EFFICIENT.

This treatise would be essentially defective in the estimation both of its author and its readers, if after so much has been advanced about instrumentality, nothing were to be said about the agency which is necessary to render it effectual for the accomplishment of its object. In all Divine operations, whether in the world of nature or of grace, God employs a chain of dependent means for the working out of his purposes and plans : but though dependent, they are appropriate.   In acknowledging, as we must do, the adaptation of these means to the production of the intended result, we do homage to God's wisdom ; while in confessing their dependence for efficiency upon his blessing, we do no less homage to his power and grace.   There is no analogy which I can borrow from the world of nature that can satisfactorily illustrate the operation of Divine grace on the human mind.   I know very well that second causes in the material universe depend for their efficiency upon Divine influence : but it is an influence of a totally different kind, and exerted altogether in a different matter from that of which I now write ; and we are very little aided in our perceptions of the nature of the Spirit's operation upon the human mind, by anything we observe in the world of vegetable or animal life.

There are two aspects in which man is to be viewed in relation to the means employed for his salvation, he is to be considered as both a rational and a sinful creature, (or as a rational creature whose reason is under the dominion of sin), and consequently, whatever method be adopted for his salvation, he must be dealt with in both these views of his condition. His fallen state as a sinner has not bereft him of his reason, will, and responsibility; but his reason and will alone will never lift him out of his condition as a fallen sinner. He cannot be dealt with otherwise than as he is, and he must be treated as a rational creature, and not as a brute or a block. His intellect must be appealed to by argument, and his heart by motives. And it will be seen that in the means of grace, and especially in preaching, there is provision for this. There is truth to be presented to the intellect, truth which represents the whole state of the case between God and the sinner, the nature and obligations of the moral law, the exceeding sinfulness of sin, the weight of the tremendous penalty of the violated precept; the wonderful love of God in the provision he has made for the salvation of the sinner, with the eternal results of misery or bliss which follow upon faith and unbelief respectively. In this, there is something in its nature adapted to engage the attention, and to interest the heart, of the sinner. It is not only the truth, but just the truth that suits his condition. In addition to this, there is, in preaching, the adaptation of the manner, as well as the matter, to his circumstances, the tendency of the living voice, ministerial solicitude, and earnest elocution, to engage the intellect and impress the heart. It will follow of course that earnestness is a part of this well-adapted system of means, and the more earnest a man is, the more likely, so far as means go, is he to do good; for if it be the matter which God blesses to change the heart, it is also the manner which he blesses to fix the attention preparatory to this change: there is as obvious an adaptation in the latter as in the former. How comes it to pass that there is greater efficiency usually attendant upon hearing the word, than there is upon reading it? Just because there is a greater adaptation to fix attention and to impress the heart; and by the same rule I argue there is more adaptation to do this in one man's manner than in that of another. Hence we see that those preachers are most successful who we might expect to be so, independently of the Divine power. This does not disprove the necessity of a Divine influence, but only shews what order of instrumentality it is that the Divine Spirit usually employs, and consequently what instrumentality we should select. As God does not usually bless ignorance, dulness, obscurity, or feebleness, we should avoid them; for to look for great results from them, is to expect not only what God has not promised, but what he very rarely bestows. God deals with us as rational creatures, by presenting to us, and requiring us to understand and believe that truth, the reception of which into the heart changes the whole character and conduct.

But there is in the heart of man, not only an indifference, but an opposition to Divine truth. "The carnal mind is enmity against God, and is not subject to the law of God, neither indeed can be." The heart so blinds the judgment that "the natural man discerneth not the things of the Spirit of God, neither indeed can he know them, because they are spiritually discerned." Therefore, however the attention may be gained by the manner of a preacher, (and gained it must be in order to conversion,) yet the heart is still opposed to the truth; and hence the need of the Spirit's influence to subdue this resistance of the heart to the truth itself. Thus the truth and the Spirit concur in conversion: it is the sinner being brought to know and love the objects presented in the truth, therefore the truth must be presented to the intellect, in order that it may be known and loved: but it never will be so loved, however theoretically understood, till the Spirit takes away the disrelish for it which is in the heart. Without the truth, there is nothing to engage the attention and employ the intellect of man as a rational being; without the Spirit there is no right disposition of the heart, when the truth is so presented. If a certain quality in an object be the ground of dislike to it, an increased knowledge of the object and of this quality, cannot in the nature of things subdue our hostility; the taste must be changed ere the object can be relished. It is precisely thus with the sinner and the truth; he dislikes the gospel for its holiness, and no increase of light will vanquish his enmity to it. Consequently, however earnest the preacher's manner, and however scriptural his matter, no saving result will follow, unless the Spirit give his blessing. Yet preaching is as necessary as if all were done by it alone, without the Spirit, because it is by this means that the Spirit usually works in the conversion of sinners. And since it is by appropriate means that he accomplishes his purposes, there is nothing in this doctrine to discourage exertion. There are means which carry in themselves the rational hope, if not the promise, of success. God will not accept the lame sacrifice, nor send down the signs of his approval on service which involves no real effort of heart or mind in his cause. The influence of the Holy Spirit comes not as a bounty upon indolence, but as a stimulus to exertion. Its office is not to give the human faculties a license to slumber, but to supply man with motives to watchfulness. Its descent upon the church is not as the torpor which betokens disease, but as an element of activity bespeaking moral and spiritual health. God is unquestionably sovereign in the dispensation of this blessed influence. He giveth it in such measures, on such occasions, and to such instruments, as it seems good to him. He that directs the course of the clouds, and causes them to drop their treasures where and when he pleases, makes the dew of his grace, and the rain of his Spirit, to fall according to the counsel of his own will. There is no such necessary connection between the exhibition of the truth and the conversion of the soul, as there is between the application of fire and the combustion of inflammable matter. The apostle says, "Who then is Paul, and who is Apollos, but ministers by whom ye believed, even as God gave to every man? I have planted, Apollus watered, but God gave the increase. So then, neither is he that planteth any thing, neither he that watereth; but God that giveth the increase." One should think it impossible to mistake the meaning of this language, or to doubt whether special Divine influence be necessary for the conversion of the soul, or whether the communication of it be a prerogative of Divine sovereignty.

Still there is every ground to expect the influence we need. It is our privilege to live under the dispensation of the Spirit, as well as under that of the Messiah. The former of these is connected with the latter: or perhaps more correctly speaking they are identical; the covenant established in Christ's blood is the economy of the Spirit. The ministry of reconciliation is the ministry of the Spirit. I do not mean to represent this divine influence as confined to the Christian economy, for since the beginning of time no soul has been converted or sanctified but by this heavenly power; but the communications of it before the coming of Christ were limited, partial, and scanty, compared with what they have been since: they constituted not the shower, but only the drops which precede it. Hence the language of the evangelist, "This spake He of the Spirit, which they that believe on him should receive, for the Holy Ghost was not yet given, because that Jesus was not yet glorified." This idea, that we are under the Spirit's economy, should enlarge our expectations of rich communications of this invaluable and essential blessing. The view I have given of Divine sovereignty is not intended, nor when rightly understood, is it calculated, to discourage hope, but simply to teach dependence. While God reserves to himself the right of bestowment, and acts upon his own rules of communication, he warrants and invites the most comprehensive requests, and the largest anticipations. Since he has promised to give the boon in answer to the prayer of faith, it would seem to be our own fault that we have it not in more abounding measure. The very recollection of our privilege in being placed under such an economy, might seem to be enough to call forth our prayers and to awaken our expectations. Instead of being surprised that so much of this Divine power accompanies our ministry in the most successful periods of our history, we should be surprised that we receive so little of it, and enquire after the obstructing cause. In a country like Egypt, where rain seldom falls, a shower is the exception, and a dry atmosphere the general rule; but in our variable climate, a long drought is the rarity, and the frequent shower is the common occurrence. The husbandman ploughs and sows in this land, with his expectant eyes upon the heavens, and feels disappointed if the fertilizing rain is withheld. So should it be with us, in reference to the shower of God's grace. We are not in the dry and arid atmosphere of the Levitical economy, but enjoy the privilege of the dew-distilling, rain-dropping dispensation of the Spirit; and with us the question should be, why we have not more of this Divine influence, and what has provoked the Lord to withhold from us the genial influences of his grace. Instead of being at any time astonished that our ministry is so much blessed, we should enquire why it is not always so. When we consider what is said, that God "willeth not the death of a sinner, but would rather that he should repent, and turn from his wickedness and live;" when we recollect what he has done for the salvation of sinners; when we add to this, that the gospel is his own truth, and preach-

ing his own institution, we are sometimes ready to
wonder that he does not pour out that influence which
is necessary to give effect to the purposes of his own
benevolence, and almost to enquire, " What does the
Lord now wait for?" In answer to this it may be
replied, " He waits for the earnest labours of his ministers, the faith of his church, and the believing prayers
of both."

It is quite perceptible that the necessity of Divine
influence is rather a dogma of faith, than a principle of
practice, both with ministers and their flocks. Did the
people really believe it, were it matter of inwrought conviction, and were there the least seriousness of spirit in
their religion, how much less dependence would there
be upon men, how much less would there be said
about talent, how much less homage would be paid to
genius and eloquence, and how much more looking up
to God by intense and persevering supplication would
there be ! Recollecting that God works by means,
and by means adapted to promote his ends, there
would be no danger of sinking into an enthusiastic and
irrational neglect of them; but on the contrary there
would be more constant and serious attendance upon
them. The knowledge that preaching, and especially
earnest preaching, is the Spirit's instrumentality, would
lead men to seek that instrumentality, in order that they
might have that blessing. How highly would it exalt
the minister to consider him as the Spirit's instrument,
and how important would it make the sermon to regard
it as God's means to bless the soul ! To view ministers
and sermons apart from the work of God is immeasurably to sink both; it is to cease to view the preacher as

an ambassador of Christ, and instead of it, to listen to him only as a lecturer on religion. With what sacred awe and with what fervent prayer would he be heard, by those who viewed him as the appointed medium of that influence, which, if received, would illuminate, renew, and sanctify their souls!

But if it be incumbent on the people to remember the dependence of means upon the Divine blessing, how much more so is it the duty of ministers? It is an article of our creed, it is often the subject of our sermons, and it is acknowledged in our prayers; but after all, is our conviction of dependence upon the Spirit so deep, practical, and constant, as to prevent us from attempting anything in our own strength, and make us to feel strong only in the Lord and in the power of his might? Do we conduct the pursuits of our studies, as well as regulate the prayers of our closets, under this conviction? Do we with child-like simplicity, and in the spirit which we inculcate upon our hearers in reference to their personal salvation, habitually give ourselves up to the guidance and blessing of this Divine Agent? Do we look up for wisdom to guide us in the selection of our texts, and the composition of our sermons? Do our eyes and our hearts go up to heaven, as we think and write for our people? Do we go to our pulpit in a praying frame, as well as in a preaching one; praying even while we preach, for our people, as well as for ourselves? Do we thus clothe ourselves with Omnipotence, and go forth as with the Lord ever before us? Do we recollect that from all that crowd of immortal souls before us, we shall gather nothing but human praise or censure, except the Lord be with us; that not one dark mind will be illumined, not one hard heart softened, not one inquiring soul directed, not one wounded spirit healed, not one uneasy conscience appeased, unless God the Spirit do it? Do we really want to accomplish those objects, or merely to deliver a sermon that will please the people, and gratify our own vanity? If the former, how entire, how confident, how believing, should be our sense of dependence upon something far higher than the best and most appropriate instrumentality! Such a feeling of dependence would cramp none of the energies of our soul, would stunt none of our powers, quench none of our fire, repress none of our intensity of manner. So far from it, we should derive from it unspeakable advantage in addressing our hearers; a seriousness, tenderness, and majesty, beyond what the greatest unassisted talent could command, would pervade our discourses; a superhuman influence would rest upon us; a Divine glory would irradiate us; and we should speak in the power and demonstration of the Spirit. "Possessed of this celestial unction, we should be under no temptation to neglect a plain gospel, in quest of amusing speculations and unprofitable novelties; the most ordinary topics would open themselves with a freshness and interest, as though we had never considered them before; and the things of the Spirit would display their inexhaustible variety and depth. We shall pierce the invisible world, we shall look, so to speak, into eternity, and present the very essence and core of religion, while too many preachers, for want of spiritual discernment, rest satisfied with the surface and the shell. We shall not allow ourselves to throw one grain of incense on the altar of vanity, and shall forget ourselves so completely, as to convince our hearers we do so; and displacing everything else from the attention, leave nothing to be felt or thought of, but the majesty of truth, and the realities of eternity."* The preacher who cherishes such a frame of mind will appear with a radiance not less dazzling perhaps than that of genius, and far more sacred heavenly and divine; and when carried to his highest pitch of earnestness and dependence, he will seem almost to reach the sublime symbol of the apocalypse, of the angel standing in the sun. "But this kind goeth not forth but by fasting and prayer." A deep, practical conviction of the need of the Spirit, would make us men of prayer, would send us to our closets, and keep us there. Here perhaps is the cause why we have not more success in our ministry, and are not more frequently and more heartily gladdened by the conversion of souls to God; we seek to be men of the pulpit merely, and are not sufficiently men of the closet. It is a mystery in God's moral government that he should make the communications of his grace for the salvation of sinners dependent in any degree upon the prayers of others; yet he does so, and we know it; and yet knowing it, how little have we been affected by it, and stirred up to prayer on this account! We have uttered our complaints of the fruitlessness of our ministry long enough before one another; but, as Dr. Wilson says in his introduction to the "Reformed Pastor," "One day spent in fasting and prayer to God, is worth a thousand days of complaint and lamentation before men."

* Mr Hall "On the Discouragements and Support of the Christian Ministry."

The author of this work can assure his brethren that it is not with any disposition to accuse them, and exalt or exculpate himself, that he writes thus. He takes his full share of blame for this deficiency of a spirit of fervent prayer, and his full share of humiliation on this account. The activities of the age, which require us to be so much in public, may furnish, if not an excuse, yet some mitigation of blame, for the too little time spent in fervid private prayer. Devotion is damped by business. Still even with this palliation, we are verily guilty, for we do not pray as if we believed we were sent to save souls from death, and that we could not be successful in a single instance without the grace of God. Who of us can read the diaries of such men as Doddridge, Brainerd, Payson, and Martyn, and very many others, and not stand reproved for our lamentable deficiency in the exercise of earnest prayer? Perhaps in modern times there was never so much of social, and never less of private, prayer. We introduce all our business transactions with prayer, but too often in a business spirit, and with a sad want of sincerity, seriousness, and deep devotion; so that the very frequency and want of reverence with which we engage in such exercises of devotion, tends to diminish the spirit of prayer. Nothing is more to be dreaded than a depression of the spirit of devotion, and nothing more intensely to be desired than its elevation. A praying ministry must be an earnest one, and an earnest ministry a praying one. Let us then feel ourselves called upon by all the circumstances of the times to abound more and more in fervent supplications. Let us, if we can in no other way command more time for prayer, take it from study or from sleep. We have neither right nor reason to expect the Spirit, if we do not ask for his gracious influence; and without him we can do nothing. Let us take care lest the bustling activity, and the endless multiplication of societies, should supplant, instead of calling forth, the feeling of intense devotion. We never more needed prayer, we were never more in danger of neglecting it. There is plausibility in the excuse that we had better abridge the time of praying than the time of acting. But it will be found in the end that doings carried on at the sacrifice of prayer, will end in confusion and vanity. Public spirit in the cause of religion, however prevalent or energetic, if it be not maintained in a feeling of dependence upon God, will be regarded by him as the image of jealousy in the temple, which maketh jealous. Our sermons are the power of man, or perhaps we might say his weakness; but our prayers are in a modified sense the power of God. Let us not slacken in preaching, but let us abound more in prayer: let us not quench a ray of intellect, but let us add to it the warmth of devotion: let us labour as if the salvation of souls depended upon our own unaided energies, and then let us feel as did the apostle when he said, "though I be nothing." The eternal destinies of our hearers hang not only upon our sermons but upon our prayers; we carry out the purposes of our mission, not only in the pulpit, but in the closet; and may never expect to be successful ministers of the New Covenant, but by this two-fold importunity in first beseeching sinners to be reconciled to God, and then beseeching God to pour out his Spirit upon them: thus we honour his wisdom in the use of the means he has appointed, and then his power by confessing our dependence upon his grace.

Baxter concludes his " Reformed Pastor" with an expression of his confidence in the usefulness of the book he had written, which it would be unwarrantable and ridiculous vanity in me to adopt in reference to mine, in any other way than that of hope and prayer; but in this spirit I borrow the language of that great and holy man, and say, " I have now, brethren, done with my advice, and leave you to the practice. Though the proud receive it with scorn, and the selfish and slothful with distaste, or even with indignation, I doubt not but God will use it, in despite of the opposition of sin and Satan, to the awakening of many of his servants to their duty, and to the promotion of a work of right reformation: and that his blessing will accompany the present undertaking for the saving of many souls, the peace of you that undertake and perform it, the exciting of his servants throughout the nation to second you, and the increase of the purity and unity of his churches. Amen."

SOME OTHER
BANNER OF TRUTH
TITLES

THE CHRISTIAN MINISTRY

Charles Bridges

The revival of the Church seems to be closely connected with the condition of its ministry. Bridges sub-titled his study of the Christian ministry, *'An Inquiry into the Causes of its Inefficiency'*, and, rightly used, it is well suited to promote a faithful and effective ministry.

Charles Bridges (1794-1869) was one of the leaders of the Evangelical party in the Church of England in the last century. He was vicar of Old Newton, Suffolk, from 1823 to 1849, and later of Weymouth and Hinton Martell in Dorset. *The Christian Ministry* is Bridges' best-known literary work, but his expositions of *Proverbs*, *Ecclesiastes* and *Psalm 119* are also highly valued.

Bridges begins by considering the general and personal causes of ministerial ineffectiveness, and goes on to examine comprehensively preaching and pastoral work. The book was one of the few which the godly Robert Murray M'Cheyne took with him to the Holy Land, and, in its field, it is without an equal.

ISBN 0 85151 087 6
400pp. Cloth-bound

AN ALL-ROUND MINISTRY

C. H. Spurgeon

One of Spurgeon's great ministries was to hundreds of preachers who had been trained in the Pastors' College founded by him. In 1865 he originated an Annual Conference for these men and during his lifetime he gave twenty-seven Presidential addresses at the Conference. The best of them were reprinted after his death in the form of this book.

While Spurgeon is always stimulating and challenging these addresses delivered in the maturest period and in a context that brought the best out of him have a unique quality. They are full of exposition, exhortation and advice gained from his own rich experience. Sparkling with wit and sanity they spring naturally from the Pastor's heart.

'For fidelity to truth, breadth of experience, warmth of spirituality, ripeness of wisdom and liveliness of style these addresses are beyond praise' — Professor G. N. M. Collins, *The Monthly Record*.

ISBN 0 85151 181 3
416pp. Paperback

THE POWER OF THE PULPIT

Gardiner Spring

Biblical preaching is the backbone of the church. Noah, Moses, Elijah, Isaiah, John the Baptist, Simon Peter and Paul the apostle were all *preachers*. But where true preaching is discounted, the people of God become weak and spiritually flabby. They lose direction, and become absorbed in secondary, rather than primary matters. By contrast, biblical preaching sets our eyes and hearts on God and his glory, exposes man in his sinfulness, and presents Christ in his grace and power.

Because the whole church is nourished by true preaching, 'the power of the pulpit' is a matter of vital concern for all Christians. Seeing the need for this, Gardiner Spring (already in the fourth decade of a ministry which spanned sixty years) penned what he hoped would be a 'few plain thoughts . . . which may be profitable to his younger brethren'. In fact he produced one of the most stirring of all books on the subject of preaching. Written with an eloquence born of knowledge and experience, *The Power of the Pulpit* covers a wide range of subjects of interest to both preachers and hearers of the Word of God.

Preachers need few things more than to be encouraged to fresh consecration of their energies to Christ in study, preparation and proclamation. Congregations need to have a vision of the kind of preaching and preacher honoured by God. *The Power of the Pulpit* provides just such encouragement and such a vision.

ISBN 0 85151 492 8
256pp. Cloth-bound

For free illustrated catalogue please write to:
THE BANNER OF TRUTH TRUST
3 Murrayfield Road, Edinburgh EH12 6EL
P.O. Box 621, Carlisle, Pennsylvania, 17013, U.S.A.